FreeHand 8

AUTHORIZED

macromedia®
PRESS

FreeHand 8 Authorized
Macromedia, Inc.

 Published by Macromedia Press, in association with Peachpit Press, a division of Addison Wesley Longman.

Macromedia Press
1249 Eighth Street
Berkeley, CA 94710
510/524-2178
510/524-2221 (fax) ·
Find us on the World Wide Web at:
http://www.peachpit.com
http://www.macromedia.com

ISBN 0-201-69691-6

Notice of Liability
The information in this book and on the CD-ROM is distributed on an "as is" basis, without warranty. While every precaution has been taken in the preparation of the book and the CD-ROM, neither Macromedia, Inc., its licensors, nor Macromedia Press shall have any liability to any person or entity with respect to liability, loss, or damage caused or alleged to be caused directly or indirectly by the instructions contained in this book or by the computer software and hardware products described herein.

Trademarks
Macromedia is a registered trademark, FreeHand, Flash, Design in Motion, Shockwave, Xtras, Extreme 3D, and the Made With Macromedia logo are trademarks of Macromedia, Inc. Insta.html is a trademark of Taylor-Kamerer, a partnership. Macintosh is a registered trademark of Apple Computer, Inc. PANTONE is a registered trademark of Pantone, Inc.

Other product names mentioned within this publication may be trademarks or registered trademarks of other companies.

Printed and bound in the United States of America

9 8 7 6 5 4 3

CREDITS

Producer
Karen Tucker, Macromedia

Authors and Instructional Designers
Thomas Faist, Craig Faist, Lori Faist, and the team at Datrix Media Group

Artwork
Julia Sifers, Glasgow & Associates
Thomas Faist and Craig Faist, Datrix Media Group
Steve Botts
Stewart McKissick

Production
Rick Gordon, Emerald Valley Graphics
Myrna Vladic, Bad Dog Graphics
Debbie Roberti, Espresso Graphics

Editor
Judy Ziajka

Indexer
Steve Rath

Thanks to the following people:
Joel Dreskin, Macromedia
Joanne Watkins, Macromedia
Tom Hale, Macromedia
Randy Varnell, Macromedia
Marjorie Baer, Peachpit Press
Amy Changar, Peachpit Press
Karen Silvey, Macromedia
Sindy Cho, Macromedia

table of contents

INTRODUCTION   1

LESSON 1 FREEHAND BASICS   6

Creating a Folder on Your Hard Drive
Creating a New Document
Exploring the Controls
Customizing Application Preferences
Working with Panels
Organizing the Workspace
Creating an Element on the Page
Changing the View
Creating Basic Shapes
Saving the Document
Applying Basic Fills and Strokes
Applying Gradient Fills
Arranging, Aligning, and Grouping Elements
Adding Other Elements
Customizing Tool Settings
Creating a Mirror Image of an Element
Rotating an Element on the Page
Getting Help
On Your Own

LESSON 2 COMBINING TEXT AND GRAPHICS   62

Creating a New Document with a Custom Page Size
Creating and Positioning a Rectangle
Creating and Aligning Ellipses
Combining Paths with the Blend Command
Precisely Rotating a Copy
Importing and Creating Colors and Tints
Applying Fills and Strokes
Cloning, Scaling, and Positioning Elements
Adding Text to the Layout
Applying a Color Fill to Text
Importing a FreeHand Graphic
Adding a Dashed Line
On Your Own

LESSON 3 WORKING WITH PATHS AND POINTS   112

Manipulating Basic Shapes
Manipulating Paths with the Freeform Tool
On Your Own
Using a Tracing Template
Manipulating Curves with Control Handles
Adding the Finishing Touches to Your Graphic
Creating the Elements for the Zoo Ad
Applying Color
Practicing Tracing Techniques
Adding a Traced Element to Another Document
Scaling and Aligning Elements
Adding Gradient-Filled Text

LESSON 4 USING LAYERS AND STYLES

Creating a New Custom-Size Document

Importing a Tracing Pattern and Moving It to a Background Layer

Defining Process Colors

Creating an Element with the Pen Tool

Rotating a Copy and Duplicating the Transformation

Combining Elements with Paste Inside

Changing Your View of the Artwork

Creating Other Foreground Layers

Creating Curved Paths with the Pen Tool

Defining and Applying Object Styles

Combining Elements with Path Operations

Creating Other Elements

Aligning Elements

Positioning Artwork and Editing Styles

Adding Elements to the Clipping Path

Scaling and Reflecting Artwork

Importing a Picture Frame

Other Layer Panel Controls

Exporting Artwork for Use in Other Programs

On Your Own

LESSON 5 MULTIPLE-PAGE DOCUMENTS

Specifying a Custom Page Size

Creating Guides for a Consistent Layout

Using the Edit Guides Command

Importing PANTONE Process Colors

Creating Text and Graphic Elements

Attaching Text to Paths

Duplicating Pages in a Document

Importing Text and Linking Text Blocks

Defining Paragraph Styles

Using the Text Editor

Importing Images

Wrapping Text around Graphics

Adding Colors from Bitmap Images to the Color List

Printing Your Document

Collecting Files for Output

On Your Own

LESSON 6   CREATING MORE COMPLEX ARTWORK   264

Creating a New Custom-Size Document
Importing and Tracing an Image
Adding a 3D Image and a Transparency Effect
Blending Multiple Shapes
Blending Shapes to Create a Reflection
Using a Template to Add a Shape
On Your Own

LESSON 7   ADVANCED TECHNIQUES   298

Creating a Composite Path
Applying Gradient Fills
Defining a Named View
Blending Shapes to Create Shading
Creating a Clipping Path
The Graphic Hose Tool
Adding Elements to an Existing Layout
Using the Envelope Xtra
Applying Lens Fills
Adding Final Touches
On Your Own

LESSON 8   BLENDING SHAPES FOR SHADING   334

Getting Started
Creating Blends
Pasting Blends Inside Paths to Create Three-Dimensional Shading
Creating Shading for the Top of a Sphere
Creating Shading for the Bottom of a Sphere
Creating Shading for a Cylindrical Ring
Adding Dimension with Radial Fills
Completing the Figure
Creating a Realistic Shadow
Creating the Finished Document
Customizing FreeHand's Toolbars and Shortcuts
On Your Own

LESSON 9 DESIGNING FOR THE WEB

370

Obtaining the Browser Software and Shockwave Flash Plug-in
Viewing Different Types of Web Graphics
Creating GIF and JPEG Files
Creating Animated Flash Graphics with FreeHand
Using FreeHand and the Insta.html Xtra to Create Web Pages
Viewing the Web Pages in a Browser

APPENDIX A WINDOWS SHORTCUTS

393

APPENDIX B MACINTOSH SHORTCUTS

397

APPENDIX C MOVING TO FREEHAND

401

INDEX

405

Macromedia's FreeHand 8 is a powerful and comprehensive drawing and layout program that provides a complete set of tools for creating dynamic graphics, illustrations, and page designs for print, multimedia, and Internet publishing projects.

This Macromedia Authorized training course introduces you to the major features of FreeHand 8 by guiding you step by step through the development of several sample projects. This 14-hour curriculum includes these lessons:

Lesson 1: FreeHand Basics
Lesson 2: Combining Text and Graphics
Lesson 3: Working with Paths and Points
Lesson 4: Using Layers and Styles
Lesson 5: Multiple-Page Documents
Lesson 6: Creating More Complex Artwork
Lesson 7: Advanced Techniques
Lesson 8: Blending Shapes for Shading
Lesson 9: Designing for the Web

Each lesson begins with an overview of the lesson's content and learning objectives, and each is divided into short tasks that break the skills into bite-size units.

Each lesson also includes these special features:

Tips: Shortcuts for carrying out common tasks and ways to use the skills you're learning to solve common problems.

Boldface terms: New vocabulary that will come in handy as you use FreeHand and work with graphics.

Menu commands and keyboard shortcuts: Alternative methods for executing commands in FreeHand 8. Menu commands are shown like this: Menu › Command › Subcommand. Keyboard shortcuts (when available) are shown in parentheses after the first step in which they can be used; a plus sign between the names of keys means you press keys simultaneously: for example, Ctrl+Z means that you should press the Ctrl and Z keys at the same time.

Appendices A and B at the end of the book provide a quick reference to shortcuts you can use on Windows and Macintosh systems, respectively, to give commands in FreeHand. Appendix C provides a quick FreeHand reference for users of other vector illustration applications.

As you complete these lessons, you'll be developing the skills you need to complete your own designs, layouts, and illustrations for print, multimedia, and the Internet. At the end of this course, you should have mastered all the skills listed in the "What You Will Learn" list in this introduction.

All the files you need for the lessons are included in the Lessons folder on the enclosed CD-ROM. Files for each lesson appear in their own folders, titled with the lesson name. You can use the lesson files directly from the CD-ROM, or you can copy the Lessons folder to your hard drive for quicker access.

Each lesson folder contains three subfolders—Complete, Media, and Start. The Complete folder contains completed files for each project so you can compare your work or see where you are headed. The Media folder contains any media elements you need to complete each lesson, such as graphics or text required to complete a layout. The Start folder contains any prebuilt files you will need to complete the lesson. The completed, media, and starting files you will need are identified at the beginning of each lesson. (Some lessons may not require starting files or media elements, so in some lesson folders, these subfolders will be empty.)

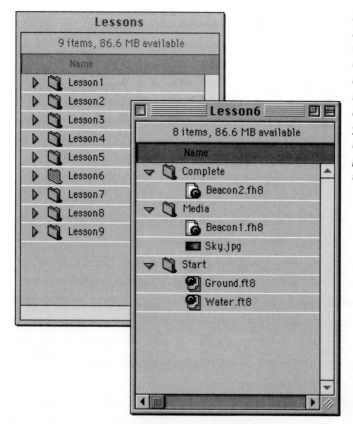

Files for each lesson appear in their own folders, titled with the lesson name. The Complete folder contains completed files for each lesson. The Media folder contains the media elements you need to complete each lesson. If a lesson requires a prebuilt file, you will find the file in the Start folder.

AUTHORIZED TRAINING FOR MACROMEDIA

Each book in the Macromedia Authorized series includes the complete curriculum of a course taught at Macromedia's Authorized Training Centers. The lesson plans were developed by some of Macromedia's most successful trainers and refined through long experience to meet students' needs. We believe that Macromedia Authorized courses offer the best available training for Macromedia programs.

The instructions in this book are designed for graphic artists, illustrators, designers, and others interested in creating stunning graphics, typography, and layouts for print, multimedia, and the World Wide Web. This course assumes you are a beginner with FreeHand but are familiar with the basic methods of giving commands on a Windows or Macintosh computer, such as choosing items from menus, opening and saving files, and so on. For more information on those basic tasks, see the documentation provided with your computer.

Finally, the instructions in this book assume that you already have FreeHand 8 installed on a Windows or Macintosh computer, and that your computer meets the system requirements listed on the next page. This minimum configuration will allow you to run FreeHand 8 and open the training files included on the enclosed CD-ROM. If you do not own FreeHand 8, you can use the training version of the software on the CD-ROM provided with this manual. You will be able to complete the lessons with the training version of the software, but you will not be able to save your work. Follow the instructions in the Read Me file on the enclosed CD-ROM to install the training version of the software.

note *Three TrueType font families included on the FreeHand 8 software CD-ROM you received when you purchased FreeHand 8 are used throughout the lessons in this course. To accurately reproduce the projects with the original fonts, install the News Gothic T, URW Garamond T Normal, and Vladimir Script font families on your system before starting the lessons. Windows users should drag those font files into the Fonts folder in the Control Panel. Macintosh users should drag those font files into the Fonts folder in the System Folder.*

If you do not install these specific fonts, simply choose other fonts available on your system and adjust type size and formatting as needed to make your projects similar in appearance to the lesson files. Working without the original fonts installed will not interfere with your ability to complete the lessons.

Welcome to Macromedia Authorized. We hope you enjoy the course.

WHAT YOU WILL LEARN
By the end of this course you will be able to:

- Create, combine, and transform graphic elements in FreeHand
- Incorporate graphics and text into your projects
- Create single- and multiple-page layouts
- Take advantage of powerful and easy-to-use special effects features
- Import and export files for easy integration with other applications
- Organize a document into layers
- Import, format, and flow text within a layout
- Prepare files for a commercial printer
- Create blends of multiple shapes

4

- Apply gradient and lens fills to enhance your illustrations
- Combine elements by joining them together or pasting them inside other paths
- Paint graphics onto the page
- Create blends for shading
- Customize your working environment
- Convert FreeHand artwork to Web page graphics
- Create Shockwave Flash graphics in FreeHand
- Use FreeHand to design and create Web pages

MINIMUM SYSTEM REQUIREMENTS

Windows

- Intel Pentium processor or faster
- Windows 95 or Windows NT 4 (with Service Pack 3) or later
- Windows 95: 16MB available RAM (24MB or more recommended)
- Windows NT 4: 24MB available RAM (32MB or more recommended)
- 30MB available disk space (60MB or more recommended)
- CD-ROM drive
- PostScript printer (recommended)
- For Lesson 9 only, a Web browser that supports Shockwave and the Shockwave Flash plug-in (see Macromedia's Web site at http://www.macromedia.com for more information about Shockwave)

Macintosh

- PowerMacintosh processor
- Mac OS 7.x or later operating system
- 16MB available RAM (32MB or more recommended)
- 30MB available disk space (60MB or more recommended)
- CD-ROM drive
- PostScript printer (recommended)
- For Lesson 9 only, a Web browser that supports Shockwave and the Shockwave Flash plug-in (see Macromedia's Web site at http://www.macromedia.com for more information about Shockwave)

a quick tour

FreeHand basics:

LESSON 1

FreeHand's drawing and layout tools can be used to develop everything from the simplest illustrations to the most complex designs. Its extensive control over graphics, colors, type, and imported artwork make FreeHand a powerhouse for any graphic design project.

FreeHand is an **object-oriented** drawing program. Object oriented means that your document is created from graphic objects, or shapes, rather than from individual pixels

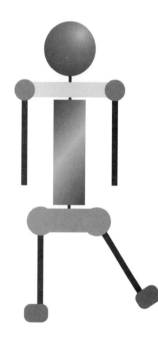

This simple robot figure is constructed from a series of shapes created with FreeHand's basic shape tools. You will see how in this lesson.

as with a **bitmap** drawing tool. Object-oriented graphics are also known as **vector** graphics. Unlike bitmap graphics, object-oriented graphics can be scaled to any size or output resolution with no loss of quality.

In this lesson, you will create a simple drawing of a robot using groups of these simple graphic objects, created using FreeHand's basic shape tools—Rectangle, Ellipse, and Line—and the Pointer tool.

If you would like to review the final result of this lesson, open Robot.fh8 in the Complete folder within the Lesson1 folder.

WHAT YOU WILL LEARN

In this lesson you will:

- Create a new document

- Identify and organize tools and controls

- Customize application settings)

- Create basic shapes such as rectangles, ellipses, and lines)

- Change the way elements look on the page by adding color and changing line thickness

- Group and align objects

- Create additional copies of existing elements

- Create a mirror image of an element or group

- Rotate elements on the page

APPROXIMATE TIME

It usually takes about 1 hour to complete this lesson.

LESSON FILES

Media Files:

None

Starting Files:

Lesson1\Start\Robot1.fh8 (optional)

Completed Project:

Lesson1\Complete\Robot.fh8

Lesson1\Complete\Robot2.fh8

CREATING A FOLDER ON YOUR HARD DRIVE

Before you begin building anything, you will create a folder to hold all the projects you will create as you work through the lessons in this book. If you are using the training version of FreeHand provided on the CD-ROM that came with this book, you do not need to create this folder because you will not be able to save files.

1] Create a folder called *MyWork* on your hard drive.
You will save all of your work in this folder.

Now you are ready to begin.

CREATING A NEW DOCUMENT

To begin working on a new project, you must first launch FreeHand and either create a new document or open an existing document.

1] Open the FreeHand application.
Open the application by double-clicking the FreeHand icon. The FreeHand toolbox, toolbars, and menu bar appear, but without an open document window. A few floating windows may appear on the screen as well; you will learn about these later in this lesson.

On Windows systems, a Welcome Wizard appears, enabling you to create a new document or open an existing file with a quick click of the mouse. If you're a new Windows user, you may find FreeHand's Wizards very useful when working with your own documents; you will learn more about the Wizards later in this lesson. If you prefer that the Wizard not appear the next time you start FreeHand, turn off this option near the bottom of the Welcome Wizard screen.

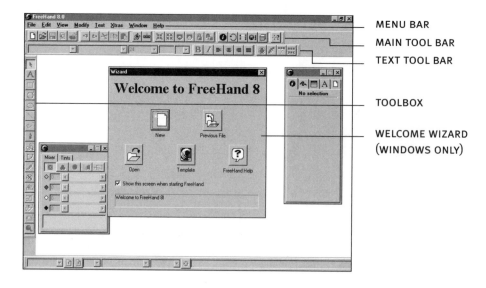

MENU BAR

MAIN TOOL BAR

TEXT TOOL BAR

TOOLBOX

WELCOME WIZARD (WINDOWS ONLY)

2] Create a new document by clicking the New button on the Welcome Wizard screen (Windows) or choosing File › New (Windows Ctrl+N, Macintosh Command+N).

A new document appears in a document window. The page is sitting on FreeHand's **pasteboard**, which is a work surface that contains all of the pages in your document. The pasteboard initially contains one page. The 222-inch by 222-inch pasteboard can hold more than 675 letter-sized pages. You will be creating a robot illustration in this window later in this lesson.

You will be learning about the elements on this screen throughout this lesson.

tip *If you cannot see the entire page, choose View > Fit to Page.*

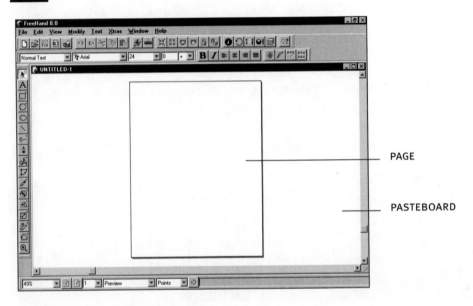

PAGE

PASTEBOARD

tip *If you see other control windows floating on your screen that are not shown here, close them by clicking the close box in each window's header bar. You will explore these panels later in this lesson.*

EXPLORING THE CONTROLS

FreeHand provides a wide variety of tools and controls for you to use to create your own artwork and graphics. In getting started with FreeHand, you first must learn where to find these controls.

1] Move the cursor over the main and text toolbars across the top of the screen. Rest the cursor over a button to see its name.

The **main toolbar** contains many of FreeHand's basic functions. The **text toolbar** contains buttons and menus for the most frequently used text commands. If you point to a button and hold the mouse still for a few moments, the button's name will appear.

The toolbar defaults are shown here. Don't worry if your toolbars do not look exactly like these. You will learn in upcoming lessons how to customize FreeHand's toolbars, toolbox, and shortcuts.

tip *If the main and text toolbars do not appear on your screen, you can display them by selecting Window > Toolbars and then Main or Text.*

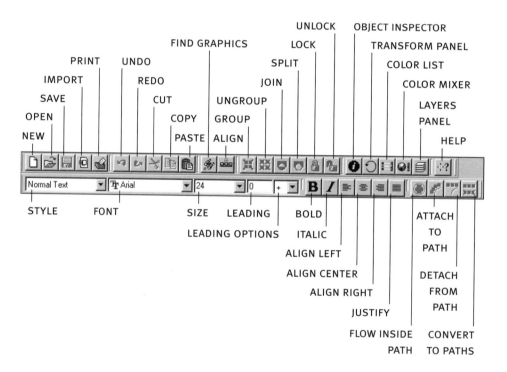

2] Move the cursor over the tools in the toolbox at the left side of your screen. Rest the cursor over a tool to see its name.

The **toolbox** contains FreeHand's drawing and transformation tools. It is **docked**, or attached, to the left edge of the screen by default.

You select a tool in the toolbox by clicking the tool once. Move the cursor into the document window to use the tool.

tip *If the toolbox does not appear on your screen, you can display it by selecting Window > Toolbars > Toolbox.*

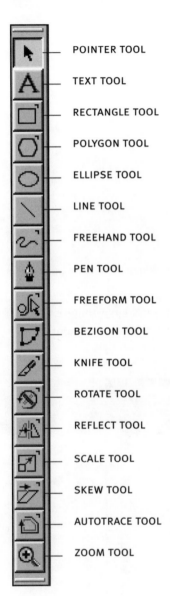

POINTER TOOL

TEXT TOOL

RECTANGLE TOOL

POLYGON TOOL

ELLIPSE TOOL

LINE TOOL

FREEHAND TOOL

PEN TOOL

FREEFORM TOOL

BEZIGON TOOL

KNIFE TOOL

ROTATE TOOL

REFLECT TOOL

SCALE TOOL

SKEW TOOL

AUTOTRACE TOOL

ZOOM TOOL

3] Move the toolbox away from the left edge of the screen by dragging the horizontal bar across the top or bottom edge of the toolbox.
When you undock the toolbox from the side of the screen, it changes shape and floats in front of your document window.

DRAG FROM HERE...   TO HERE

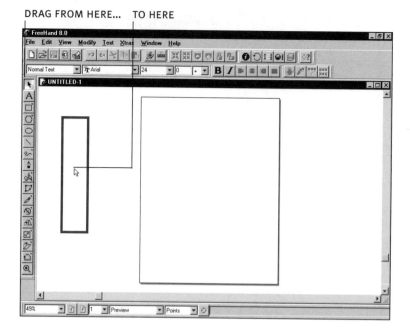

4] Change the size of this floating toolbox by dragging the size box at the bottom-right corner of the toolbox.

You can resize this floating toolbox the same way you can resize any window. This is one of the ways FreeHand enables you to organize your working environment to suit your individual preferences.

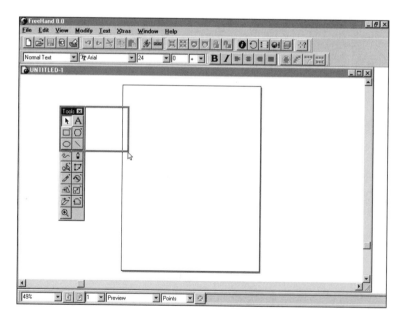

5] Dock the toolbox against the left edge of the screen again by dragging the header bar at the top of the floating toolbox window to the left edge of the screen.
FreeHand automatically resizes the toolbox and attaches it to the left edge of the screen. You can move the tools up and down along the left edge of the screen by dragging.

tip   *You may find it convenient to use the toolbox in the docked position, because here it is not floating over your document window where it may hide part of your artwork as you work.*

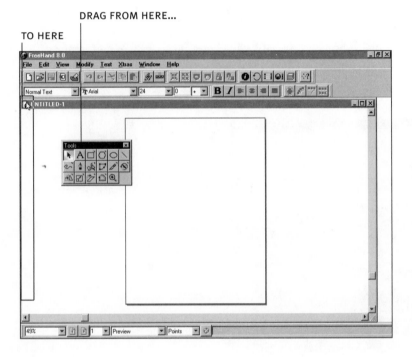

tip   *The main and text toolbars can also be undocked from the top of the screen to become floating windows in the same manner. Dragging them back to the top edge of the screen will dock them again.*

CUSTOMIZING APPLICATION PREFERENCES

FreeHand lets you set a wide array of preferences for customizing your working environment. You can customize the way elements are displayed, the number of Undo levels, and the way text and graphics can be edited, among many other settings.

Before beginning work with FreeHand, you will change one preference setting that will make it easier to learn the program and see your results clearly.

1] Choose File › Preferences to display the Preferences dialog box. Select General from the preference categories and make sure your General Preferences options are set as shown here.

In the Preferences dialog box that appears, you choose a category of preferences from the tabs at the top (Windows) or the list on the left side (Macintosh). The options in the dialog box change with the category you select.

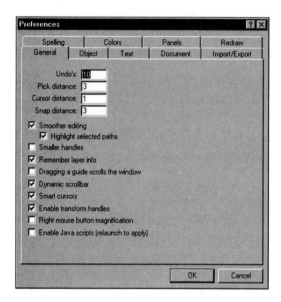

2] Select Redraw from the preference categories. Make sure that the option High-Resolution Image Display is turned on (checked).

This will give you a better screen display of imported images. On some systems, this option can slow down screen redrawing significantly when you are working with very-high-resolution images, but it should not cause any problems for the images you will use in these lessons. The Redraw options apply only to the display and do not have any effect on your printed results. The default settings of the other Redraw Preferences options are shown here.

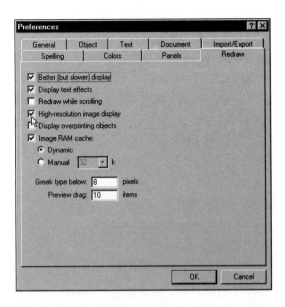

3] Click OK to close the Preferences dialog box.

You will not see the results of the High-Resolution Image Display preference setting until you start working with images on the page.

WORKING WITH PANELS

Many FreeHand drawing settings can be set in **panels**: floating collections of tools and formatting controls that you can open, close, customize, and move around on your desktop. Unlike dialog boxes, FreeHand's panels can remain on the screen as you work so you can quickly and easily edit document settings.

Earlier in this lesson you learned that undocking the toolbox turns it into a floating panel. In this section, you'll be introduced to some other useful panels: the Inspectors, Color Mixer, and Color List. You will use these panels often in the lessons that follow.

1] Display the Object Inspector by clicking the Inspector button on the main toolbar or by choosing Window > Inspectors > Object.

OBJECT INSPECTOR

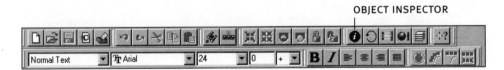

FreeHand's Inspector panels are grouped together by default; when you open the Object Inspector, you see them all. Two or more panels combined in this way are called a **panel group**.

The Inspector panels display current information regarding selected objects and allow you to change the characteristics of those objects. No information is displayed in the Object Inspector at this time, because no element is selected.

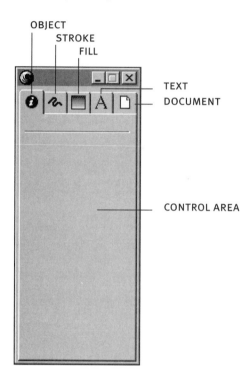

OBJECT
STROKE
FILL
TEXT
DOCUMENT
CONTROL AREA

> **tip** *The five Inspectors (Object, Stroke, Fill, Text, and Document) contain important controls for editing FreeHand graphics. Virtually every FreeHand drawing task involves one or more of these Inspectors. These Inspectors are on movable panels and can be arranged to suit your individual preference.*

2] Click the tab for the Document Inspector to activate that set of controls (bringing that Inspector to the front of the group).

The Document Inspector contains controls for specifying page size and orientation and for adding or removing pages from the document. You will work with each of these controls in later lessons.

You can change to any of the other Inspectors by clicking its tab at the top of the panel group.

tip *In addition to the toolbar controls, you can display any of FreeHand's Inspectors by selecting Window > Inspectors and choosing the Inspector you want to use.*

3] Hide the Inspector panel group by clicking the close box in the header bar at the top of the panel.

You can display and hide panels as needed.

Now look at the Color Mixer panel.

4] Display the Color Mixer by clicking its button on the main toolbar or by choosing Window › Panels › Color Mixer.

COLOR MIXER

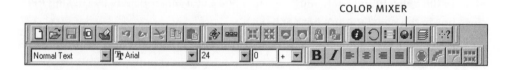

The Color Mixer enables you to create and modify colors that can be applied to elements throughout the document. You will see how this tool works later in this lesson.

The Color Mixer is initially grouped with the Tints panel. The Tints tab can be seen at the top of this panel group.

5] Click the Tints tab at the top of this panel group.

The Tints panel comes to the front of the group, hiding the Color Mixer. The Tints panel enables you to create **tints**, which are lighter shades of a color, expressed as a percentage of the base color. (Tints are also referred to as **screens**.)

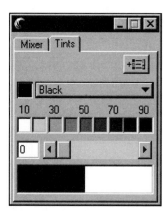

6] Hide the panel group containing the Tints and Color Mixer panels by clicking the close box in the panel group's header bar.

Each panel group can be displayed or hidden as needed when working on a project.

7] Display the Color List by clicking its button on the main toolbar or by choosing Window › Panels › Color List.

The Color List appears, showing the names of the colors that have been defined for this document. Adding colors to the Color List makes it easy to apply those colors to other elements in the document without having to re-create them in the Color Mixer for each use.

The Color List is grouped with the Layers and Styles panels by default. The Layers and Styles tabs can be seen at the top of this panel group.

8] Click the Layers tab at the top of this panel group.

The Layers panel comes to the front of the group. In an upcoming lesson, you will use Layers to organize artwork in a more complex illustration than the robot drawing you create in this lesson.

19

9] Drag the Layers panel out of this panel group by pointing to the name _Layers_ on the tab at the top of the panel and dragging the tab out onto the pasteboard. Then release the mouse.

Layers now appears as a separate panel, so you can access the Color List at the same time as Layers. You have **ungrouped** these two panels.

10] Drag the Layers tab onto the Color List panel and release the mouse.

This combines the two panels into a panel group again. As you can see, panels can be separated or combined by dragging their tabs.

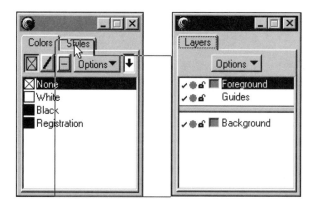

11] Click the Colors tab to bring the Color List to the front of the panel group. Then hide the Color List by clicking the button on the main toolbar again.

You can also hide panels as needed using the buttons on the toolbar.

tip *In addition to using the toolbar controls, you can display any of FreeHand's panels by selecting Window > Panels and choosing the panel you want to use.*

ORGANIZING THE WORKSPACE

Next you will see how you can align panels to one another and connect panels together to customize your working environment.

1] Display the Color List and Color Mixer panels again by clicking the two buttons on the main toolbar.

FreeHand has built-in capabilities to help you align panels to keep your working environment organized.

2] Move any edge of the Color List panel toward an edge of the Color Mixer panel by dragging the header bar at the top of the Color List panel.

Notice that as you move the Color List close to the Color Mixer, it **snaps** into position so that the two panels are aligned. These panels are not connected together, but are neatly aligned at the edges. When you drag a panel or group by its header bar to within 12 pixels of another panel or group, FreeHand automatically aligns them with one another. Panels snap to the top, bottom, or sides of other panels when you move any edge of a panel to within 12 pixels of another panel.

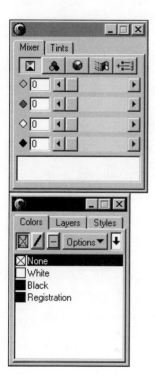

You can also align panels to the edge of your workspace by dragging them to within 12 pixels of the monitor border or to the border of the application.

3] Move the Color List away from the Color Mixer and release the mouse. Then hold down the Shift key and move the Color List back toward the Color Mixer. Release the Shift key.

The panels do not snap together. Pressing Shift while dragging a panel (Shift-drag) temporarily disables snapping. Panels automatically snap to one another when you move panels without holding down the Shift key.

4] Move the top of the Color List toward the bottom of the Color Mixer by dragging the Color List's header bar while holding down the Control key (on both Windows and Macintosh computers).

This **docks** the panels, connecting them together so they behave as if they are one. Unlike a panel group, docked panels are all displayed at the same time. Notice the **panel dock**, a small bar connecting the two panels together.

22

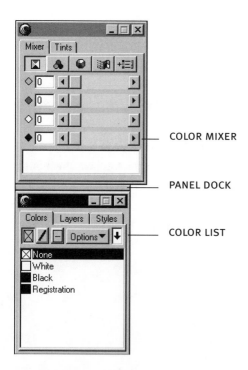

COLOR MIXER

PANEL DOCK

COLOR LIST

5] Try moving one of the docked panels. Then collapse one of the docked panels by clicking the Minimize button (Windows) or Zoom box (Macintosh).

Docked panels move and collapse together, making it easier to work with several panels at once.

Docked panels also are displayed and hidden together, so hiding or displaying either the Color List or Color Mixer while the panels are docked will hide or display both docked panels.

6] Expand the collapsed panels and then undock them by clicking the panel dock between the two panels.

The panels are now independent again. You can also undock the panels by holding down Control while dragging the header bar of a docked panel away from its adjacent panel.

7] Close all open panels.

As you work with FreeHand, you can position, group, dock, and collapse panels as desired. Remember that you can also show and hide panels quickly with the buttons on the main toolbar.

The flexibility that FreeHand offers with panels makes it easy for you to organize FreeHand's controls in a way that is comfortable for you.

CREATING AN ELEMENT ON THE PAGE

In creating any great masterpiece, the most important step is getting started. Here you will begin by creating a rectangle on the page.

1] Select the Rectangle tool near the upper left of the toolbox by clicking it once.

2] Position your cursor anywhere on the page. Hold down the mouse button and drag diagonally downward and to the right to create a rectangle. Release the mouse when your rectangle is about the size of a playing card.

The rectangle you created appears on the page with a border and no fill. (If your rectangle looks different, don't worry. You will be changing its characteristics shortly.)

Small boxes, called **selection boxes**, appear at the corners, indicating that this element is selected.

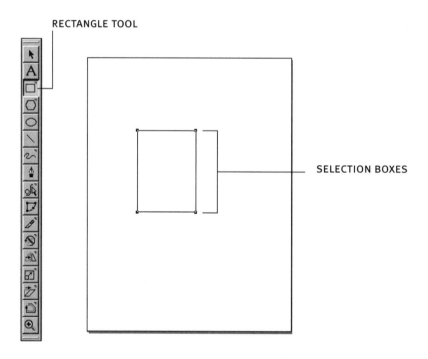

There are five different actions you can apply to any selected element. In the next few steps, you will learn how to move, resize, duplicate, and delete a selected element and how to change its appearance.

tip   *If the selection boxes do not appear at the corners of the object, click once on the object's border with the Pointer tool to select the object.*

First you will move the rectangle to a new position on the page.

24

3] Select the Pointer tool in the toolbox. Position the cursor on the border of the rectangle (but not on one of the selection boxes) and drag the mouse approximately two inches to the right.

Dragging from the middle of the selected element's border will move the rectangle to a new position on the page. This rectangle is empty, so there is nothing to grab inside the border when you want to move the object. Filled objects can be moved by grabbing anywhere in the middle of the object and dragging the mouse. You will learn how to fill an object later in this lesson.

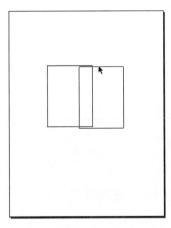

Next you will change the size of the selected element.

4] Position the tip of the Pointer tool on the bottom-right corner selection box of the rectangle. Hold down the mouse button, drag downward about an inch, and release.

The height of the rectangle has been increased about one inch. Dragging any selection box enables you to resize an object.

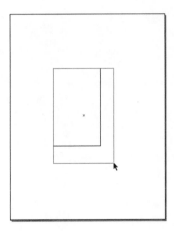

25

It may help to remember Move = Middle (drag the middle to move an object) and Size = Selection box (change an object's size by dragging a selection box).

Now you will create duplicates of a selected object.

5] With the rectangle still selected, choose Edit › Copy. Then choose Edit › Paste to add a duplicate of the rectangle to the page.

The pasted item appears in the center of the screen. You can duplicate a selected item with the Copy and Paste commands. You can paste duplicates of the most recently copied object into the current document or into other FreeHand documents as needed.

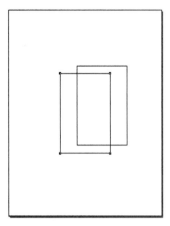

6] Choose Edit › Duplicate to add another copy of this rectangle on the page.

Duplicate is a one-step command you can use when additional copies of the selected element are needed in the same document. The duplicate is positioned down and to the right of the object duplicated.

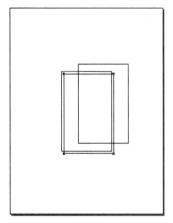

In the next step, you will learn how to delete unwanted elements from the page.

7] With one of the rectangles still selected, press the Delete key.
The selected object is deleted, leaving the other two rectangles on the page.

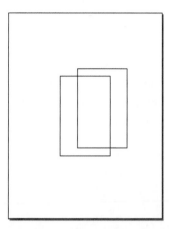

Now you can create and manipulate elements on the page. You will learn how to change the appearance of elements a bit later in this lesson.

8] Use the Pointer tool to move one of the new rectangles off the page onto the pasteboard. Then move the other rectangle off the page as well.
If these two actions are mistakes, or if you simply change your mind, you can use FreeHand's Undo command, which reverses the most recent changes.

9] Choose Edit › Undo to reverse the most recent change. Then choose Edit › Undo once more to reverse the next most recent change.
Both of the rectangles should be restored to their original positions on the page. FreeHand supports multiple levels of Undo. The default setting is 10 levels of Undo, but you can specify the number of Undo operations by selecting File > Preferences > General and entering a new value.

CHANGING THE VIEW

As you work on your FreeHand documents, you may find it helpful to zoom in to see the artwork in more detail or zoom out to see the entire illustration. FreeHand offers several features for viewing your artwork on the screen.

1] Select the Zoom tool at the bottom of the toolbox by clicking it once. Then point to one of the rectangles on your page and click to zoom in on that spot.
Clicking with the Zoom tool magnifies the spot where you click. Another way to zoom in is to hold down the mouse button and drag the Zoom tool cursor to surround the desired area with a **marquee**, a dotted line that surrounds the area you define by dragging the mouse; when you release the mouse, FreeHand will zoom in on the surrounded area.

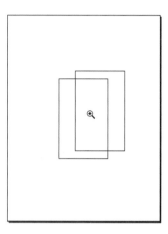

2] Press and hold the Alt (Windows) or Option (Macintosh) key and click with the Zoom tool to reduce the view. Then choose the Pointer tool from the toolbox.

tip *It is often helpful to change to the Pointer tool when you complete your work with the Zoom tool (and any other tool as well). This prevents an accidental click of the mouse from zooming you in somewhere in the workspace after you had just changed to the perfect view. You cannot use Undo to return to a previous view.*

The Zoom tool displays a plus or minus sign to indicate whether it will magnify (+) or reduce (−) the view. If the magnifying glass cursor appears without either a plus or minus sign, you are zoomed in or out as far as possible. FreeHand supports a zoom range of from 6 to 25,600 percent of the drawing size, so you shouldn't see the empty cursor very often. Notice that the magnification value appears in the lower-left corner of the screen.

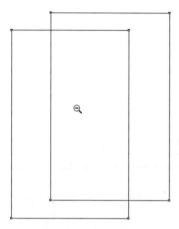

3] Choose View › Fit to Page to see the entire page again (Windows Ctrl+Shift+W, Macintosh Command+Shift+W).

The top three choices on the View menu allow you to change your view of the page immediately with specific results. Fit Selection zooms to fill the document window with any selected element (or elements), Fit to Page resizes the view so you can see the entire page, and Fit All reduces the view so you can see all of the pages in your document at once. (Right now, Fit All and Fit to Page would have the same results, because your current document contains only one page.)

4] Choose Edit › Select › All (Windows Ctrl+A, Macintosh Command+A) to select both of the rectangles on your page. Then choose View › Fit Selection.

This zooms the view so that the selected rectangles fill the document window. The Select All command allows you to select all of the elements on the page at one time.

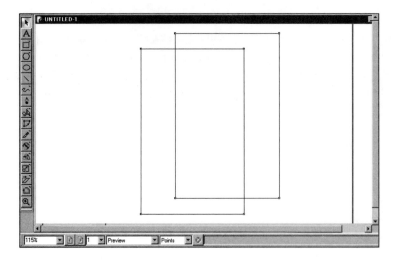

5] With both rectangles still selected, press the Delete key to remove both of the rectangles from the page.

Your page should now be empty again.

6] Point to the arrow in the lower-left corner of the document window and hold down the mouse button to display the magnification menu. Select 100% and release the mouse button.

This menu contains popular preset magnification values. Instead of typing a value in the magnification value field, you can select a value from this menu.

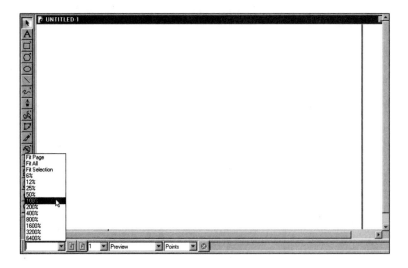

As you can see, FreeHand offers several ways for you to achieve the same results, so you can work in the way that is most convenient for you.

CREATING BASIC SHAPES

Now you will begin creating your first project: a simple drawing of a robot. This next task will introduce concepts you will use in every FreeHand project

If you prefer to re-create the robot more closely, you can work from the template provided. Choose File > Open and open Robot1.fh8 in the Start folder within the Lesson1 folder. This document contains gray outlines of the robot's elements for you to follow. Remember, though, that your main goal in this lesson is to learn to use the drawing tools, not to match the sample exactly. Don't worry if your version of the robot looks a little different from the one shown here.

You will start by creating a rectangle for the torso.

tip *Make sure that your magnification is set to 100% so you can create these elements at actual size.*

1] With the Rectangle tool, create a rectangle of any size on the page.

The rectangle appears on the page with a border and no fill. (If your rectangle looks different, don't worry. You will be changing its characteristics shortly.)

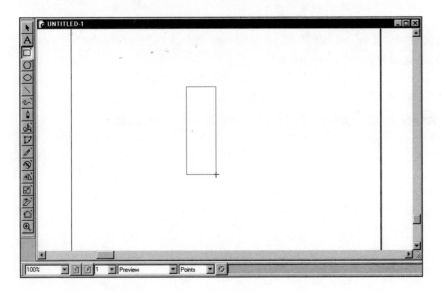

Rather than manually adjusting the size of the rectangle as you did earlier in this lesson, you will use the Object Inspector to specify a precise size for this element.

tip *Zoom in to see the artwork clearly as you work.*

2] Display the Object Inspector by clicking its button on the main toolbar.

The position and size of the selected element are displayed in the Object Inspector.

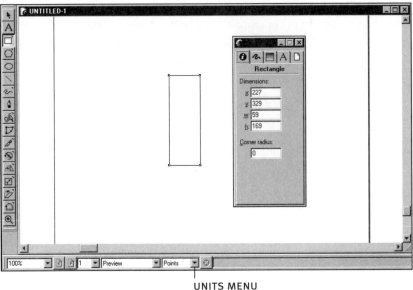

UNITS MENU

3] Change the unit of measure for this document to Inches by using the Units menu at the bottom of the document window.

This menu defines the unit of measure used throughout the document (except for the type size, which is always measured in points). Notice that now the values in the Object Inspector representing the position, width, and height of the selected object are displayed in inches.

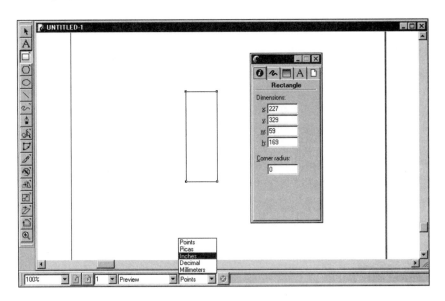

4] In the Object Inspector, select the current *w* value and type a width of *0.75*. Press the Tab key to highlight the *h* value and type a height of *2*. Press the Enter key to apply these changes.

This will change the size of the selected rectangle to the desired size for the robot's torso.

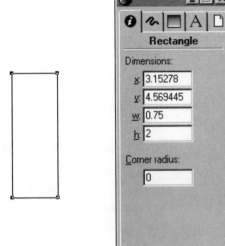

> **tip** *When this book says to press Enter, you can press the Enter key on the numeric keypad. PC users can also press Enter on the main keyboard, and Macintosh users can also press Return. For simplicity, this book refers only to the Enter key.*

5] Create another rectangle above the torso for the shoulders. Make this rectangle wider than it is tall, as shown here. Then use the Pointer tool to move the shoulder element by pointing to the edge of the rectangle (not on a selection box), holding down the mouse button, and dragging. Visually position the shoulders over the torso.

The precise size of this rectangle is not important, and don't worry if your elements are not centered perfectly above one another; you will fix that shortly.

> **tip** *Remember that to move this element, you must point to the border of the element (without pointing to a selection box) and drag. Because this rectangle is empty, there is nothing to grab inside the border when you want to move the object.*

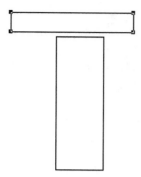

6] Select the Ellipse tool and use this tool to create a perfect circle for the head by holding down the Shift key as you drag diagonally. Then move the circle into position over the shoulders using the Pointer tool.

Holding down Shift enables you to draw perfect circles with the Ellipse tool and perfect squares with the Rectangle tool and constrains lines created with the Line tool to 180-, 90-, and 45-degree angles. Make sure that you release the mouse button *before* you release the Shift key, or the constraints Shift provides will be released.

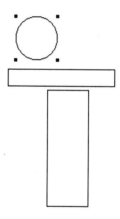

7] Draw another horizontal rectangle below the torso for the hips of the robot. Then use the Line tool to draw a vertical line connecting all of these shapes; this is the spine of the robot. Make sure to hold down the Shift key to keep the line vertical.

You now have five elements on your page.

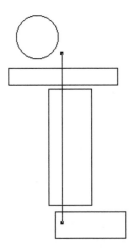

8] Choose the Pointer tool in the toolbox.

It is always a good idea to return to the Pointer tool when you finish with other tools. Then an accidental click will not add a tiny rectangle, line, or ellipse, change your view, or perform any other operation on your artwork.

SAVING THE DOCUMENT

Saving your work frequently is a good habit. You should save at least every 15 minutes or each time you finish a task. This will prevent you from losing hours of work if a power outage or computer malfunction occurs.

1] Choose File › Save to display the Save As dialog box (Windows Ctrl+S, Macintosh Command+S). Alternatively, you can click the Save button on the toolbar.

Because this is the first time you have saved this document, FreeHand will ask for a location and name for the file.

2] Select the location where you want to save this document. In this case, choose the MyWork folder you created on your hard drive.

If you are using the training version of FreeHand supplied on the CD-ROM that came with this book, you will not be able to save your work.

3] Type a name for the document, such as *MyRobot*, and click Save.

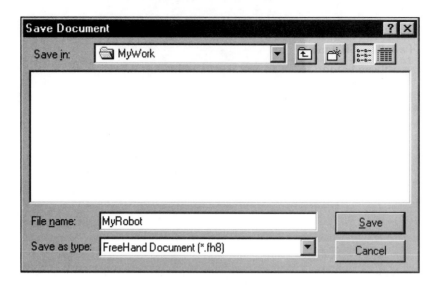

When FreeHand is finished saving the file, the name you entered will appear in the title bar at the top of the document window.

tip   *Always choose the location before entering a name for a document. This ensures that you know exactly where your document is saved.*

APPLYING BASIC FILLS AND STROKES

The circle and rectangles you have created are empty shapes with thin black outlines. In this task, you will fill in each of these empty shapes with one or more colors or shades. Applying colors to the inside of an element is called applying a **fill**. You will also change the border, or **stroke**, of each element.

1] Open the Color Mixer by choosing Window › Panels › Color Mixer or by clicking the Color Mixer button on the main toolbar.

You will use the Color Mixer to create new colors to apply to elements in your documents. The buttons across the top allow you to select the type of color you want to define.

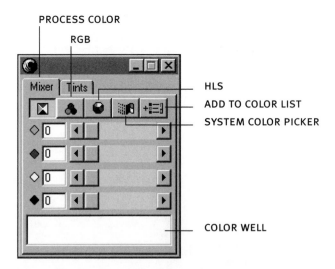

PROCESS COLOR

RGB

HLS

ADD TO COLOR LIST

SYSTEM COLOR PICKER

COLOR WELL

2] Click the top-left button in the Color Mixer to display the four color controls—Cyan, Magenta, Yellow, and Black—used to define process colors (if they are not already visible in the Color Mixer). Drag the sliders to create a green color, such as 100 Cyan, 0 Magenta, 100 Yellow, and 0 Black.

You can define a color by dragging the sliders or entering values for each color component directly and pressing Enter.

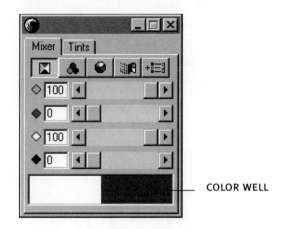

COLOR WELL

3] Point to the color well at the bottom of the Color Mixer, hold down the mouse button, and drag a color swatch out from the well. Drop this swatch inside the bottom rectangle of your robot (the hips).

You can drag and drop any color from the Color Mixer onto any element in your document.

37

You can drag and drop a color inside any of the closed shapes in your drawing to apply a basic (solid) fill. If the stroke changes instead of the fill, you dropped the swatch on the stroke; choose Edit > Undo and try again.

tip *It is often easier to drop color inside a small shape if you first zoom in on the element.*

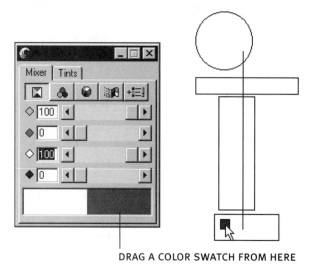

DRAG A COLOR SWATCH FROM HERE

You will use this drag-and-drop technique to fill the remaining shapes in the robot.

4] Fill the torso rectangle and the head with the same color as the hips.

Next you will create and apply a screen, or tint, of a color to the shoulder rectangle.

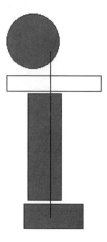

5] Click the Tints tab at the top of the Color Mixer panel group to display the Tints panel and then select Black from the Color List menu.

The Tints panel displays a strip of tints, in small squares called **swatches**, in 10 percent increments of the base color—in this case, black. This panel also provides a custom tint control (with an entry field and slider) for creating other tint values.

The Color List menu in the Tints panel enables you to directly select any color that currently exists in the Color List panel as a base color for a tint.

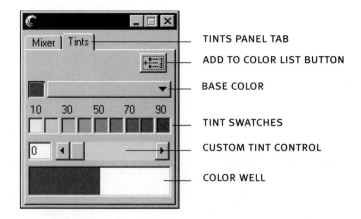

6] Drag the 30 percent swatch and drop it inside the shoulder rectangle of your robot.

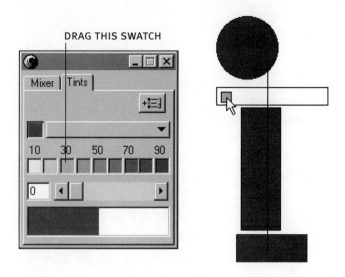

tip   *If the stroke color changes instead of the fill, use Edit > Undo and try again. Zooming in closer will often make filling small objects easier.*

Next you will change the thickness of the robot's spine.

7] Select the spine line with the Pointer tool. Select the Stroke Inspector by choosing Window > Inspectors > Stroke or Modify > Stroke. Alternatively, you can select the Stroke Inspector by clicking the Inspector button on the toolbar and then clicking the Stroke tab.

The Stroke Inspector appears. With this Inspector, you can control the stroke (line) characteristics of the selected object.

STROKE TAB

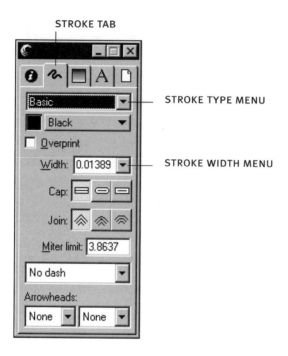

STROKE TYPE MENU

STROKE WIDTH MENU

8] At the top of the panel, make sure that the Basic and Black stroke options are selected. Change the width to 4 points either by entering *4 pt* in the Width field and pressing Enter or selecting 4 from the adjacent menu.

The selected line should now appear thicker, representing the increased stroke width.

tip   *Because you set the unit of measure for this document to inches earlier, you must type* pt *after the value in the width field so FreeHand will properly apply a 4-point stroke. Entering a 4 without the* pt *and pressing Enter will result in a stroke that is 4 inches wide! (The Stroke Width menu is always displayed in points for convenience.)*

9] Select the torso with the Pointer tool. Hold down the Shift key and click the head, shoulder, and hip elements. In the Stroke Inspector, change the stroke type to None on the Stroke Type menu. Then press the Tab key to deselect all elements.

You have now removed the outlines from the robot elements.

You can add to a selection by holding down the Shift key and clicking additional objects. Selecting the four elements together enabled you to change the stroke for all four at once.

You can apply a thick or thin stroke to any selected graphic, or you can remove the stroke all together.

tip   *To deselect all objects, press the Tab key. You can also deselect all objects by clicking the Pointer tool on an empty part of the page or pasteboard. Windows users: If a panel is active, you must first activate the document window by clicking it before you can use the Tab key to deselect all objects.*

APPLYING GRADIENT FILLS

You will now change the fill inside two of the elements from a solid shade, called a **basic** fill, to one that changes from one shade to another, called a **gradient** fill. FreeHand enables you to define your own gradient fills or to select from a library of predefined styles.

1] Display the Styles panel by choosing Window › Panels › Styles.

Styles are collections of visual characteristics for graphics or text that can save you time and help you achieve design consistency by letting you apply or edit attributes for several objects in one quick step. As you will see in upcoming lessons, you can also use the Styles panel to apply your own fill and stroke settings to objects or to apply paragraph formatting (font, size, leading, and so on) to text quickly and easily throughout your documents.

The Styles panel initially displays two default styles—one each for text and objects. FreeHand also provides a collection, or **library**, of gradient presets that make it as easy to apply a complex gradient fill to an element as it is to apply a solid-color fill with the Color Mixer.

2] Choose CMYK Styles from the Options menu at the top of the Styles panel. Select the gradient style named Reds by clicking it. Then click Import.

This style now appears in the Styles panel. In this display of styles, you can see the style name plus an icon for each style that indicates the style type: object or text.

tip *Since these style presets can be customized, this specific style may not be available on your system. If Reds is not available, select another that you like and use it instead.*

3] Choose Options › Hide Names in the Styles panel.

Now the Styles panel displays icons for each style that show the visual characteristics of the individual styles.

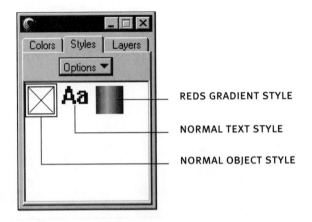

REDS GRADIENT STYLE

NORMAL TEXT STYLE

NORMAL OBJECT STYLE

4] Drag the Reds gradient swatch from the Styles panel and drop it inside the torso rectangle.

The gradient fill is immediately applied to the rectangle.

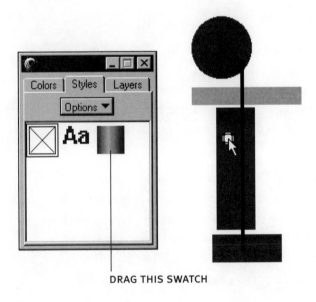

DRAG THIS SWATCH

To modify this gradient slightly, you will use the Fill Inspector.

5] With the Pointer tool, select the torso rectangle. Click the Fill tab in the Inspector panel group to display the Fill Inspector. Alternatively, you can choose Window › Inspectors › Fill or Modify › Fill.

The Fill Inspector appears. With this Inspector, you can control the characteristics of the fill inside an element. Notice that the Fill Type menu at the top of the Fill Inspector indicates that this element already has a Gradient fill.

A sample of the gradient is displayed in a **color ramp** on the left side of the Inspector. There are seven color swatches defining this gradient. These appear as swatches attached to the right edge of the color ramp: the starting color for the gradient appears at the top of the color ramp, the ending color appears at the bottom, and the five other colors appear in between. Gradient fills can contain up to 32 color swatches anywhere along the color ramp.

Two types of gradient are available, and you can change from one to the other by clicking the Graduated or Radial button in the Inspector panel. A **graduated** fill changes color in a straight line across the graphic. The direction of this color change is determined by the Direction control at the bottom of the panel. A **radial** fill changes color from a center point outward in all directions. When you click the Radial button, the options in the Fill Inspector change to enable you to reposition the center point of the radial fill.

6] Change the direction of this linear gradient by dragging the Direction control at the bottom of the Inspector to point down and to the right.

You can also adjust the direction by typing a value in the Direction Angle field.

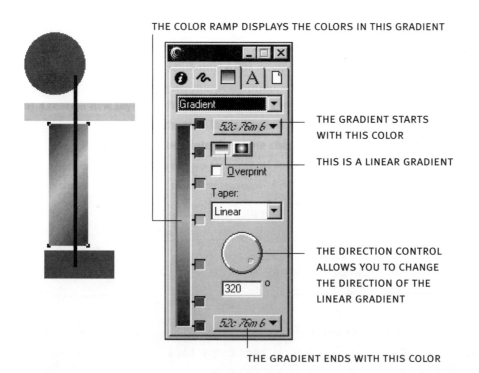

THE COLOR RAMP DISPLAYS THE COLORS IN THIS GRADIENT

THE GRADIENT STARTS WITH THIS COLOR

THIS IS A LINEAR GRADIENT

THE DIRECTION CONTROL ALLOWS YOU TO CHANGE THE DIRECTION OF THE LINEAR GRADIENT

THE GRADIENT ENDS WITH THIS COLOR

Next you will define your own gradient for the robot's head.

7] Select the circle and change the fill type from Basic to Gradient in the Fill Inspector. Then click the Radial button in the Fill Inspector. Move the center of the radial fill up and to the right by dragging the center point in the Fill Inspector.

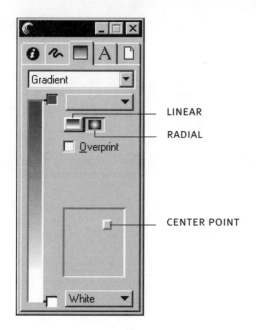

LINEAR

RADIAL

CENTER POINT

The circle is now filled with a radial fill, which helps create the appearance that the robot's head is a sphere instead of a flat circle.

Next you will make the robot's head a bit more colorful by changing the colors in the gradient to the same ones used in the gradient style you applied to the torso rectangle. The colors in this gradient style were automatically added to the Color List when you imported the style from the library. These colors were given names that describe their cyan, magenta, yellow, and black components.

8] Change the starting color of this gradient to brown by choosing 52c 76m 69y 18k in the starting color menu at the top of the color ramp. Now change the ending color to orange by choosing 0c 26m 76y 0k in the ending color menu at the bottom of the color ramp.

The robot's head is now filled with a radial gradient that radiates out from the center point from orange to dark red.

9] Display the Color List by clicking its button on the main toolbar. Drag an orange swatch, 1c 57m 83y 0k, from the Color List and drop it anywhere on the color ramp in the Fill Inspector to add a new color to this gradient.

You can drag the swatch up and down along the ramp to reposition it in the gradient. If you want to remove a color from the gradient, simply drag the swatch to the right away from the color ramp and release the mouse.

Your robot should now look similar to the following illustration.

10] Save your document with File › Save.

tip *Remember to save frequently as you work.*

ARRANGING, ALIGNING, AND GROUPING ELEMENTS

FreeHand arranges elements on the page in the order that they are created, which is why the spine of the robot is in front of the other body parts. You will rearrange the elements to make the robot look better.

1] Select the spine with the Pointer tool and choose Modify › Arrange › Send to Back.
The spine is now behind all of the other elements. The Arrange submenu offers four commands you can use in different situations. Use Send to Back or Bring to Front to move an object behind or in front of all of the other elements. Move Forward and Move Backward move a selected object forward or backward one element at a time.

Next get all the elements in your robot into proper alignment so the body looks symmetrical.

2] Select all of the elements by choosing Edit › Select › All. Choose Window › Panels › Align or Modify › Align.
The Align panel appears. This panel provides several choices for both horizontal and vertical alignment.

47

tip *Alternatively, click the Align button on the main toolbar.*

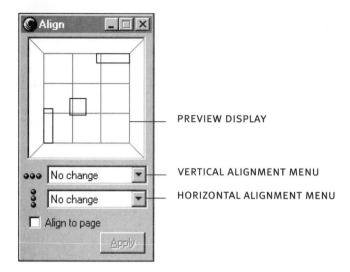

PREVIEW DISPLAY

VERTICAL ALIGNMENT MENU

HORIZONTAL ALIGNMENT MENU

3] On the Vertical Alignment menu, select No Change. On the Horizontal Alignment menu, select Align Center.

The preview display in the Align panel should show the desired results: elements centered left and right and not aligned up or down.

4] Click Align to Page in the Align panel to turn on this option.

The elements will now be centered horizontally on the page as well as centered horizontally on one another. (Because Vertical Alignment is set to No Change, the elements will not be adjusted vertically on the page.)

5] Click the button at the bottom of the Align panel to align your elements.

All five elements are now aligned accurately and centered horizontally on the page. To keep them aligned to one another and prevent accidental changes, you can group the elements.

6] With all five elements still selected, choose Modify › Group (Windows Ctrl+G, Macintosh Command+G).

This ties all the selected elements together into one group. One set of selection boxes now appears around the group, instead of individual selection boxes appearing around each element. Now you can move, resize, and modify all of these elements as one.

7] Save your work.

ADDING OTHER ELEMENTS

Next you will add arms and legs to complete the robot. The two arms are identical, so you can create one and make a copy for the second. The legs are identical also, but the feet point in opposite directions. For this effect, you will create a mirror image of the leg.

First you will create an arm. Then you will perform a simple copy-and-paste operation to create the second arm.

1] Choose the Ellipse tool and position the cursor about halfway up the left edge of the shoulder. Hold the Alt (Windows) or Option (Macintosh) key and the Shift key and draw a circle just a bit larger than the height of the shoulder box. Fill the circle with 50 percent black using the Tints panel and set the stroke to None in the Stroke Inspector.

Holding Shift creates a perfect circle. Holding Alt or Option draws an object from the center. Notice that the cursor changes from the standard crosshair to a crosshair in a circle to indicate that you are drawing the circle from the center. These keys work the same way with the Rectangle tool.

tip *Remember that you can choose Undo if you don't like your first attempt. Also, once the ellipse is on the page, you can use the Pointer tool with Shift and the Alt or Option key to resize the circle from the center.*

2] Draw a vertical line from the middle of the circle downward to form the arm. Using the Stroke Inspector, change the width of this line to 8 points.

For this robot, the arm should not reach as low as the hips.

tip *Remember to return to the Pointer tool.*

3] Bring the circle to the front by selecting the circle and choosing Modify › Arrange › Bring to Front (Windows Ctrl+F, Macintosh Command+F).

The arm is almost ready to be duplicated, but it would be easier to work with if the two elements were grouped together.

4] Select the circle and the line at the same time by clicking either element with the Pointer tool and then holding down the Shift key and clicking the other element.

Holding down Shift and clicking additional elements allows you to select multiple objects. Shift-clicking a selected item deselects it while leaving all other selected elements selected.

5] Group the selected elements by choosing Modify › Group.

Now you can work with the arm as if it were a single element.

6] With the arm still selected, choose Edit › Copy.

This puts an electronic copy of the selected artwork onto the clipboard.

7] Choose Edit › Paste to paste a second copy of the arm on the page.

FreeHand will paste the duplicate arm on the page in the center of your screen.

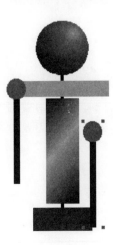

You now need to move the duplicate arm into position.

8] Use the pointer to move the second arm into position on the other shoulder Then select both arm groups and use the Align panel to align both arms vertically.
In the Align panel, select Top from the Vertical Alignment menu, select No Change from the Horizontal Alignment menu, and turn off Align to Page. Choose Edit > Undo if something goes wrong.

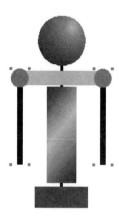

9] Repeat steps 1 through 3 to create one leg by drawing a circle and a line. Fill the circle with any fill and set the stroke of the line to 8 points.
You will add a foot in the next task before duplicating this leg.

10] Save your work.

CUSTOMIZING TOOL SETTINGS

The robot's feet are rounded rectangles, which you can draw after making an adjustment to the way the Rectangle tool works. Notice that the Rectangle tool in the toolbox is one of several tools that has a small mark in the upper-right corner. This mark indicates that preferences can be set for this tool. Double-clicking these tools displays a dialog box where you can change the settings.

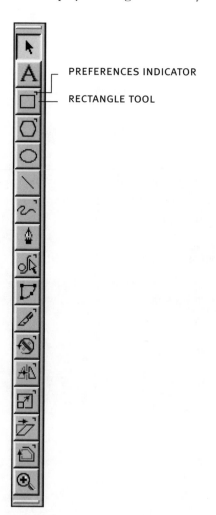

PREFERENCES INDICATOR

RECTANGLE TOOL

1] Double-click the Rectangle tool in the toolbox.

A dialog box appears where you can specify a radius for rounded corners. By default, the Rectangle tool uses a radius of zero, which draws rectangles with sharp, right-angle corners and no rounding.

2] Set the radius to 9 points by typing *9pt* in the radius field. Then click OK.

The radius value determines how rounded the corners of your rectangle will be. A radius value of zero creates rectangles with angled corners; increasing the value creates larger curves at each corner of the rectangle. If you specify a value greater than half the length of any of the sides of your rectangle, those entire sides will be curved.

Dragging the slider in this dialog box also enables you to adjust this radius value. Since the unit of measure for this document is set to inches, the radius values are displayed in inches rather than points if you drag the slider.

3] Draw a small rounded rectangle at the bottom of the robot's leg. Fill it with any tint of black and remove the stroke.

Notice the rounded corners on the rectangle. Reposition the foot as needed with the Pointer tool.

54

4] Complete the leg by selecting all three pieces and grouping them together with Modify > Group.

Remember that you can select several elements at the same time by holding down the Shift key.

5] Save your work.

The robot is nearly complete.

CREATING A MIRROR IMAGE OF AN ELEMENT

Duplicating the leg is a bit more challenging than duplicating the arm because the new leg must face the opposite direction. You will use the Mirror tool, which is one of FreeHand's **Xtra** tools. Xtras are plug-in software extensions that enhance FreeHand's capabilities. Some Xtras are provided with FreeHand, but you can purchase many others from third parties. (Go to www.macromedia.com/software/xtras/ for more details.) Each Xtra adds a specific feature or group of features. Xtras providing additional tools are located in the Xtra Tools panel.

1] Choose Window > Xtras > Xtra Tools to display the Xtra Tools panel.

This panel contains additional drawing, manipulation, and special-effect tools.

A wide variety of Xtras are included with FreeHand and are installed when you install the program.

MIRROR TOOL

2] With the grouped leg still selected, click once on the Mirror tool in the Xtra Tools panel.

By default, this tool will create a mirror image of a selected object.

3] Position the cursor on the spine of the robot and then click the mouse.

A mirrored duplicate is positioned on the other side of the body, so your robot now has two legs.

Clicking the spine with the Mirror tool sets a vertical reflection axis at that point. This reflection axis works like a mirror, reflecting a selected item an equal distance on the opposite side of the axis.

56

tip   *The robot's spine is in the exact center of the figure. Clicking the Mirror tool on this center line ensures that the new leg is the same distance from the spine as the old leg.*

ROTATING AN ELEMENT ON THE PAGE

The robot is so happy to have all of its parts—now help it kick up its heels.

1] With the Pointer tool, double-click the new leg.

A new set of **transform** handles appears around the selected item, and the center of transformation appears as a hollow circle in the center of these transform handles. Double-clicking an element in the workspace enables you to rotate, scale, and transform elements without having to switch to the specific transformation tools. As you rotate this element, it will revolve around the center of transformation.

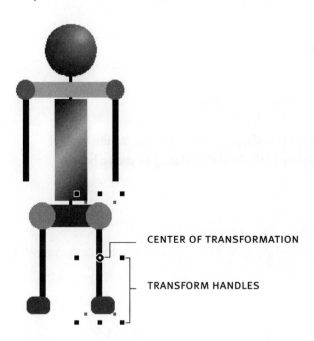

CENTER OF TRANSFORMATION

TRANSFORM HANDLES

2] Move the center of transformation by dragging the hollow circle in the center of the transformation handles to visually center the hollow circle on the circle at the top of the leg.

Next you will rotate the leg around this center point.

3] Position the mouse outside the transform handles surrounding the leg and drag out to the right and up slightly until the leg is rotated as shown here.

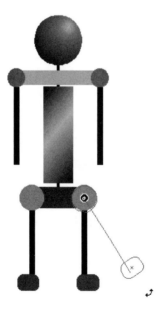

As you move the mouse over and around the control handles, the cursor will give you feedback to indicate what type of transformations you can apply, such as the rotation you applied to this element.

4] Double-click the leg again to hide the transform handles.

You can access these transform handles at any time by double-clicking an object or group on the page. When the transformation is complete, double-click the object again to hide the controls.

FreeHand also offers tools to perform specific transformations, including the Rotate, Reflect, Scale, and Skew tools in the toolbox, which you will explore in upcoming lessons.

The last step in creating this robot is to group all of its pieces together so they can't accidentally be disturbed.

5] Choose Edit › Select › All. Then choose Modify › Group or click the Group button on the main toolbar. Save your document.

Congratulations. You have just created your first piece of original art with FreeHand.

GETTING HELP

There will be times when you just cannot remember a specific technique and need a quick and easy resource for more information. In addition to the manuals that come with the application, FreeHand offers an online help system for quick reference while you're working. For assistance in FreeHand, choose Help > FreeHand Help. A map of FreeHand's help system appears, providing you with point-and-click navigation to help you find the answers you need.

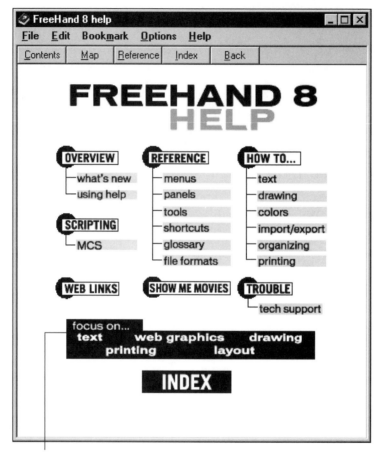

FOCUS ON TOPICS

Experiment with the help system by looking up some topics in the help index or searching for help on a particular command or feature. Explore the Focus On topics, which present easy access to information on five dynamic focus areas within FreeHand: text, web graphics, drawing, printing, and layout.

The help system offers several additional features designed to help you get the most out of FreeHand. These include movie clips demonstrating hard-to-describe features and Tell Me How guides that provide step-by-step information on how to perform specific tasks. Take a look at these features—they're like having an instructor inside your computer.

If you have an Internet connection and a Web Browser, you can find up-to-the-minute technical information at the Macromedia Web site (http://www.macromedia.com/support).

ON YOUR OWN

Create a companion for your robot using techniques you have learned in this lesson. Move the existing robot to one side of the page or onto the pasteboard to make room for the companion. You can create your own robot, or open a sample document and re-create the companion robot to match the sample. To see this example, choose File > Open and open Robot2.fh8 in the Complete folder within the Lesson1 folder.

WHAT YOU HAVE LEARNED

In this lesson you have:

- Opened FreeHand and created a new document [*page* **8**]
- Been introduced to FreeHand's tools, toolbars, and panels [*page* **10**]
- Customized application and tool preferences [*page* **14**]
- Duplicated elements with the Copy and Paste commands [*page* **26**]
- Created basic shapes with the Rectangle, Ellipse, and Line tools [*page* **31**]
- Applied basic and graduated fills and adjusted stroke width [*page* **36**]
- Aligned and grouped elements together [*page* **47**]
- Aligned elements to the page [*page* **47**]
- Used one of FreeHand's Xtra tools to create a mirror image of a selection [*page* **55**]
- Rotated a selection by double-clicking it to access the transform handles [*page* **57**]

and graphics

combining text

LESSON 2

The basic drawing tools you used in the last lesson are good for more than drawing playful robots. In this lesson, you will use the same tools, along with FreeHand's text tool, to create a graphic identity for a corporate letterhead. You will use the same basic shape tools you worked with in Lesson 1: the Rectangle, Ellipse, and Line tools. Here you will combine the elements in new ways, apply color for fills and strokes, and add text to create the completed design.

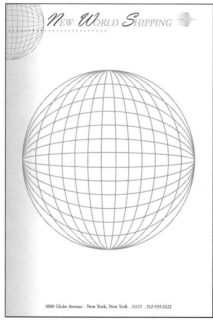

This corporate letterhead was created from scratch using FreeHand's drawing and text tools.

Designed by Julia Sifers of Glasgow & Associates.

If you would like to review the final result of this lesson, open World.fh8 in the Complete folder within the Lesson2 folder.

WHAT YOU WILL LEARN

In this lesson you will:

- Set a custom page size

- Specify measurement units

- Create and combine more basic shapes

- Change the appearance of objects

- Practice rotating elements

- Design the layout for printing with two ink colors

- Practice aligning and grouping elements

- Enter and format text

- Import a FreeHand graphic created elsewhere

APPROXIMATE TIME

It usually takes about 1 hour and 30 minutes to complete this lesson.

LESSON FILES

Media Files:

Lesson2\Media\Plane.fh8

Starting Files:

None

Completed Project:

Lesson2\Complete\World.fh8

CREATING A NEW DOCUMENT WITH A CUSTOM PAGE SIZE

In this lesson, you will design the letterhead for New World Shipping. You will create this letterhead for an Executive-size page, which measures 7.25 by 10.5 inches. Your first task is to create a page with these dimensions.

1] Choose File > New to create a new document (Windows Ctrl+N, Macintosh Command+N).

A new document window will appear containing one page on the pasteboard.

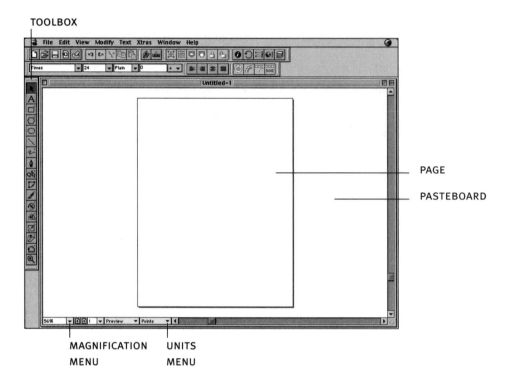

2] Change the unit of measure for this document to Inches using the Units menu at the bottom of the document window.

This menu defines the unit of measure used throughout the document (except for the type size, which is always measured in points).

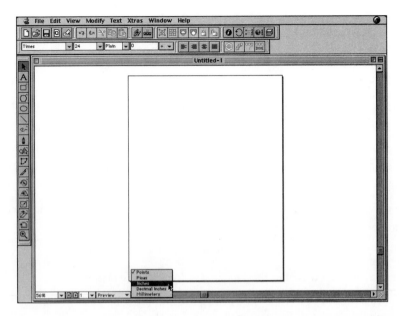

The only visible indication that the units have changed is that the Units menu now displays Inches instead of Points.

3] Choose Window › Inspectors › Document to display the Document Inspector.

The Document Inspector contains controls that enable you to change the size, orientation, and number of pages within your document.

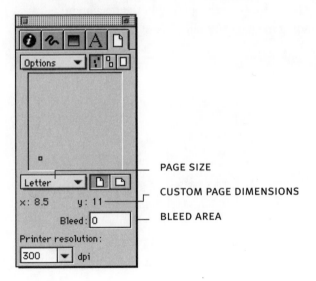

PAGE SIZE

CUSTOM PAGE DIMENSIONS

BLEED AREA

65

4] Use the Page Size menu in the Document Inspector to change from Letter to Custom.

You will now be able to edit the page dimensions to change the page size to match the size of an Executive page.

You will also need to specify the **bleed** area, the amount of space that elements will print beyond the edges of the layout. On a printing press, layouts that require color extending to the edge of the page must be printed on larger sheets of paper than the document requires, and the color must extend beyond the boundaries of the layout. Then when the paper sheets are cut to the correct page size, the color will extend beyond the cut—even if the paper shifts a bit on the press so the ink is not placed exactly in the same position on each sheet, there will be no strips of paper color showing at the edge of the page where the ink did not reach.

You can set the size of the bleed area in the Document Inspector, which defines the distance around the page that FreeHand will print. The default value is zero, which means nothing beyond the edge of the page will print. Your letterhead includes elements that extend to the edge of the layout, so you need to specify a bleed area.

5] Select the value in the *x* field and type a new width of *7.25*. Press the Tab key to highlight the *y* field and type a height of *10.5*. Press Tab again to highlight the Bleed field and type a value of *0.125* inch. Press Enter to apply these changes.

This will change the page to the size of an Executive page and give the document a bleed area of one-eighth inch all around. (One-eighth inch is the standard bleed size used by most printers.) The new page size is now displayed in the document window. The dotted line surrounding the page indicates the bleed area.

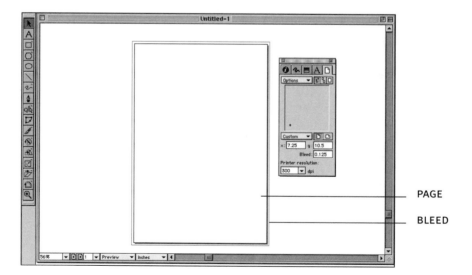

PAGE

BLEED

6] Close the Document Inspector. Save your document as *MyWorld* in your MyWork folder on your hard drive.

The page is now ready for you to begin creating the artwork.

CREATING AND POSITIONING A RECTANGLE

In the previous lesson, you adjusted the size and position of selected elements directly using the Pointer tool. FreeHand also offers you precise control over the size and position of elements with the Object Inspector. In this task, you will create a rectangle running along the left edge of the page from top to bottom. This will eventually contain the yellow gradient fill that bleeds off the left of the page.

You will start by creating a rectangle somewhere on the page and then adjust the size and position numerically.

1] Select the Rectangle tool and draw a small rectangle of any size anywhere on the page.

When you are finished with the Rectangle tool, the rectangle you drew will be selected. With the rectangle selected, you can enter specific width, height, and position values using the Object Inspector.

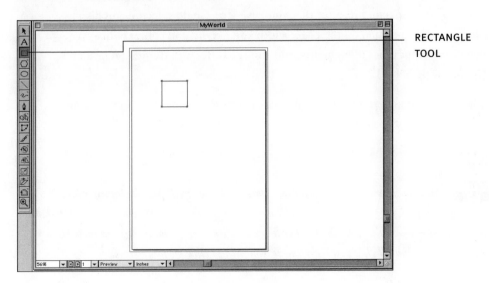

RECTANGLE TOOL

67

What should you do if the rectangle you create has rounded corners? This could happen if Changing Objects Changes Defaults is turned on in the Object Editing Preferences dialog box (under File > Preferences). If that happens, choose Edit > Undo and then double-click the Rectangle tool to set the corner radius to zero.

tip *Any time a tool does not behave as you expected and the wrong element is created, remember to use the Undo command by clicking the Undo button on the main toolbar, by choosing Edit > Undo, or by using the keyboard shortcut (Windows Ctrl+Z, Macintosh Command+Z).*

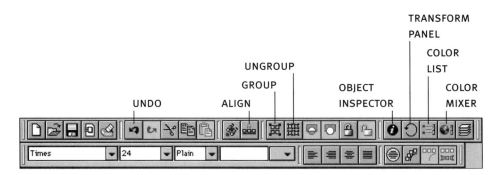

2] Choose Window › Inspectors › Object to display the Object Inspector.

The Object Inspector indicates that you have a rectangle selected and displays the rectangle's position on the page, width and height, and corner radius. When you select other types of elements, you will see different information in the Object Inspector.

The measurements shown in the Object Inspector are in inches because you changed the unit of measure for this document to inches.

These values will change as you move or resize the rectangle.

tip *An element must be selected for the Object Inspector to display its information. If nothing is selected, the Object Inspector will not display any values. To select an object, point to a solid part of that object with the Pointer tool and click. For example, this rectangle has a black stroke but no fill. To select this element, you need to click the black stroke.*

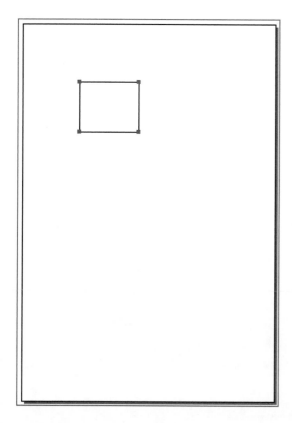
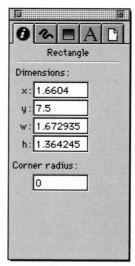

3] Select the Pointer tool from the toolbox. Position the tip of your cursor along a side of the rectangle, hold down the mouse button, and drag the shape to the bottom center of the page.

Notice that the values for *x* and *y* have changed. These indicate the distance from the zero point (which by default is at the lower-left corner of the page) to the lower-left corner of the rectangle. The *x* value is the distance from the zero point to the left edge of the rectangle, and the *y* value is the distance from the zero point to the bottom of the rectangle.

Notice that the *w* and *h* values did not change; you changed only the position of the rectangle, not its size.

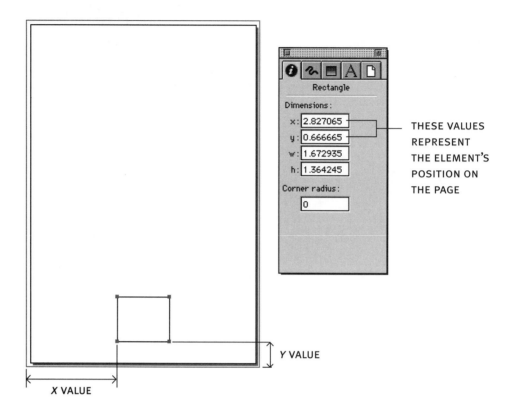

THESE VALUES REPRESENT THE ELEMENT'S POSITION ON THE PAGE

4] Watch the *x* and *y* values in the Object Inspector as you choose Edit › Undo to return the rectangle to its previous position.

You can use the Undo and Redo commands when you make a mistake or simply to compare before and after views.

5] Position the Pointer tool on the top-right corner selection box and drag the mouse upward and to the right about an inch to make the rectangle larger.

The width (*w*) and height (*h*) values increase as you make the rectangle larger. The position values did not change because you did not change the position of the bottom-left corner of the rectangle (the point on the rectangle from which FreeHand measures).

The corner radius is the value you specified to create a rectangle with rounded corners for the foot of the robot in the previous lesson. For this layout, you can leave this value set to zero to create sharp corners on your rectangle, not rounded ones.

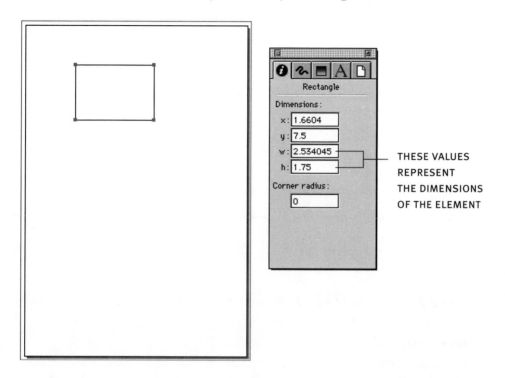

THESE VALUES REPRESENT THE DIMENSIONS OF THE ELEMENT

Now you are ready to move this rectangle to the desired position in the letterhead layout. This box will be filled with the yellow gradient and should extend (bleed) off the left side, top, and bottom of the page. You will start by precisely positioning the rectangle with the Object Inspector.

6] Select the value for *x* in the Object Inspector. Change this value by typing a negative value, –*.125*, and pressing Enter.
Enter a negative value by typing a minus sign before the number. This negative value moves the box beyond the left edge of the page. It now extends off the page and aligns with the bleed area you defined for this document.

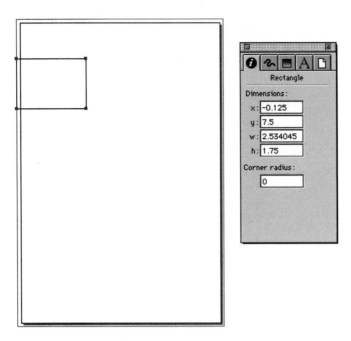

7] Select the *y* value and type *–.125*. Press the Tab key to select the width and type *1.625*. Press Tab again to select the height and type *10.75*. Press Enter to apply these values.

The rectangle now extends off the top and bottom edges of the page, as well as off the left edge. The rectangle has a width of 1.5 inches plus the left bleed of 0.125 inch, and it has a height of 10.5 inches plus the top bleed of 0.125 inch and the bottom bleed of 0.125 inch.

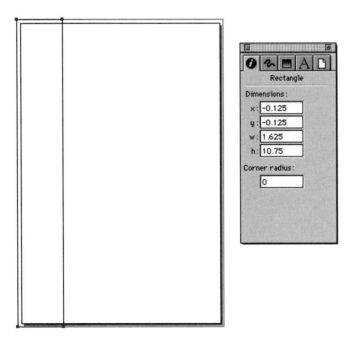

72

8] Save your work.

> **tip** *As you work, you may need to open and close panels, depending upon the size of your monitor. If the following instructions call for you to open a panel you already have displayed on your screen, you will not need to issue the command to open it again. You may also use the buttons on the main toolbar to open and close panels instead of choosing commands from the Window menu.*

CREATING AND ALIGNING ELLIPSES

Although it looks complex, the globe on the letterhead will not be difficult to create. You will start by creating two ellipses and aligning them so that one is centered over the other. To ensure consistent results, you will precisely size each of the ellipses using the Object Inspector.

1] Select the Ellipse tool in the toolbox. Position the cursor anywhere on the page, hold down the mouse button, and drag in a diagonal direction to draw any size of ellipse. Use the Object Inspector to change this ellipse into a perfect circle 6 inches across by changing the width value to *6* and the height value to *6*. Then press Enter.

Your first ellipse is a perfect circle 6 inches in diameter.

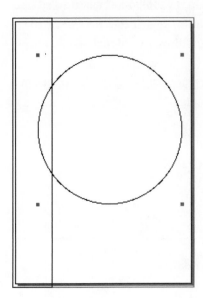
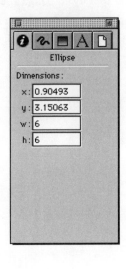

2] Draw a second ellipse with the Ellipse tool anywhere on the page. In the Object Inspector, change the width value to *0.5* and the height value to *6*.

These two ellipses are the elements you need to create the globe graphic.

73

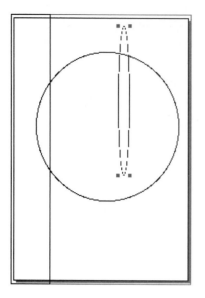

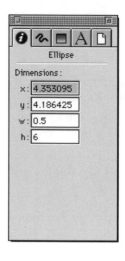

Next you will select both ellipses at once so you can use the Align panel to center one over the other.

3] Change to the Pointer tool by clicking that tool in the toolbox. The narrow ellipse may already be selected. If not, click once on its outline to select it. Hold down the Shift key and click once on the outline of the larger ellipse to add that element to the selection.

Both of the ellipses are selected at the same time. The Shift key enables you to add elements to a selection without deselecting a previous selection.

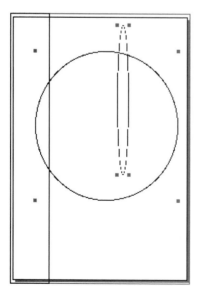

74

4] Choose Modify › Align to display the Align panel. Click the center of the preview grid to set both vertical and horizontal alignment to Align Center. Be sure Align to Page is checked. Then click Align.

The ellipses are now centered on one another and centered on the page. Clicking any part of the Align panel's preview grid enables you to specify alignment options, just as you can using the Vertical and Horizontal Alignment menus in the Align panel. In this example, clicking the center of the grid sets both vertical and horizontal alignment to Align Center.

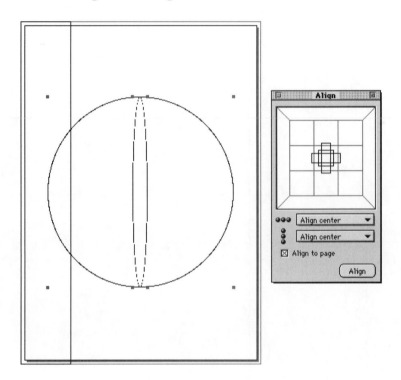

5] Save your work.

Next you will have FreeHand blend these two shapes together.

COMBINING PATHS WITH THE BLEND COMMAND

FreeHand graphics are made up of **paths**. A path is simply a line containing at least two **points**. Paths can be curved or straight, open or closed. An element created with a basic shape tool (a rectangle or ellipse) is actually a **grouped path** (a path grouped by itself). In this task, you will learn how to create a **blend** between individual paths that creates intermediate steps between the original paths. You will use that feature to automatically create the new paths that will form the latitude and longitude lines of the globe.

The Blend feature in FreeHand combines paths by creating intermediate shapes—paths that fit between the original paths to create a transition with respect to shape, stroke, and fill. You will now create a blend between the small ellipse and large ellipse.

1] Both ellipses should still be selected. (If they are not selected, click one with the Pointer tool and then hold down Shift and click the other one.) Choose Modify ›Ungroup to see the points and paths that make up these elements.

You can now see that each of these elements is made up of four points. (The top and bottom points of each path are directly on top of one another.) To create a blend between the two paths, you first will select the top point on each path.

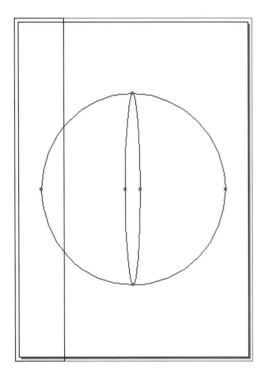

2] Using the Pointer tool, position the cursor above and to the left of the point visible at the top of the paths. (Make sure that you are not pointing to any other object, such as the rectangle, because you do not want to move or change another element on the page.) Hold down the mouse button and drag downward and to the right until the dotted rectangle surrounds the top point. Then release the mouse button.

The dotted rectangle is called the **selection marquee**. It should surround only the topmost point on each path.

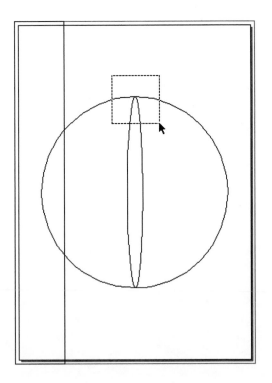

When you release the mouse button, the top point appears as an outlined box, indicating that the point is selected. That point, and the points to its right and left along the path, have sprouted handles. You will learn what those are for in the next lesson.

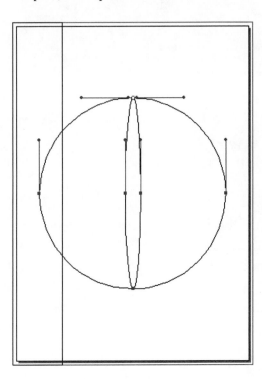

3] Choose Modify › Combine › Blend.

FreeHand creates intermediate paths between the two original ones. However, there are many more paths than you want for this graphic.

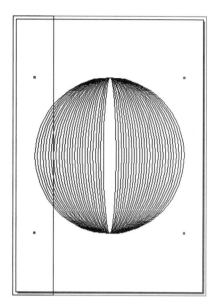

4] Choose Window › Inspectors › Object to display the Object Inspector. Change the number of steps in this blend to *5* and press Enter to apply the change.

Blends create a transition between two or more paths with respect to shape, stroke, and fill. The number of steps determines the number of intermediate paths. All of the paths in the blend are also automatically grouped together.

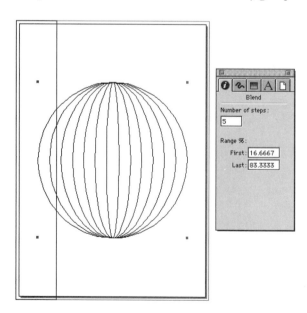

5] Save your work.

PRECISELY ROTATING A COPY

You have created the longitude lines for the globe. Now you need to add the latitude lines. To add these lines and complete the globe, you will make a duplicate of the blend directly on top of the original and precisely rotate it 90 degrees around its center to position it at a right angle to the original.

Your first step will be to **clone** the blend. Cloning creates a duplicate of the selected object directly in front of the original object. (It's like copy and paste, but it always positions the new copy directly in front of the original selection.)

1] Select the blend and then choose Edit › Clone.

A copy of the object, now selected, is placed precisely on top of the original.

2] Double-click the Rotate tool in the toolbox to display the Transform panel, which contains the rotation controls.

You will use the Transform panel to precisely rotate the clone. (You can also select the Transform panel by choosing Window > Panels > Transform.)

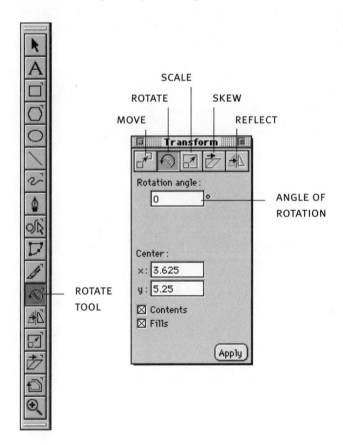

79

3] Type *90* in the Rotation Angle field and click Rotate (Windows) or Apply (Macintosh).

By default, the Transform panel rotates the selected element around its center, so this clone is rotated into a horizontal position. (In Lesson 4 you will define a different center of rotation using the Transform panel.) Positive values rotate the selection counterclockwise; negative values rotate the selection clockwise.

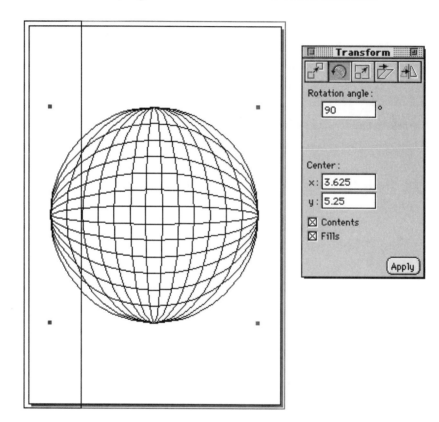

Now you need to group the two blends together.

4] Close the Transform panel and change back to the Pointer tool. Then choose Edit > Select > All.

This selects everything on the page, including the rectangle, which you do not want to group with the globe.

80

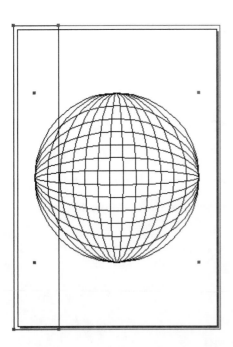

5] Hold down the Shift key and click the edge of the rectangle to deselect that element.

Earlier you held down Shift to add elements to a selection. Holding down Shift also deselects selected elements without deselecting any other elements.

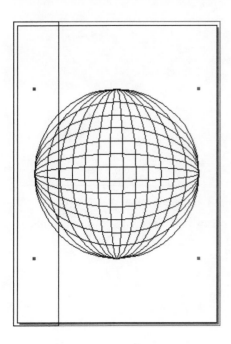

6] Choose Modify › Group to tie the globe components together.

The globe graphic is complete.

7] Save your work.

IMPORTING AND CREATING COLORS AND TINTS

You will use two additional colors and tints of those colors in your layout. You will add these colors to the Color List.

1] Choose Window › Panels › Color List (or click the Color List button on the main toolbar) to display the Color List.

This panel displays the named colors currently available for this document. You need to add two colors to this list.

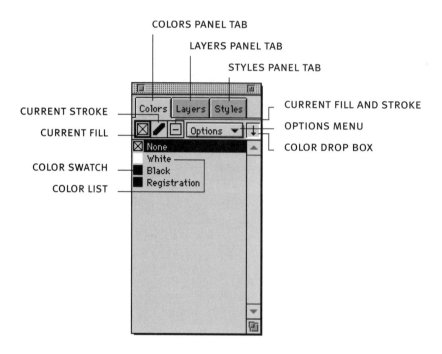

For projects that will be printed on a printing press, there are several industry-standard color selection systems for which printed swatch books of actual ink colors are available to help you choose colors accurately.

2] Select PANTONE® Coated from the Options menu at the top of the Color List.

This opens a color library containing the colors in the PANTONE Coated color-matching system. These colors are each identified by a unique number that corresponds with a number in the PANTONE Coated printed swatch book and a color of PANTONE ink.

FreeHand allows you to choose colors from PANTONE Coated and PANTONE Uncoated color libraries by using the Color List Options menu. The Uncoated color library shows the colors printed on standard (uncoated) paper. The Coated color library shows the same colors printed on coated paper, which has a thin coating of clay that has been polished to create a very smooth surface. Colors generally appear more brilliant on coated paper because the ink is not absorbed by the paper the way it is by uncoated paper. If you don't know what kind of paper your artwork will be printed on, your printer can advise you. For this lesson, it will not make any difference which of these two systems you choose.

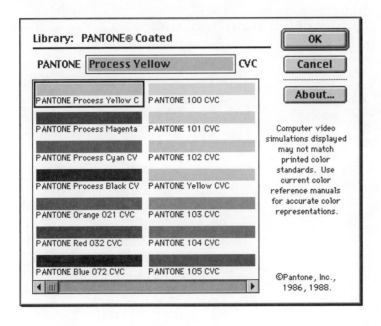

3] Type *135* to select PANTONE 135 and then click OK.

The golden color, PANTONE 135 CVC, is added to the color list.

4] Select PANTONE Coated from the Options menu again and add PANTONE 285 to the color list.

The blue color, PANTONE 285 CVC, is added to the color list. You now have two PANTONE colors in the list.

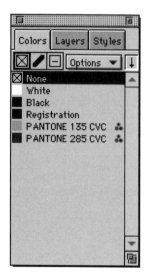

84

5] Display the Tints panel by clicking the Color Mixer button on the main toolbar and clicking the Tints tab at the top of the panel group.

A tint is a lighter shade of a color expressed as a percentage of that color. The Tints panel displays a range of tints for the base color in 10 percent increments as well as a custom adjustment for creating tints at other values. You will use this panel to create a tint of each of the PANTONE colors in your document.

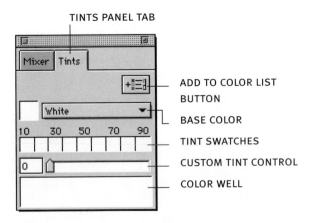

TINTS PANEL TAB

ADD TO COLOR LIST BUTTON

BASE COLOR

TINT SWATCHES

CUSTOM TINT CONTROL

COLOR WELL

6] Drag the color swatch next to PANTONE 135 in the Color List and drop it on the base color swatch at the top of the Tints panel.

Tints for that color now appear in the panel.

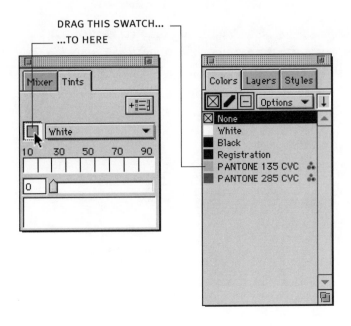

DRAG THIS SWATCH...

...TO HERE

7] Drag the 40 percent tint swatch from the Tints panel and drop it on the color drop box at the top of the Color List.

Dropping a swatch on the **color drop box** adds that color or tint to the Color List. You could also drop the swatch on an open spot in the color list, but be careful not to drop it on another color swatch or you will change that color to this tint.

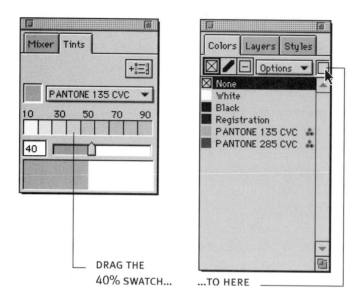

DRAG THE
40% SWATCH...   ...TO HERE

The tint will be added to the Color List with the name 40% PANTONE 135.

8] Use the Base Color menu at the top of the tint controls to select PANTONE 285. Drag the Custom Tint Control slider to the right until the value 15 appears in the field just to the left of the slider. Click the Add to Color List button at the top of the tints panel and then click OK to accept the default name for this color.

The Color List will now have the colors and tints needed for this lesson.

ADD TO COLOR LIST BUTTON

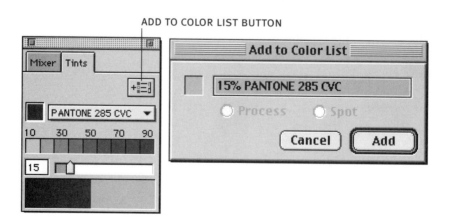

9] Close the Tints panel. Save your work.

You just added the two colors and tints that will be used for the elements of this document.

APPLYING FILLS AND STROKES

Now that the colors you need are in the Color List, you will use the Fill and Stroke Inspectors to apply those colors to the elements on your page.

1] Select the rectangle on the page with the Pointer tool. Display the Fill Inspector by choosing Window › Inspectors › Fill. Using the Fill Type menu at the top of the Inspector, choose Gradient as the type of fill for this element.

The rectangle is now filled with a gradient.

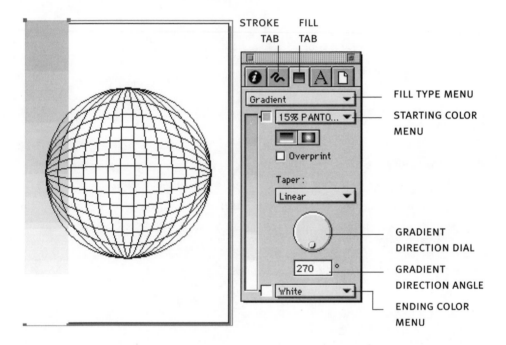

2] Drag the swatch for 40% PANTONE 135 from the Color List and drop it on the swatch at the top of the Fill Inspector. Change the gradient direction angle to *0* degrees and press Enter to complete the fill.

The bottom color in the Fill Inspector is White. The direction of the gradient is 0 degrees, which results in a gradient fill that goes from 40% PANTONE 135 on the left to White on the right.

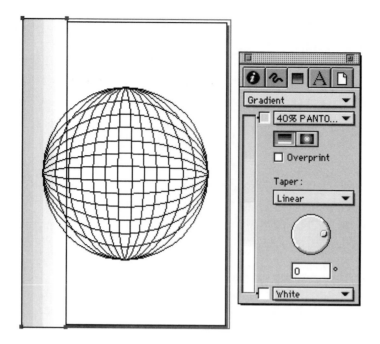

The rectangle would look better if there were no line around it.

3] Click the Stroke tab at the top of the Inspector panel group to display the Stroke Inspector. Change the option on the Stroke Type menu to None.

The stroke is removed, and the rectangle is finished.

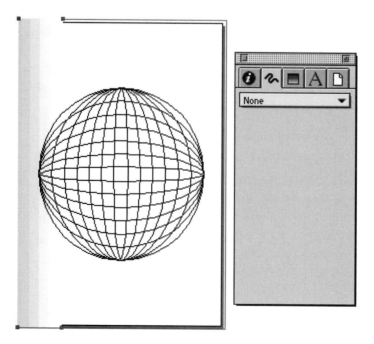

88

Now change the color and stroke of the globe.

4] Select the grouped globe by clicking it with the Pointer tool. Make sure that the option on the Stroke Type menu is set to Basic. Use the Stroke Color menu to select 15% PANTONE 285. Then change the stroke width by selecting 2 pt from the Width menu.

The globe now has a 2-point stroke of 15% PANTONE 285. Because the units for this document are set to inches, the stroke width of 2 points is shown as 0.02778 inch in the Stroke Inspector.

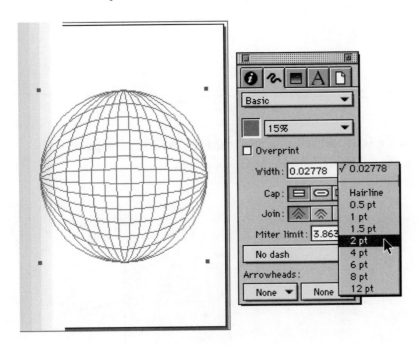

5] Close the Color List and Stroke Inspector for now. Save your work.

CLONING, SCALING, AND POSITIONING ELEMENTS

In this task, you will create a second globe on the page that is 40 percent of the original globe's size. Creating this smaller version is easy with the Transform panel. You will then position this smaller globe in the upper-left corner of the layout.

1] Select the globe and choose Edit › Clone.

This creates a duplicate globe directly on top of the original. The duplicate remains selected.

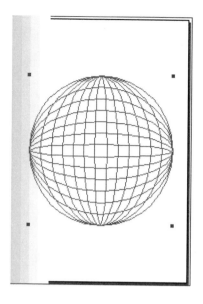

2] Double-click the Scale tool in the toolbox to display the Transform panel.

The Transform panel is displayed with the scale controls.

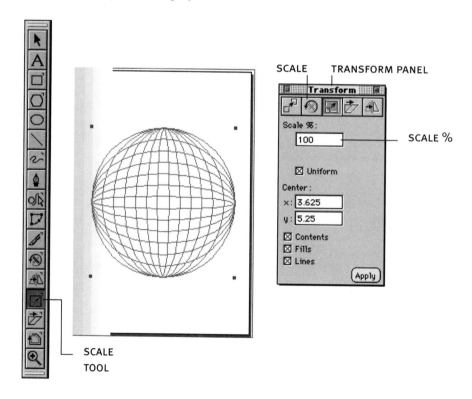

SCALE   TRANSFORM PANEL

SCALE %

SCALE
TOOL

3] Type *40* in the Scale % field and click Scale (Windows) or Apply (Macintosh).

The copy of the globe is reduced to 40 percent of its original size.

If the Uniform box is checked, when you scale an object, it keeps its proportions. If you turn uniform scaling off, you can scale the *x* and *y* values at different percentages, distorting the proportions as you scale the object. In this task, you want uniform scaling turned on.

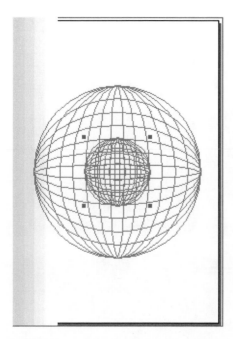
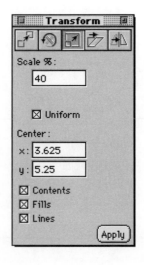

4] Close the Transform panel. Using the Pointer tool, move the smaller globe so that it extends off the top and left edges of the page.

Position the artwork similar to the example shown here. This artwork extends beyond the bleed area, but FreeHand will print only the portion that appears within the bleed area defined by the dotted line that surrounds the page.

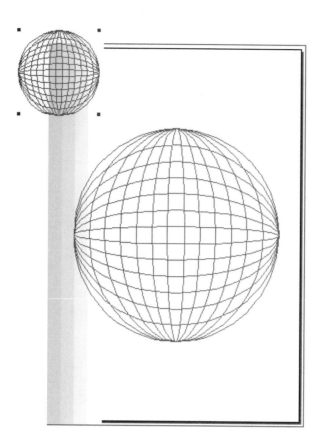

5] Save your work.

Now you are ready to add the company name and address.

ADDING TEXT TO THE LAYOUT

FreeHand has a full array of features for entering, editing, and formatting text. In the next several tasks, you will use these features to position text in your layout and set the font and fill. First, of course, you need to enter the text.

1] Select the Text tool from the toolbox and click once at the top of the page to begin a new text block.

You will see a blinking insertion point on your page where text typed on the keyboard will appear. The arrows that appear above the blinking cursor are used to set custom tabs for the type. These tabs provide formatting controls that are not necessary for this lesson.

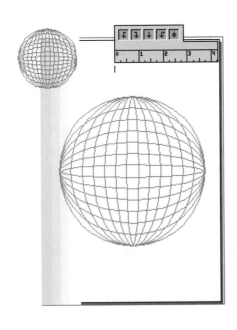

2] Type the company name, *New World Shipping*.

The text block automatically adjusts to the amount of text you enter. Once you start typing text in the text block, the text ruler will also appear. This ruler is needed to set custom tabs.

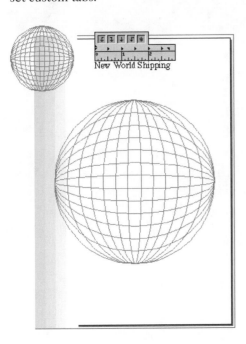

3] Select the Pointer tool and click once on the words you just typed to select the entire block of text.

When the text block is selected with the Pointer tool, you can specify formatting that will apply to all of the text.

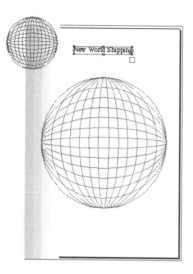

4] Choose View › Magnification › 100% to see the selected text at actual size.

When you change your view using the magnification commands, FreeHand automatically centers the view on the element (or elements) you have selected.

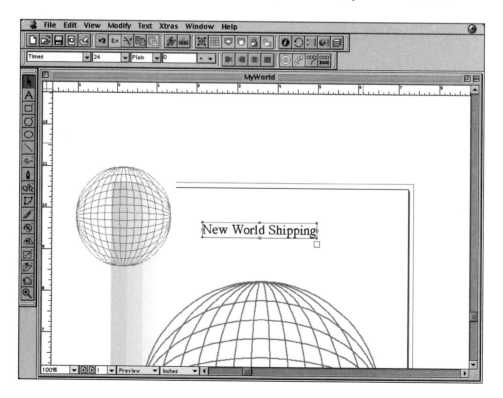

5] Using the controls on the text toolbar near the top of your screen, change the font to URWGaramondTMed, the style to Italic, and the size to 24 points. Choose Text › Convert Case › Upper to change all of the text to uppercase characters.

The URWGaramondTMed font is on the FreeHand 8 software CD-ROM. If you don't have it, you can just use a font you already have installed.

The Convert Case commands enable you to change the capitalization of characters in selected text. The controls for changing the font, size, and style of the text can also be found on the Text menu and in the Text Inspector.

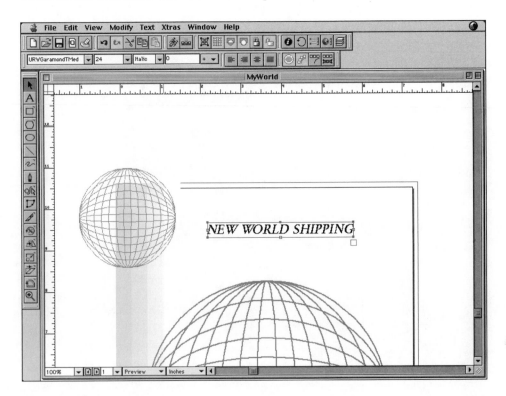

You've entered the basic text. Next you will give it some flair.

6] Save your work.

APPLYING A COLOR FILL TO TEXT

You will now change the black fill of this text to something more subtle, add more text, and position the elements on the layout.

1] Choose Window > Panels > Color List to display the Color List. Change the fill color of the text by dragging the color swatch next to PANTONE 135 in the Color List and dropping it directly on the text.

All of the characters should now be filled with yellow. (By default, text has a stroke of None.) When you change the color of text using the drag-and-drop method, all of the text in the text block will automatically change regardless of what is currently selected or what tool you are using. You will make some additional changes to just a few of these characters next.

 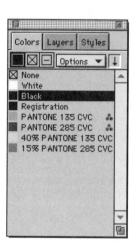

tip *If the background of the text block, rather than the characters, changes to the color you selected, you did not drop the swatch directly on a character, but instead dropped it on the text block background. This is easy to correct: Simply choose Edit > Undo to return to the previous state and then drag the swatch onto the text again. Take care to release the swatch when the tip of the arrow is touching a character of text.*

2] Select the Text tool and click inside the text block to open the block for editing. Highlight the *N* in *NEW* by dragging over it with the Text tool. Change the font to VladimirScrD, the style to Plain, and the size to 48 points using the text toolbar.

This changes only the selected character to the new character formatting.

The VladimirScrD font is on the FreeHand 8 software CD-ROM. If you don't have it, you can just use a font you already have installed.

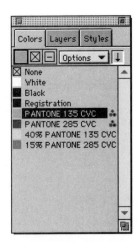

3] Change the fill color of the selected _N_ to PANTONE 285 by dragging the color swatch for that color from the Color List and dropping it onto the selected character.

Dropping a color on a text selection changes the color of the selected text only.

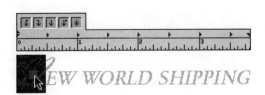

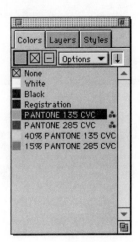

4] Repeat steps 2 and 3 for the _W_ in _WORLD_ and the _S_ in _SHIPPING_. Then click the text block with the Pointer tool and close the Color List.

Your artwork should appear similar to the artwork shown here. Now you are ready to move the text block into position.

5] Display the page rulers by choosing View › Page Rulers (Windows Ctrl+Atl+M, Macintosh Command+Option+M). Choose View › Fit to Page to see the entire page in the document window (Windows Ctrl+Shift+W, Macintosh Command+Shift+W).

The rulers will help you position the elements on the page.

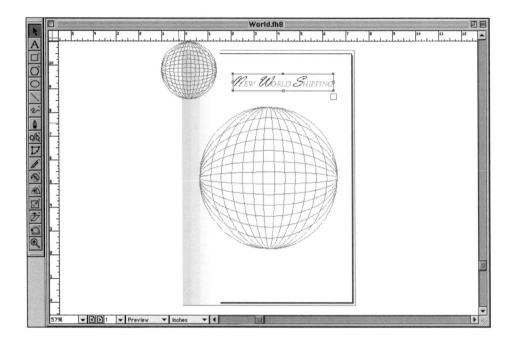

6] Position the Pointer tool on the text, near the middle of the block, and drag the block to visually center the text from left to right on the page approximately one-quarter inch down from the top of the page.

Make sure to move the text block by dragging from the middle of the block. If you were to drag the selection boxes for the text block, you would be resizing, not moving, the block and possibly reformatting the text. As you move, dotted lines in the rulers, corresponding to the edges of the selected objects, will follow the selected element, helping you identify when you are in the correct position. Use this example as a guide to position your text.

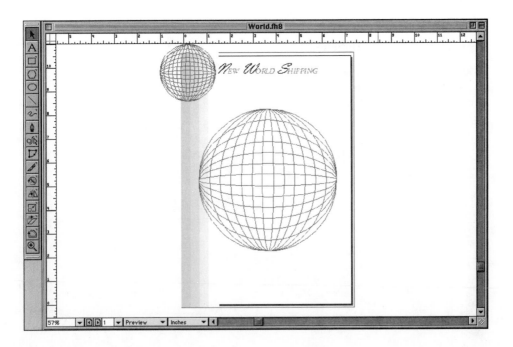

Now add the address line at the bottom of the layout. You'll want this text to be less prominent than the company name.

7] Click the Text tool at the bottom of the page. Change the font to URWGaramondTMed, the style to Plain, and the size to 12 points using the text toolbar controls.

You can change the formatting before or after entering the text. This text block is waiting for the text to be entered.

The URWGaramondTMed font is on the FreeHand 8 software CD-ROM. If you don't have it, you can just use a font you already have installed.

8] Choose View › Magnification › 100% to see the text you are about to type and then type the following address:

1000 Globe Avenue . New York, New York . 11111 . 212-555-2222

Enter a space, a period, and another space between the street, city/state, zip code, and phone number.

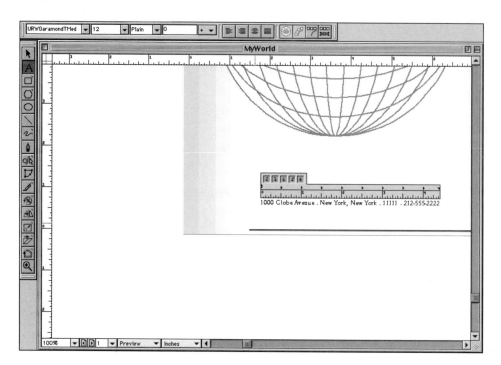

9] Select the text block with the Pointer tool and display the Color List by clicking the Color List button in the toolbar. Change the fill color to PANTONE 285 by dragging the swatch for that color and dropping it on the text on the page. Then close the Color List.

Formatting applied while the text block is selected with the Pointer tool will apply to all characters in the block. Using the Text tool to select text allows you to apply formatting to specific words or characters within the text block.

10] Choose View › Fit to Page to see the entire page. Using the Pointer tool, position the text block so it is visually centered horizontally and approximately one-quarter inch up from the bottom of the page.

Watch the ruler on the left side as you move the text block into position.

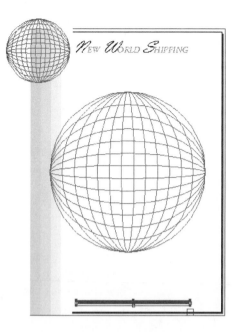

You do not have to rely on visual judgment to position text. FreeHand provides an easier (and more precise) way.

11] Using the Pointer tool, select the text at the top of the page. Hold down the Shift key and click the large globe and then the text at the bottom of the page to select all three elements. Choose Modify › Align to display the Align panel.

Using this panel, you will align these elements to center them horizontally without changing their vertical positions on the page.

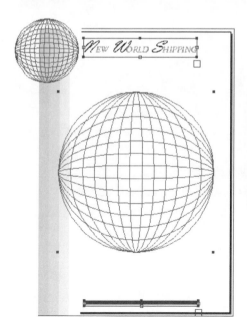

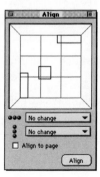

12] On the Horizontal Alignment menu in the Align panel, choose Align Center. The Vertical Alignment menu should be set to No Change. Make sure that Align to Page is turned off. Then click Apply (Windows) or Align (Macintosh).

Your text elements and globe are aligned together.

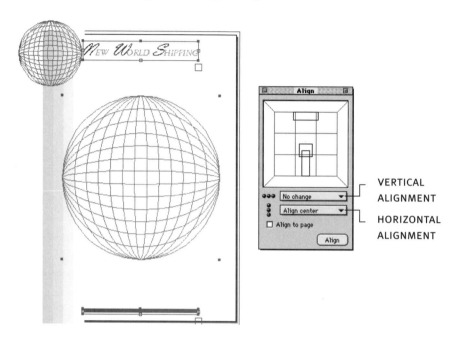

VERTICAL ALIGNMENT

HORIZONTAL ALIGNMENT

tip   *In the Align panel, remember that the Vertical Alignment menu is the top menu and is identified by three spheres that are aligned vertically. The Horizontal Alignment menu is the bottom menu and is identified by three spheres that are aligned horizontally.*

13] Save your work.

IMPORTING A FREEHAND GRAPHIC

To add some visual interest to your letterhead, you will add a small airplane graphic to the layout. The graphic has been created for you in a separate FreeHand document. You will need to import it into the document you are creating.

1] Choose File › Import (Windows Ctrl+R, Macintosh Command+R). Select Plane.fh8 from the Media folder within the Lesson2 folder and click Open.

Your cursor will change to the import cursor, which represents the top-left corner of the graphic.

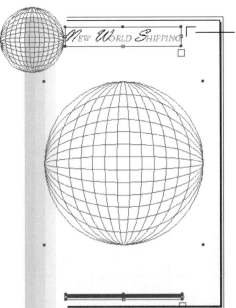

IMPORT CURSOR

2] Position the cursor on the page just to the right of the company name and click the mouse.

The graphic appears on the page in this position.

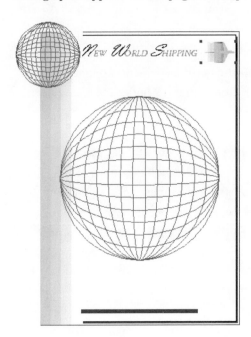

tip *Be careful not to drag the mouse when clicking to position an imported graphic, as this will resize the graphic.*

103

3] Choose View › Magnification › 200%.

This zooms in the view to two times actual size, with the screen centered on the selected graphic.

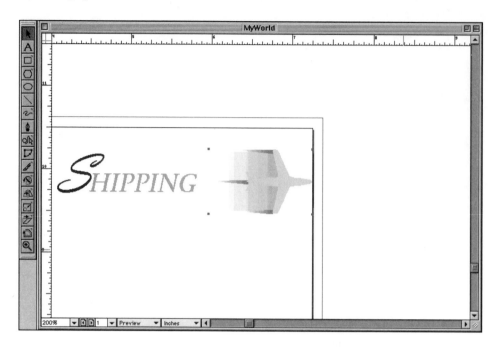

To help position the graphic element so the lower edge is aligned with the baseline of the company name text, you will use a **ruler guide**. Ruler guides are nonprinting lines you can use in your documents to help you position elements accurately. To add a guide with the page rulers active, drag from either the horizontal or vertical page ruler.

4] Pull a ruler guide onto the page by pointing to the horizontal page ruler at the top of the page and dragging the mouse downward. Position this guide at the bottom of the letter *I* in *SHIPPING* and then release the mouse.

If you position a ruler guide in the wrong place, point to the guide and drag it to a new position. (Be careful to point to a spot on the guide away from other elements on the page, so you do not select those elements by mistake.) To remove a guide, drag it off of the page and release the mouse.

This guide is positioned along the **baseline** of the text, the imaginary line on which the characters rest. If this text had uppercase and lowercase characters, the descenders for characters such as *g* and *y* would extend below the baseline.

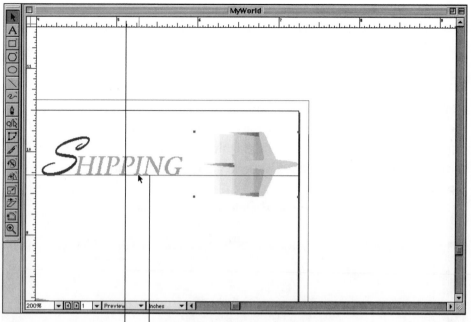

POINT AND CLICK HERE...   ...AND DRAG DOWNWARD TO ADD A GUIDE

5] Using the Pointer tool, move the graphic so the bottom of the airplane rests on the ruler guide and the left edge of the graphic is just to the right of the last character, *G*.

Notice that the cursor displays a small alignment icon when the graphic is snapped to the guide.

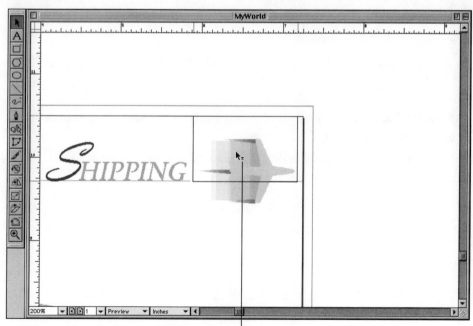

CURSOR DISPLAYS A SMALL ALIGNMENT ICON

105

Now you will make the graphic smaller to more closely match the height of the largest text characters. Because the bottom and left edges of the graphic are positioned correctly, you will want to resize the graphic by dragging the selection box at the upper-right corner of the airplane.

6] Pull a new ruler guide down from the top ruler and position it at the top of the *S* in *SHIPPING*. Using the Pointer tool, hold down the Shift key and drag the top-right selection box of the airplane graphic downward and to the left to make the graphic smaller. Release the mouse when the top of the graphic aligns with the top ruler guide.

Use as many ruler guides as you need while working on your projects.

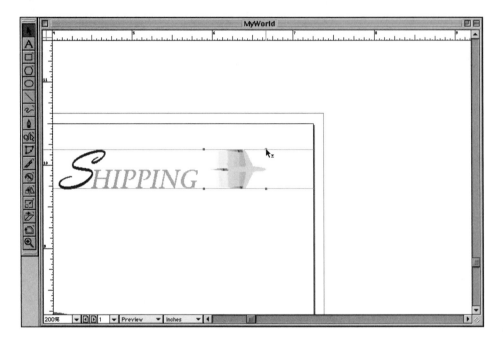

7] Press the Tab key to deselect all of the elements on the page. Then choose View › Fit to Page. Save your work.

You need to add only one more basic element to make your layout complete.

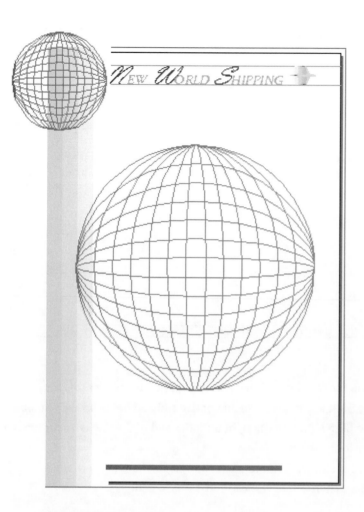

ADDING A DASHED LINE

To make your layout look more dynamic, you will add a dashed line at the top of the page.

1] Using the Zoom tool, click the _N_ in _NEW_ at the top of the page. Then click the _N_ a second time to zoom in closer. Adjust your view so you can see the left edge of the page and the text _New World_.

Clicking the Zoom tool enlarges the view of the page. To zoom out, hold down the Alt (Windows) or Option (Macintosh) key and click with the Zoom tool.

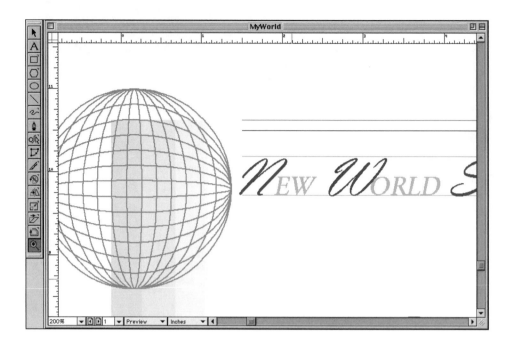

2] Use the Line tool in the toolbox to draw a horizontal line below the company name. Hold down the Shift key to keep the line horizontal and begin on the left side at the left edge of the bleed. Drag to the right until the end of the line is under the *R* in *WORLD*. Then release the mouse.

A solid line appears on the page. Holding down Shift while dragging with the Line tool constrains the line to horizontal, vertical, and 45-degree angles.

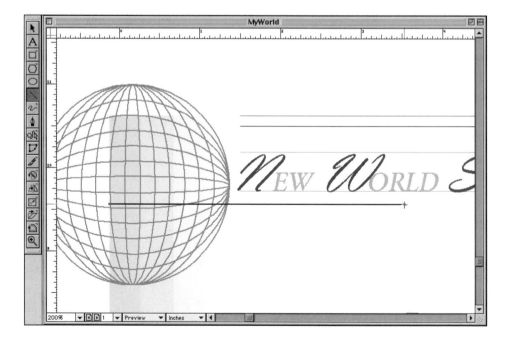

3] Choose Window › Inspector › Stroke to display the Stroke Inspector. Select Basic from the Stroke Type menu and set the color to PANTONE 285 by selecting it from the Stroke Color menu in the upper portion of the Inspector. Change the width to 2 points using the Stroke Width menu.

Because the document's unit of measure is inches, the 2-point stroke width is displayed as 0.02778 inch.

STROKE TYPE MENU

STROKE COLOR MENU

STROKE WIDTH MENU

4] Select the sixth type of dash from the Dash Type menu in the Stroke Inspector.

The line becomes a dashed line.

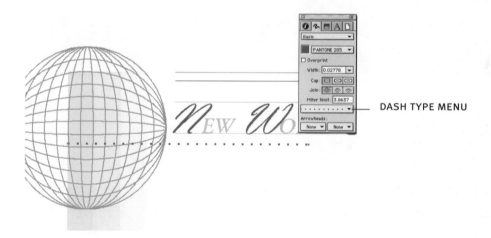

DASH TYPE MENU

109

5] Press the Tab key to deselect all elements and choose View › Fit to Page. Save your work.

Congratulations—the corporate letterhead is complete!

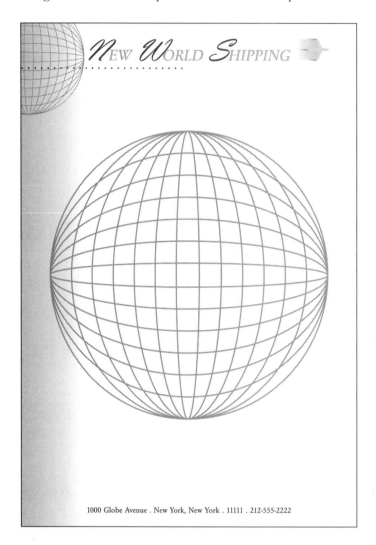

ON YOUR OWN

Create a new document and construct your own personal or business letterhead page. Make it similar to the one you just completed in this lesson or design something new.

Make sure to enter all of your own information, including your name, address, phone number, and e-mail address.

WHAT YOU HAVE LEARNED

In this lesson you have:

- Used the Page Inspector to set a custom page size and a bleed [*page* **64**]

- Changed the measurement units for a document [*page* **64**]

- Practiced creating, modifying, and combining basic shapes [*page* **67**]

- Created shapes with precise dimensions [*page* **73**]

- Created a blend between two shapes [*page* **75**]

- Selected multiple items by dragging a selection area with the Pointer tool [*page* **76**]

- Used the Transform panel to rotate and scale elements [*page* **79**]

- Practiced grouping individual elements together [*page* **80**]

- Used PANTONE colors and tints [*page* **82**]

- Practiced using the Fill Inspector, Stroke Inspector, Tints panel, and Color List panel to apply fills, strokes, and colors [*page* **87**]

- Entered text and changed the font, size, and other text formatting [*page* **92**]

- Practiced using the Align panel to position elements relative to one another [*page* **101**]

- Imported a graphic from another FreeHand document [*page* **102**]

- Used ruler guides to align elements on the page [*page* **104**]

- Created a dotted rule [*page* **107**]

paths and points

working with

LESSON 3

In this lesson you will complete an advertisement that has already been started for the Greenville Zoo. In the process, you will work directly with the points and paths that make up the graphic elements in FreeHand documents.

As you learned in Lesson 2, graphics in FreeHand consist of paths, which are lines defined by points. The span between two points, either straight or curved, is called a **path segment**. As you will see in this lesson, you can manipulate these paths, also

The animal shapes at the bottom of this advertisement were created by tracing patterns with FreeHand's Bezigon tool and then manipulating the resulting paths. Special text effects like the gradient and striped fills used here can be added by turning text outlines into paths. You will learn how to apply these techniques in this lesson.

Designed by Julia Sifers of Glasgow & Associates.

known as **Beziér curves,** to create virtually any shape and to make precise adjustments to those shapes.

In the first part of this lesson, you will experiment with basic shapes and tracing templates to learn how to create and modify paths and points. Then you will apply these new skills by tracing elements that will complete the zoo advertisement.

If you would like to review the final result of this lesson, open Zoo.fh8 in the Complete folder within the Lesson3 folder.

WHAT YOU WILL LEARN

In this lesson you will:

- Manipulate basic shapes
- Create and modify paths to create objects of any shape
- Use existing artwork as tracing templates)
- Copy artwork into different documents
- Create gradient-filled text

APPROXIMATE TIME

It usually takes about 1 hour and 45 minutes to complete this lesson.

LESSON FILES

Media Files:

Lesson3\Media\Howl.ft8 (optional)

Starting Files:

Lesson3\Start\Trace1.ft8

Lesson3\Start\ZooStart.ft8

Lesson3\Start\Wolf.ft8

Lesson3\Start\Angel.ft8

Completed Project:

Lesson3\Complete\Zoo.fh8

MANIPULATING BASIC SHAPES

In this lesson, you will learn how to create and modify paths using the Bezigon and Freeform tools to create all kinds of paths: from prickly shapes with pointed corners to smooth, fluid curves. In Lesson 4, you will learn how to create paths using the Pen tool. Both the Bezigon and Pen tools can be used to create points and paths, and the choice between the two is a personal one. The Bezigon tool is often easier to learn and has the advantage of creating points that automatically adjust the path as you trace. The Pen tool can be used to create the same paths, but it requires you to make every adjustment manually. If you do not have experience using the Pen tool in earlier versions of FreeHand or in other applications, you may find it easier to learn after you are comfortable with the Bezigon tool.

You will start by creating a basic shape. You will then ungroup the paths in this shape and manipulate them in several ways.

1] Create a new document by choosing File › New (Windows Ctrl+N, Macintosh Command+N).

A new document window containing one page will appear.

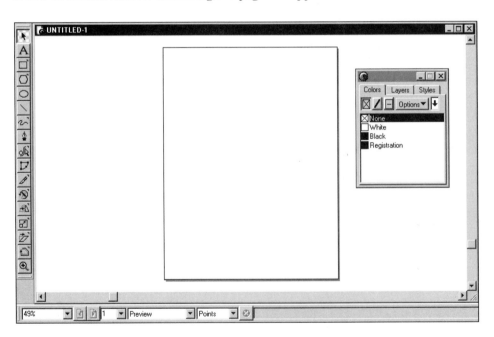

2] Use the Rectangle tool to draw a medium-size rectangle on the page.

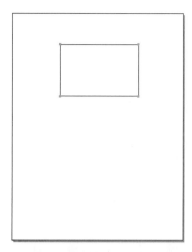

3] Resize the rectangle by dragging a corner handle with the Pointer tool.

The size of the rectangle changes as you drag the handle with the Pointer tool. The basic shapes you create in FreeHand (rectangles, ellipses, and lines) are actually grouped paths. This means that you cannot manipulate the individual points that create these shapes. These grouped paths will continue to behave as basic shapes until they are ungrouped.

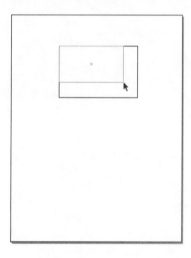

4] With the rectangle still selected, click the Ungroup button on the main toolbar or choose Modify › Ungroup.

Notice that the display changes slightly to show that the path and points are now selected. When a group is selected, the path is not displayed as a selection; only the corner selection handles indicate that this group is selected. You will soon see how differently the ungrouped selection behaves when you manipulate it.

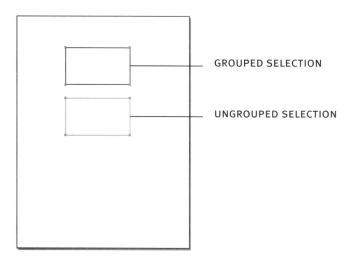

GROUPED SELECTION

UNGROUPED SELECTION

5] With the Pointer tool, drag the bottom-right corner point a short distance to the right.

This time, dragging does not change the size of the rectangle. Instead, it moves that individual point by itself, modifying the path.

In addition to moving the existing points, you can also add new points to this path. You can add a point to the path with either the Bezigon tool or the Pen tool. For this example, you will select the Bezigon tool and click once along the path to add a point.

6] Select the Bezigon tool in the toolbox, position the cursor in the middle of the bottom segment of the selected path, and then click the mouse to add a new point.

A new point will be added to the path where you clicked.

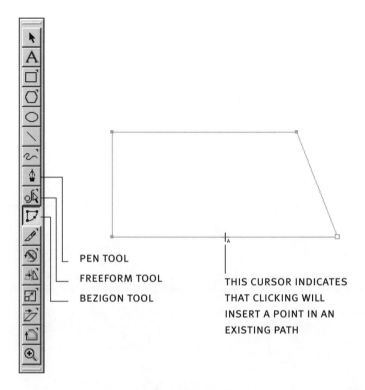

PEN TOOL

FREEFORM TOOL

BEZIGON TOOL

THIS CURSOR INDICATES
THAT CLICKING WILL
INSERT A POINT IN AN
EXISTING PATH

7] Choose the Pointer tool from the toolbox and click once on a segment of the path.

All of the points on this active path are displayed as solid squares. This indicates that these are **corner points** and are not selected. FreeHand uses three different kind of points—**corner points**, **curve points**, and **connector points**—which are used at different places on a path and are displayed in different ways on an active path.

To more simply demonstrate the process of creating paths, these lessons work with only corner and curve points. You can create any type of path using just these two types of points.

CLICK PATH SEGMENT

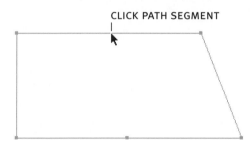

Corner points are represented by squares, and curve points are represented by circles on an active path

8] Use the Pointer tool to move the new corner point up toward the middle of the shape.

After you move the point and release the mouse, the corner point you moved appears as an outlined square, indicating that it remains selected.

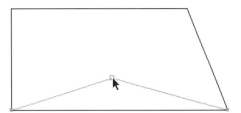

Now you will transform this corner point into a curve point.

9] Display the Object Inspector by choosing Window › Inspectors › Object. Change the selected corner point to a curve point by clicking the Curve Point button in the Object Inspector.

The point now appears as a circle on the path, but the path did not change—yet.

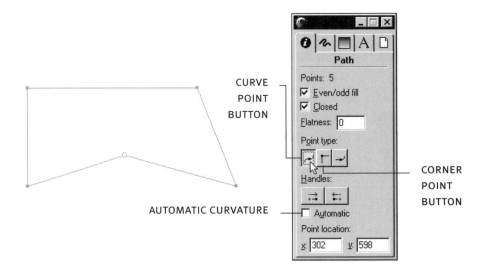

CURVE POINT BUTTON

CORNER POINT BUTTON

AUTOMATIC CURVATURE

10] Click Automatic in the Object Inspector.

The Automatic setting adjusts the path as it passes through this point with respect to the position of the preceding and following points. The path now follows a smooth curve through your curve point, with two **control handles** appearing across the point. Curve points have two control handles that are connected to one another, like a long lever.

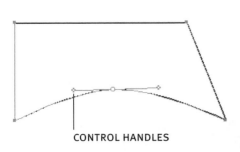

CONTROL HANDLES

Next you will see how to use these control handles to manipulate the shape of the curve.

11] With the Pointer tool, grab the left control handle and pull down, causing the right control handle to go up.

The distance and direction you move the control handle influences the direction of the path as it passes through the selected point. The distance you pull the control handle from the point determines how far the curve extends in that direction.

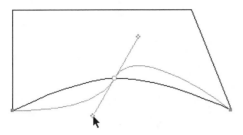

12] To remove the curve point from the path, select the curve point with the Pointer tool and press the Delete key.

To remove any point from a path, simply select the unwanted point with the Pointer tool and press Delete.

119

tip *If your entire path was deleted, simply choose Edit > Undo and make sure that an individual point is selected before pressing the Delete key.*

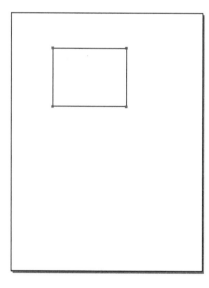

13] Choose File › Close to close the document without quitting FreeHand. Don't save the changes.

Your work here was just for practice; you don't need to save it. If FreeHand asks if you want to save changes to Untitled, click the Don't Save button.

MANIPULATING PATHS WITH THE FREEFORM TOOL

The Freeform tool enables you to modify paths interactively, by directly pushing or pulling the path.

1] Create a new document and draw a rectangle anywhere on the page.

You will now use the Freeform tool to change the shape of this rectangle. The Freeform tool can be used to make adjustments to basic shapes or custom paths.

2] **Choose the Freeform tool from the Toolbox. Position the cursor in the center of the rectangle on the page. Hold down the mouse button, drag the tool slowly against the right side of the rectangle until you have pushed the path segment out approximately one inch, and then release the mouse.**

The rectangle now has a circular bulge on the right side where you pushed the Freeform tool against it.

While the mouse button is held down, the cursor is surrounded by a circle that indicates the size of the Freeform tool. The default mode of the Freeform tool is Push/Pull, which enables you to directly alter path segments by pushing the tool against them.

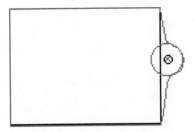

You can change the size of the Freeform tool while you are using it by using the arrow keys on the keyboard.

3] **Again position the Freeform tool cursor in the center of the rectangle. Hold down the mouse button and press the right arrow key to make the tool larger, or press the left arrow key to make the tool smaller. Then use the tool to make the right side of this path circular.**

The right side of the rectangle is now a rounded path.

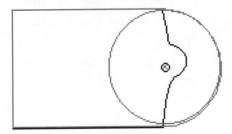

Now you will change the tool preferences and experiment with the Reshape Area operating mode.

4] Double-click the Freeform tool in the toolbox to display the Freeform tool options. Change the Tool Operation mode to Reshape Area and then click OK.

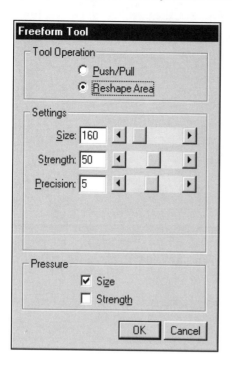

The Push/Pull mode enables you to directly alter the shape of a path segment by pushing the edge of the Freeform tool against it. In the Reshape Area mode, you can adjust the size of the area that the tool influences. This influence is strongest near the center of the tool and diminishes toward the outer edge of the tool. This area of influence is indicated by the circles displayed when you are using the tool.

5] Position the cursor in the center of the rectangle once again and hold down the mouse button. Use the right arrow key to enlarge the area and then drag the tool across the left side of the rectangle and release the mouse.

Notice the difference between the right and left sides of this path that was a rectangle. The Push/Pull mode directly modifies a path by deforming it to match the edge of the Freeform tool.

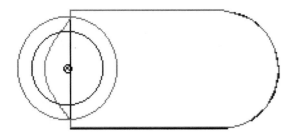

As you work with paths in FreeHand, the Freeform tool offers an easy way to directly alter the shapes of those paths.

tip *When you are getting started with the Freeform tool, remember that the Undo feature is available if something goes wrong!*

6] Choose File › Close to close the document without quitting FreeHand. Don't save the changes.
This was another practice document, so you don't need to save it. If FreeHand asks if you wish to save changes to Untitled, click the Don't Save button.

ON YOUR OWN

You have seen that basic shapes are actually grouped paths, and you can gain precise control over any path by adding, deleting, moving, and modifying points along that path. You have also learned how to modify paths directly with the Freeform tool.

Create other new documents and experiment further with these techniques. Alter paths with the Freeform tool and practice using both operating modes. Ungroup a basic shape such as a rectangle, ellipse, or line. Add new points, change points from one type to another, and manipulate the control handles until you understand how the handles act upon the paths.

USING A TRACING TEMPLATE

To simplify the creation of several graphics, you will open an existing template document that contains patterns you will trace with the Bezigon tool. This task is designed to develop your ability to create all types of paths.

1] Choose File › Open, select Trace1.ft8 in the Start folder within the Lesson3 folder, and click Open.

A page appears containing tracing patterns that you will use to practice creating different types of paths. Tracing these simple shapes will help you learn how you can create any type of curve or straight line by positioning corner and curve points.

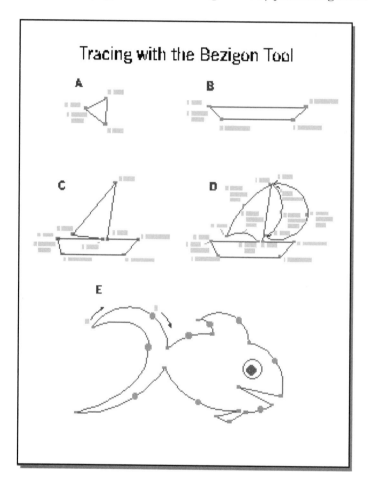

tip *The filename extension in these sample files indicates the type of FreeHand file you are opening. FreeHand documents are identified with the .fh8 extension, and templates are identified by .ft8. When you open a template file, FreeHand actually opens a copy of the file instead of the original. That way, the template remains unaltered for future use.*

2] Select the Zoom tool in the toolbox. Position your mouse above and to the left of the first pattern, the triangle, at the upper left of the page. Drag downward and to the right until a selection marquee surrounds that pattern. Then release the mouse.

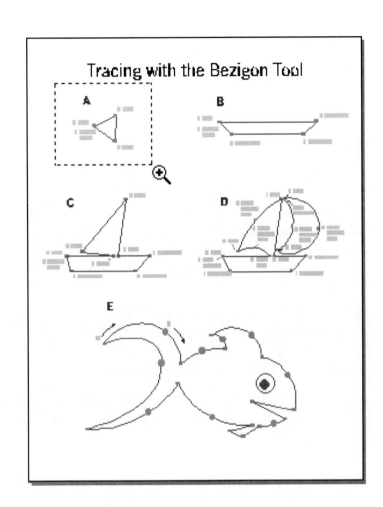

Tracing pattern A is now clearly visible. Next you will trace the triangle pattern by placing corner points with the Bezigon tool.

3] Select the Bezigon tool in the toolbox. Position the cursor on point 1 and click once to create the first corner point. Move the cursor to point 2 and click and then move the cursor to point 3 and click to create the other two corner points. Close the path by clicking once more on the starting point for this path.

You have created a closed path that matches the triangle tracing pattern.

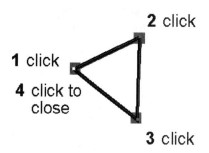

tip *Watch the cursor as you create paths. The crosshair cursor is displayed with an empty square alongside it when you are ready to create a new path. The crosshair appears with a small carat beside it when you can add points to an active path. A solid square appears near the crosshair when the mouse is positioned over the first point in the path, so you know that clicking that point will close the path. If it is difficult to see these cursors as you trace this pattern, create another small triangle on an empty part of the page so the cursors will be easier to see. Make sure to close the path before you continue.*

4] Save the document as *MyShapes* in your MyWork folder.

Each time you complete something successfully, save it!

5] Choose View › Custom › B to see tracing pattern B.

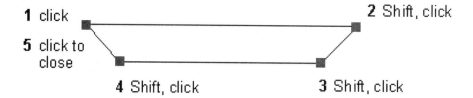

Instead of manually scrolling or zooming to find this part of the document, you jumped to this view using a custom view that has been saved with this template. Custom views enable you to save any view of your document by choosing View > Custom > New. You can enter a name for the view, and then you can switch back to this view at any time.

Shape B is also a shape you will create using corner points. This path contains segments that should be horizontal and at 45-degree angles.

Just as you can use the Shift key to constrain ellipses and rectangles to create circles and squares, you can also use it to constrain the position of points as you trace. When you want to position the next point to create a segment that is horizontal, vertical, or at a 45-degree angle, hold down Shift while you click the mouse.

6] Using the Bezigon tool, click corner 1 to begin tracing this shape. To keep the top segment horizontal, hold down the Shift key and click point 2 at the top-right corner. The next segment should be at a 45-degree angle, so hold down Shift and click point 3. Hold down Shift and click point 4 and then click again on the starting point to close the shape.

The only segment that Shift will not constrain is the very last one—the one that closes the shape when you click the starting point—because the last segment must extend from the last point to the first point at whatever angle may be required. If your last segment is not oriented properly, you can use the Pointer tool to reposition one of the points.

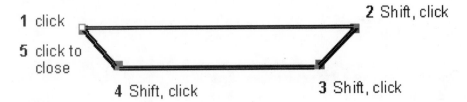

tip   *You can use the arrow keys to nudge a selected element or point a small amount in any direction. For example, select a point on the last path—when selected, the point should appear as an outlined square. Now instead of using the mouse to move the point, press the right arrow key several times and watch the point move slightly to the right each time you press. This approach works the same way when you select a path, group, or block of type with the Pointer tool. The default movement is 1 point, although this amount, called the cursor distance, can be customized in the General Editing category of the Preferences dialog box.*

Now try pattern C.

7] Choose View › Custom › C. Trace this simple sailboat using the Bezigon tool, beginning at point 1 on the template. Hold down the Shift key when the next point you want to add should create a segment that is perfectly horizontal, vertical, or at a 45-degree angle.

Follow the steps as shown in the tracing template. If you are not happy with the position of any point as you work, press the Delete key to delete that point and then continue.

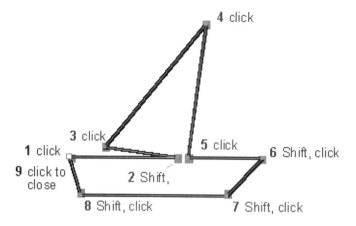

Now you should be ready to create pattern D. This looks complex, but you can see that it's based on the patterns you've already created.

8] Change to custom view D to see tracing pattern D.

This pattern consists of two separate shapes, which you will trace as two paths. Each of these paths consists of both corner and curve points. Corner points should be positioned where the path forms a corner, and curve points should be placed at the outermost part of each curve.

You will first trace the billowing sail on the right. Small squares at the top and bottom tips of the sail indicate that corner points are needed in these positions. The circles positioned at the outermost parts of the curved segments identify the positions of the curve points required.

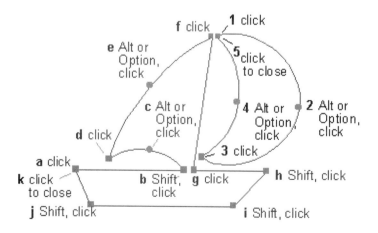

9] Click the Bezigon tool on point 1 to start the path with a corner point at the top of the sail. Add a curve point at position 2, the outermost point of the sail curve, by holding down the Alt (Windows) or Option (Macintosh) key and clicking the mouse.

The path does not look like a curve yet, and the curve point you added at point 2 has control handles sticking out the wrong way. Do not stop to make adjustments—continue tracing the path, and the points will automatically adjust once the next point is added.

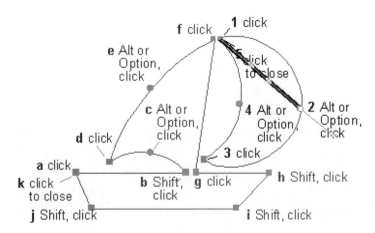

10] Click to add a corner point at the bottom tip of the sail (point 3).

Because this should be a corner point, click without pressing Alt or Option.

The curve point automatically adjusts the control handles to balance the curve between the points on either side.

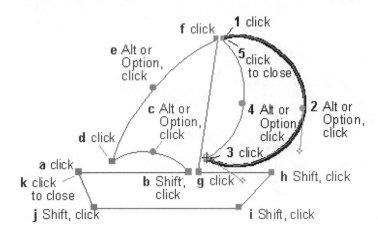

11] Finish the sail by adding a curve point (point 4) and then click the original point again to close the path.

Because the final point should be a corner point, do not hold down the Alt or Option key for the final click.

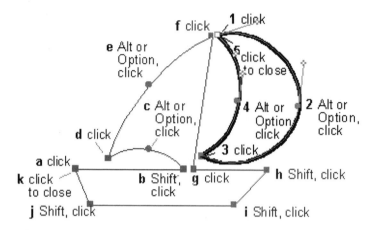

The billowing sail is finished; now you will trace the other parts of this boat.

12] Starting at point *a*, trace the boat pattern using the same techniques as before. Hold down the Shift key to control the direction of segments and the Alt (Windows) or Option (Macintosh) key to add curve points as indicated by the pattern.

Follow the alphabet and read the instructions as you trace. Position corner points where the path should form an angled joint. Place curve points at the outermost spot along a curved part of the path.

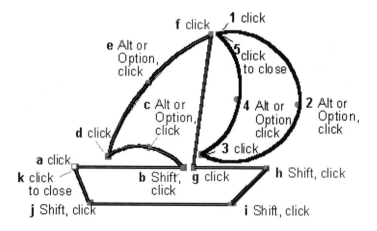

This is such a nice drawing; complete it by adding some color.

13] Click the Pointer tool on an empty part of the page or pasteboard to deselect all elements in the document. Choose Window › Panels › Color Mixer and use the Mixer controls to create any color you want, such as a bright green. Drag a swatch from the color well at the bottom of the Mixer and drop it inside both of the shapes you created for this boat to fill the shapes.

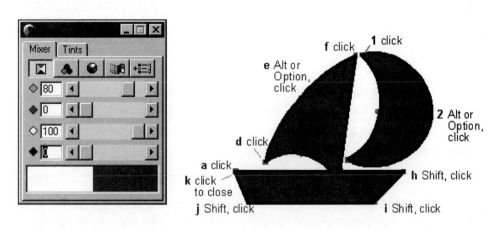

You can also select the elements with the Pointer tool and change the stroke to None in the Stroke Inspector, if you like.

14] Save your work.

MANIPULATING CURVES WITH CONTROL HANDLES

Now you are ready to create the fish that appears at the bottom of the page of templates.

1] Change to custom view E to see the fish.

This graphic consists of three elements: two circles (that make up the eye) and a closed path for the body. The tracing path for the body has squares positioned to indicate corner points and circles positioned to indicate where curve points should be located.

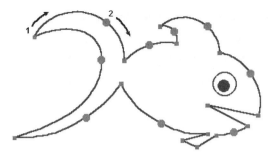

2] Using the Bezigon tool, start by adding a corner point at the top-left tip of the fish's tail. Then hold down Alt (Windows) or Option (Macintosh) and click to create a curve point at position 2. Continue to trace around the body in a clockwise direction, adding curve and corner points as needed.

It is important to trace around the shape—do not jump across the fish's body.

Don't stop to make adjustments as you trace. Simply put each point in position as you work around the figure. The path may not perfectly match the pattern, but you can easily make adjustments once all of the points are in position and the path has been closed. The following graphic shows the partially traced fish. Notice that you can tell that the curve point at the bottom of the fish was the last point added because this point is selected.

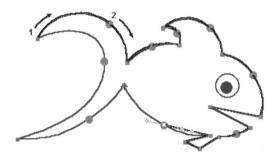

tip *Don't worry if the path does not match the template as you trace. It is easier to create the entire path first and then adjust the points or control handles.*

3] After adding all of the points on the fish, close the path by clicking the starting point.

The path will not follow the template along the inner curve of the tail. You will need to make adjustments to this path with the Pointer tool.

4] Select the last curve point you added, in the center of the tail, with the Pointer tool. Adjust the top control handle for this point to make the control handles vertical.

This adjustment aligns the segment of the path above the curve point much more closely to the tracing pattern. The segment of the path below the curve point still does not look very good.

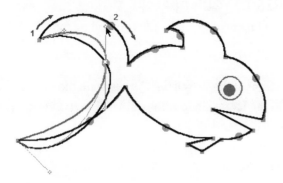

Every point on a path can have two control handles—even corner points. The handles are visible when the point is selected. When a point is selected, control handles for the preceding and following points, which also control the selected point's path segment, will also appear. Note that the corner point at the bottom tip of the tail has a control handle pointing down and to the right, which is causing the path to dip down.

5] Select the corner point at the bottom tip of the tail with the Pointer tool. Point to the control handle that extends downward to the right from this point. Drag this handle up toward the direction you want the path to follow.

The path should now follow the pattern much more closely. You can move the control handle closer to or farther away from the point to adjust the path as needed.

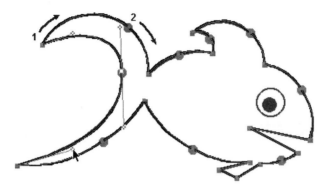

6] Save your work.

The body of the fish is complete.

ADDING THE FINISHING TOUCHES TO YOUR GRAPHIC

You can complete the fish graphic by adding two circles for the eyes, filling the shapes, and grouping the elements together.

1] Use the Ellipse tool to create the larger of the two circles. Then create the smaller circle using the same tool. Fill the larger circle with white and keep the black stroke. Fill the smaller circle with black.

Zoom in closer if you have difficulty filling either shape. If the small circle disappears when you fill the larger one, simply send the larger circle to the back with Modify > Arrange > Send to Back.

tip *To draw an ellipse from the center out, hold down Alt (Windows) or Option (Macintosh) when drawing with the Ellipse tool. If you would like this shape to be a perfect circle drawn from the center out, hold down the Shift key as well as Alt or Option.*

2] Fill the body with a Gradient fill, using any colors you wish. Set the stroke to None.

If the eye elements are not visible, send the body to the back.

tip *If the fill does not appear in your fish, the path may not be closed. Select the fish with the Pointer tool and display the Object Inspector to see if the fish is a closed path. If it isn't, click the Closed box in the Inspector. The fill should now appear inside the fish.*

3] Select the small circle, hold down Shift and click the larger circle and then the body of the fish, and group the elements together.

It is often helpful to group elements together when a graphic is complete. This will make it easier to move, resize, or duplicate the entire graphic.

4] Save your work.

CREATING THE ELEMENTS FOR THE ZOO AD

Now that you have explored how to add and adjust points and paths, you will begin to create the elements you will add to the Greenville Zoo ad. You will be putting all your tracing skills learned thus far to use here.

1] Close your MyShapes document and open Wolf.ft8 in the Start folder within the Lesson3 folder. Adjust your view as needed so you can clearly see the tracing pattern.

This document contains a tracing pattern for a wolf.

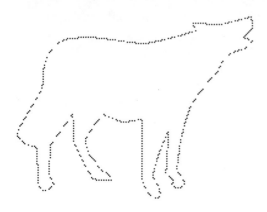

2] Save the document as *MyWolf* in your MyWork folder.

Save frequently while you work.

3] Trace the wolf using the Bezigon tool. Start by putting a corner point at the tip of the nose. Work your way around the shape, adding curve points at the outermost spot along curved sections and corner points where appropriate. Make sure to close this shape by clicking the first point again after tracing the entire path.

Don't worry if your path does not follow the template precisely. In the next step, you will use the Freeform tool to fine-tune the path as necessary. Use the following illustration to get an idea of the types and locations of the points you might use to create this shape.

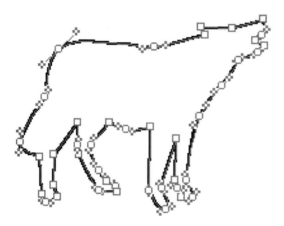

tip *If you make a mistake as you trace the shape, press the Delete key. Use the Alt (Windows) or Option (Macintosh) key when placing curve points. Don't worry if the path does not match the template as you trace; you can adjust points and control handles with the Pointer tool after completing your path.*

4] Use the Freeform tool to make adjustments to the path, as necessary.

Before you use this tool, you can double-click the Freeform tool in the toolbox to select the Push/Pull or Reshape Area adjustment mode. As you work, use the left and right arrow keys to decrease or increase the size of the tool.

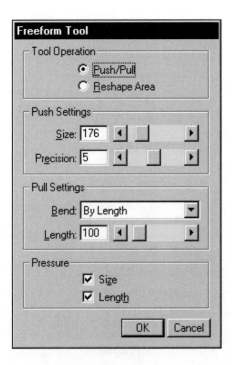

5] Save your work.

In the next few tasks, you will mix a color and fill the path. Then you will copy the wolf and paste it into an unfinished ad layout document.

You can see a finished version of this wolf by opening Howl.fh8 in the Media folder within the Lesson3 folder.

APPLYING COLOR

This task explores the process of creating new colors, adding them to the Color List, and applying these colors to elements on the page—in this case, to the wolf drawing.

1] Make sure that nothing is selected by clicking the Pointer tool on an empty part of the page or pasteboard. Choose Window › Panel › Color List to display the Color List and then display the Color Mixer by choosing Window › Panel › Color Mixer.

The Color List displays the named colors currently available for this document. The Color Mixer provides controls to create new colors and tints to apply to elements and add to the Color List.

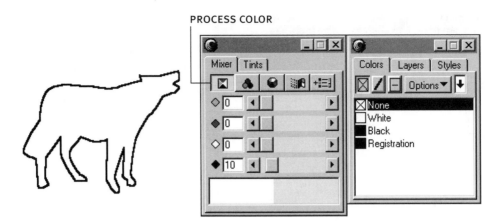

2] Select the Process Color button at the top left of the Color Mixer to create a color using the process ink colors.

The panel displays four sliders, one for each of the process ink colors: cyan (C), magenta (M), yellow (Y), and black (K). Tints of these four ink colors can be used in printing to create a broad range of colors. Now you will create a new color by mixing these four primary colors. Process colors are also referred to as CMYK colors.

3] Using the CMYK controls in the Color Mixer, create a color with 27 percent cyan, 56 percent magenta, 4 percent yellow, and 13 percent black by dragging the sliders or entering values in the Color Mixer fields.

As you enter information, a new purple color is displayed in the color well at the bottom of the Color Mixer panel. This is the color that results from combining these four inks in these percentages.

When entering values such as these color percentages into a group of fields, select the value in the first field and type a new value. Then press the Tab key to select the next field automatically. For example, if you type 56 in the Magenta field and then press Tab, the Yellow field will be selected and ready to accept a new value. Press Enter after you type the last value to apply the settings.

4] Click the Add to Color List button at the top of the Color Mixer, specify a name for this color by typing *Wolf*, and press Enter.

ADD TO COLOR LIST

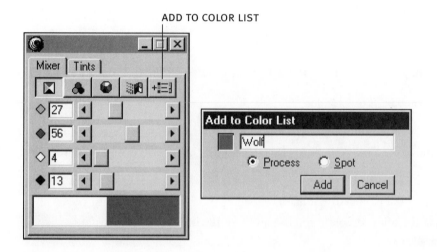

Your new color will automatically be named and added to the list.

5] Close the Color Mixer. Drag the color swatch for your new color from the Color List and drop it inside the wolf path on your page. Then drag the swatch for None and drop it on the path to set the stroke around the wolf to None.

Next you will group the wolf path by itself, which will make it more difficult to accidentally alter the path.

6] Select the wolf path with the Pointer tool and choose Modify › Group (Windows Ctrl+G, Macintosh Command+G).

The wolf is now ready to use in the Zoo layout.

7] Save your work.

PRACTICING TRACING TECHNIQUES

Another tracing pattern is provided to help you practice your tracing skills.

1] Open Angel.ft8, which is located in the Start folder within the Lesson3 folder.

2] Trace the angelfish using the Bezigon tool.

Begin at a corner point for easier tracing. The tip of a fin would be a good starting point. If you make a mistake, press the Delete key. Use the Alt (Windows) or Option (Macintosh) key when placing curve points.

Don't worry if the path does not match the template as you trace. Adjust points or control handles after completing your path. Use the illustration for assistance in the placement of points.

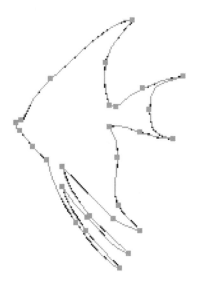

3] Fill the fish as desired and save the document as *MyFish* in your MyWork folder. Close this document when you are finished working on the fish.

ADDING A TRACED ELEMENT TO ANOTHER DOCUMENT

You need to place the wolf you created in the zoo ad. You will do this by simply copying and pasting.

1] In your MyWolf document, select the wolf with the Pointer tool. Copy this element to the clipboard by choosing Edit › Copy.

Next you will open the ad layout and paste a copy of the wolf into that document.

tip *If the MyWolf document is not visible, choose it from the bottom of the Window menu, where all open documents are displayed. If you do not see it in the Window menu, it may have been closed. Use File > Open to open it again.*

2] Open ZooStart.ft8, located in the Start folder within the Lesson3 folder.

ZooStart.ft8 has many of the elements of this layout already completed and in position on the page. You will add your wolf and some text to the layout.

Notice that several colors are already defined in the Color List.

 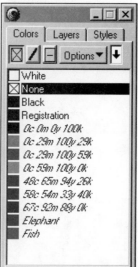

3] Save the document as *MyZoo* in your MyWork folder.

Now paste the wolf into the zoo ad.

4] Choose Edit › Paste.

The wolf is pasted into this document in the center of the page, because it was the last thing you copied to the clipboard. The Wolf color has also been added to the Color List.

However, your wolf is a bit large for this layout, don't you think?

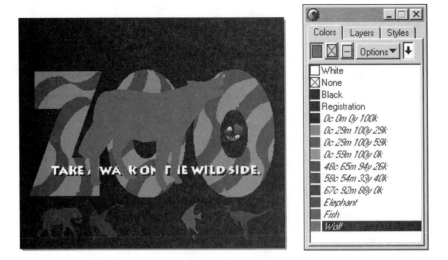

SCALING AND ALIGNING ELEMENTS

You will now reduce the size of the wolf and align it to fit evenly between the illustrations of other wildlife at the bottom of the page.

1] Display the Transform Panel by choosing Window › Panels › Transform. Select the Scale tool in the Transform panel. Type a scaling percentage of *25*, make sure Uniform is checked, and click Scale (Windows) or Apply (Macintosh).

This will scale your artwork to match the size of the other creatures at the bottom of this ad.

SCALE PERCENTAGE

UNIFORM
SCALING

tip *For information on other scale options, consult the* FreeHand User's Guide *that is included with the software.*

2] Using the Pointer tool, point to the middle of the wolf and move this figure to the open spot between the bird and fish figures. Then close the Transform panel.

You will next use FreeHand's align features to precisely distribute the wildlife figures across the bottom of the page. To distribute these objects, all five figures need to be selected.

3] Because the wolf is still selected, hold down the Shift key while you click the elephant, bird, fish, and kangaroo. Display the Align panel by choosing Window › Panel › Align. Set the vertical alignment to Align Center and the horizontal alignment to Distribute Widths. Click Apply (Windows) or Align (Macintosh).
This will evenly space the objects across the bottom of the ad as well as align the centers of the objects vertically.

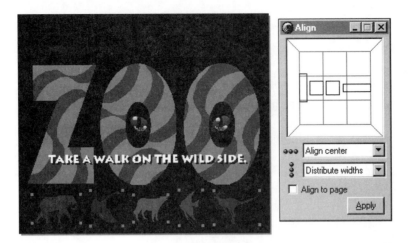

4] Save your work.

ADDING GRADIENT-FILLED TEXT

You will now add the name *GREENVILLE* to the top of the ad and apply a gradient fill inside of this text.

1] Scroll up so that you see part of the pasteboard above this ad. With the Text tool, click once on the pasteboard to start a new text block.

You will move this text onto the ad after you have created the effect you want. Right now, though, the text will be easier to see and work with on the pasteboard.

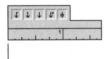

2] Press Caps Lock and type the name *GREENVILLE*.

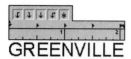

GREENVILLE

tip   *You can use the Convert Case commands on the Text menu if you mistakenly type this text in uppercase and lowercase characters. Note that your text may not look just like the text shown here because the default font may be different on your machine.*

Now you will change the font and size of this text.

3] Select the text using the Pointer tool. Using the controls on the text toolbar near the top of your screen, change the font to URWGaramondT.

Selecting a text block with the Pointer tool lets you change all the characters within that block. When selecting a font from the menu, you will notice that as you position your cursor over any font name in the menu, a sample of the selected text is displayed in that particular font.

tip   *The fonts specified in the lessons in this book are on the FreeHand 8 software CD-ROM. If you do not have these specific fonts installed, simply choose other fonts available on your system and adjust the type size and formatting as needed to make your projects similar in appearance to those in the lesson files.*

145

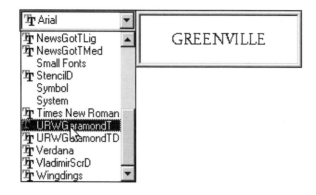

4] Change the type size to 56 points by selecting the type size in the text toolbar, typing _56_, and pressing Enter.

Entering a value in the Type Size field and pressing Enter enables you to specify sizes that are not available in the Type Size menu.

You want to fill this text with a gradient fill, but FreeHand allows only basic fills in text. In the next step, you will convert this text to paths, just like the paths you created with the Bezigon tool. Once the characters are paths, you will be able to fill them with a gradient.

5] With the text block still selected, choose Text › Convert to Paths.

When you convert text to paths, each letter is converted to a path consisting of corner and curve points. You do not see the points at this time because all of the character paths are grouped together. You will now be able to place a gradient fill inside the word.

6] With the text group selected, change the fill type in the Fill Inspector to Gradient. Select Wolf in the color menu at the top of the Inspector and White in the color menu at the bottom of the Inspector. Set the direction of the gradient to 270 degrees.

The text now is filled with a gradient that ranges from the Wolf color at the top to White at the bottom. If the text had not been converted to paths and was selected with the Pointer tool, the text *block*, not the text, would now be filled with a gradient.

7] Using the Pointer tool, move the text onto the top of the ad so that it is positioned above the word *ZOO*. If you cannot see the entire page, choose View › Fit to Page.

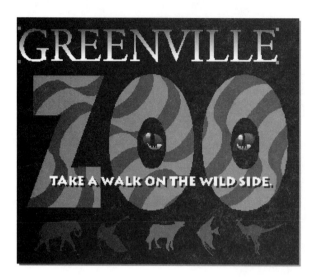

8] With *GREENVILLE* still selected, display the Align panel by choosing Window › Panel › Align. Set the vertical alignment to No Change, set the horizontal alignment to Align Center, and turn on Align to Page. Click Apply (Windows) or Align (Macintosh).

This will center the type on the page.

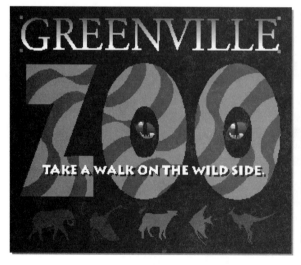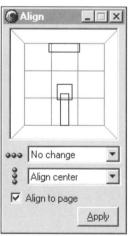

9] Save your work.

Congratulations! The advertisement is now complete.

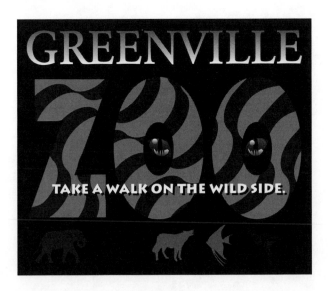

WHAT YOU HAVE LEARNED

In this lesson you have:

- Ungrouped basic shapes and edited the paths [*page* **115**]

- Created and modified points on Beziér curves [*page* **116**]

- Adjusted paths with the Freeform tool [*page* **120**]

- Used templates as patterns to trace [*page* **124**]

- Changed the view using custom views [*page* **126**]

- Created and named colors for process color printing [*page* **137**]

- Combined artwork from different documents by copying and pasting [*page* **141**]

- Practiced scaling and aligning artwork for a layout [*page* **142**]

- Converted text to paths to apply a gradient fill [*page* **144**]

and styles

using layers

Layers and styles are among FreeHand's most powerful features for organizing and simplifying your documents and making it easier to apply and modify the look of an element. **Layers** are transparent planes or overlays that help organize objects and control how they stack upon each other in an illustration. A **style** is a set of graphic attributes such as color, fill, and stroke or a set of text attributes such as font, style, space before and after, indents and tabs, and alignment.

Creating a complex illustration, like this picture of a country sunset, is made easier by FreeHand's ability to combine and manipulate different layers, as you will learn to do in this lesson.

Designed by Julia Sifers of Glasgow & Associates.

You will apply these features to the creation of a stylized drawing of sunbeams radiating above a hillside. As you work, you will use the Pen tool, perform and duplicate transformations, work with layers and styles, apply path operations, and use the powerful Paste Inside command. You will also export your artwork so it can be imported into other applications.

If you would like to review the final result of this lesson, open Sunbeams.fh8 in the Complete folder within the Lesson4 folder.

WHAT YOU WILL LEARN

In this lesson you will:

- Import tracing patterns to help you accurately create paths and elements

- Organize a document into layers

- Create paths with the Pen tool

- Create and duplicate transformations

- Create an object style so you can easily apply and modify visual characteristics

- Trim unwanted portions from graphics

- Import another FreeHand document

- Export artwork for use in other applications

APPROXIMATE TIME

It usually takes about 2 hours to complete this lesson.

LESSON FILES

Media Files:

Lesson4\Media\Pattern1.tif
Lesson4\Media\Pattern2.tif
Lesson4\Media\Pattern3.tif
Lesson4\Media\Frame.fh8

Starting Files:

None

Completed Project:

Lesson4\Complete\Sunbeams.fh8
Lesson4\Complete\Sunbeams.eps

CREATING A NEW CUSTOM-SIZE DOCUMENT

You will begin working on the artwork for this lesson in a new document.

1] Create a new document by choosing File › New (Windows Ctrl+N, Macintosh Command+N).

A blank page appears, which you will now adjust to the page size needed for this illustration.

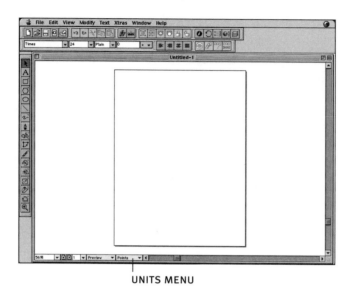

UNITS MENU

2] Change the unit of measure to Inches using the Units menu at the bottom of the screen. Choose Window › Inspectors › Document to display the Document Inspector.

The Document Inspector shows the current page dimensions and orientation.

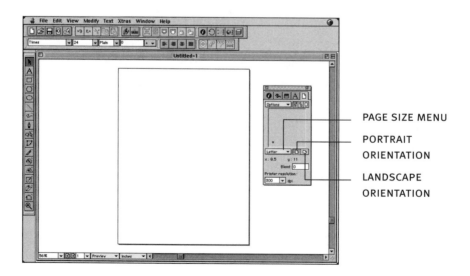

PAGE SIZE MENU

PORTRAIT ORIENTATION

LANDSCAPE ORIENTATION

3] In the Document Inspector, select Custom on the Page Size menu, enter the dimensions *6.125* by *4.875* inches, and click the icon for Landscape orientation.

Landscape orientation displays the page so that the height is the smaller dimension and the length is the larger dimension.

Your page is now the correct size, but it appears small in the document window.

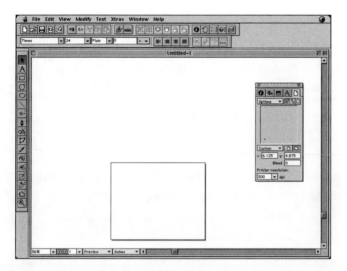

4] Close the Document Inspector and choose View › Fit to Page (Windows Ctrl+Shift+ W, Macintosh Command+Shift+W) to make the document larger in the window.

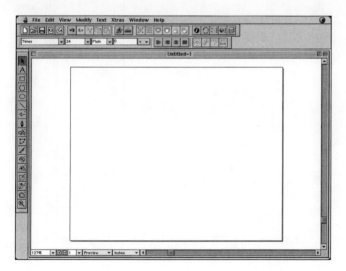

5] Save the document as *MySun* in your MyWork folder.

The page is now ready for you to begin creating the illustration.

IMPORTING A TRACING PATTERN AND MOVING IT
TO A BACKGROUND LAYER

As you learned in the last lesson, a good way to accurately create paths and elements is to trace an existing image of the desired layout or artwork. For example, you can use a scanned image of a pencil sketch or other printed source as a pattern for tracing in FreeHand.

In the last lesson, you opened a template containing a tracing pattern. Here you will import an image called Pattern1.tif to use as a tracing pattern in the drawing you will be creating. This pattern will become the basis for the sunbeams.

You will want this pattern in the background so you can trace over it, but you will not want it to print. You will accomplish this by using layers. By placing elements on layers, you can control the visibility and printing of individual elements.

1] Choose File › Import (Windows Ctrl+R, Macintosh Command+R). Select Pattern1.tif from the Media folder within the Lesson4 folder and click Open. Align the cursor with the top-left corner of the page and click the mouse to position the artwork accurately on the page.

An image of a rectangle enclosing a circle with one ray appears.

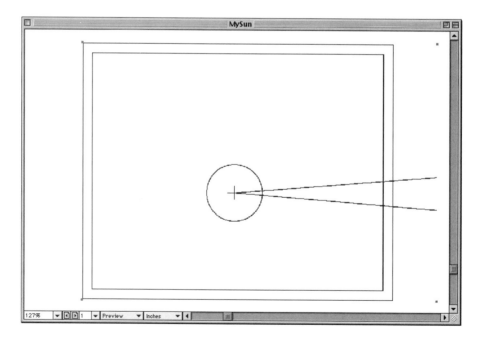

If the image does not look very clear on the page, you should check your preference settings. Choose File > Preferences to display the Preferences dialog box and click Redraw. Make sure that the High-Resolution Image Display option is turned on and then click OK. The imported image should now be displayed much more clearly.

Now place this pattern on a layer so you can move it into the background.

2] Choose Window › Panels › Layers to display the Layers panel.

Three layers initially appear in the Layers panel: Foreground, Guides, and Background. These are preset layers in every FreeHand document. Notice that the Background layer appears below a separator line in the panel.

You can add additional layers in any FreeHand document, and you can use these layers to organize elements and control the visibility and printing of the elements on each particular layer. You can move graphic elements from one layer to another, except for the Guides layer, which holds all of the guides you use for aligning elements in your document. As you learned when you used guides in Lesson 2, the Guides layer does not print. Any other layer that appears above the separator line in the panel is a printing layer and is considered a foreground layer. Any layer appearing below the separator line is a nonprinting background layer.

In this first use of layers, you will move the pattern image into the background so it will be visible to trace over, but will not print.

3] With the image still selected, click the name Background in the Layers panel.

The lines in the image will dim, indicating that this artwork is now on a nonprinting background layer.

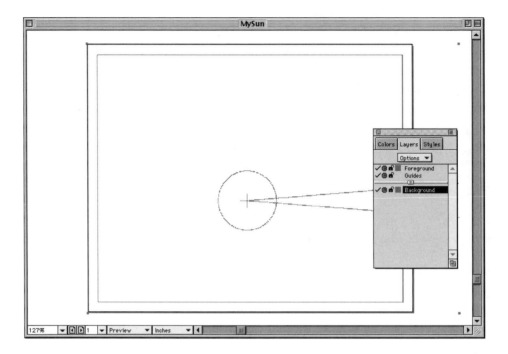

4] Lock the Background layer by clicking once on the Lock icon next to the layer name in the panel.

This will prevent accidental changes to the layer as you work. It also prevents you from accidentally adding the next elements you create to the Background layer. Notice that the Foreground layer is selected in the panel. This indicates the current active layer, where the next elements will be added.

156

5] Save your work.

Creating the elements of the sky will be much easier now that the tracing pattern is in place.

6] Create a new layer by choosing New from the Options menu in the Layers panel. Double-click the name of the new layer, Layer-1, and type *Sky* as the new name for this layer. Press Enter to complete the name change.

You can see that the Sky layer is a foreground (printing) layer because it appears above the separator line in the Layers panel. This new layer is now the active layer, so the artwork you create next will be added to this layer.

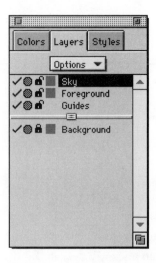

7] Using the Rectangle tool, create a rectangle that matches the size and position of the large rectangle visible in the background.

This rectangle will define the edges of your picture and will appear behind all of the other artwork.

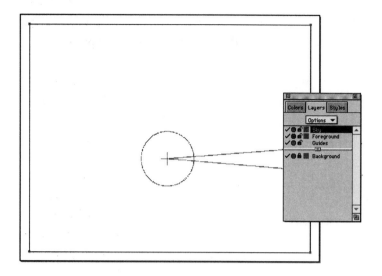

8] Save your work.

You will assign a gradient fill to this element, but first you need to import the colors you will use for this illustration.

DEFINING PROCESS COLORS

When defining colors in FreeHand, you must determine whether to create **spot colors** or **process colors**. Spot colors match the color of the specific ink that will be used on a printing press to print that color in a FreeHand illustration. For example, to use green and red in your document, you could use a green ink and a red ink. In that case, you would define the red and green colors in your document as spot colors, as you did for the letterhead elements in Lesson 2.

Alternatively, you could define every color you use as a process color, a combination of cyan, magenta, yellow, and black inks, as you did for the wolf in Lesson 3. The majority of full-color printed pieces you see use process color printing.

Why choose one rather than the other? If you have fewer than four colors in your document, printing with spot color can be cheaper, since it uses fewer inks. You can also match colors precisely with spot color and choose from a wider variety of colors than CMYK colors can reproduce. On the other hand, if your artwork contains many colors, it is much cheaper to use process color, which can create almost any color you need using the same four ink colors. (The exceptions are some very bright colors and specialty inks, such as flourescents and metallics, which CMYK cannot reproduce.)

Most (if not all) color computer monitors cannot represent colors as they will appear when printed on a printing press. FreeHand includes libraries of spot and process colors for use in your artwork, including PANTONE for spot color (which you used in Lesson 2), PANTONE for process color, Trumatch, Focaltone, Toyo, and Munsell. You will be importing colors from the PANTONE Matching System for process colors in this lesson.

1] Choose Window › Panels › Colors to display the Color List. Choose PANTONE Process from the Options menu in the Color List panel.

This displays the colors available in the PANTONE Process color library. You will select several colors from this library to import into your document.

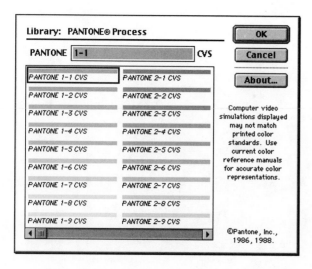

2] Click the color named 1-5. Then scroll to the right. Hold down the Ctrl (Windows) or Command (Macintosh) key and click 18-7 to add it to the selection. Continue to hold down the Ctrl or Command key while adding 31-5, 161-6, 221-5, and 289-1 to the selection. Then click OK.

This imports all six of these colors into the Color List panel.

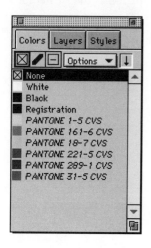

tip *FreeHand displays the names of process colors in italic type, while the names of spot colors are displayed in roman characters.*

3] Display the Fill Inspector by choosing Window › Inspectors › Fill. Select the rectangle on your page with the Pointer tool (if it is not already selected). Change the fill to Gradient, with PANTONE 221-5 (light blue) at the top and PANTONE 1-5 (yellow) at the bottom.

The entire rectangle should be filled with a gradient from blue at the top to yellow at the bottom. Because the filled rectangle is on the topmost layer, no other elements are now visible.

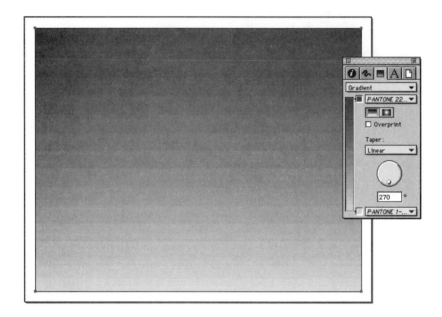

4] Display the Stroke Inspector by clicking the Stroke tab at the top of the Inspector panel group. On the Stroke Type menu, select None.

Another way to display the Stroke Inspector is to choose Window > Inspector > Stroke.

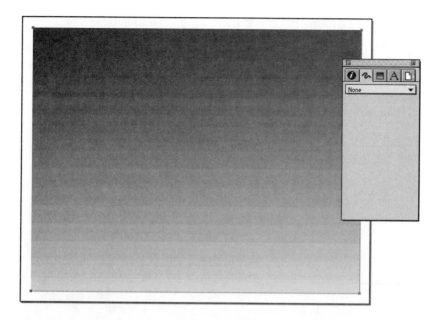

5] Press the Tab key to deselect all elements. Hide the Inspector and display the Layers panel.

6] Now create a new layer by choosing New from the Options menu in the Layers panel. Double-click the default name, type the new name *Sun*, and press Enter.
On this layer, you will trace the sun and sunbeams. However, the sky is blocking your view of the tracing pattern. To solve that problem, you will temporarily hide the artwork on the Sky layer while creating new elements on the Sun layer.

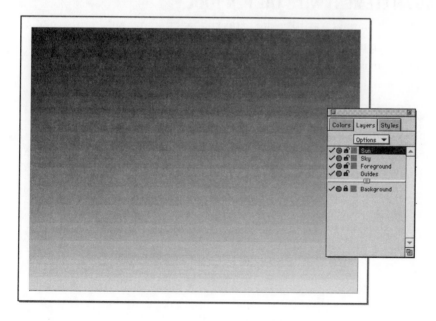

161

7] Hide the Sky layer by clicking the check mark to the left of the name Sky in the Layers panel to remove it. Then save the document.

You can use the check mark to display or hide the contents of any layer whenever it is helpful to do so. The Sun layer should be the active layer at this time, as indicated by the layer name Sun reversed out of a black bar in the Layers panel.

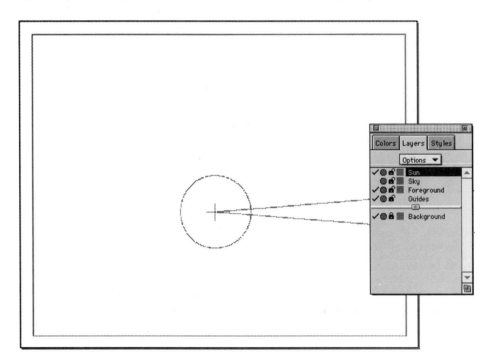

CREATING AN ELEMENT WITH THE PEN TOOL

The Pen tool offers another way to create paths and points and is an alternative to the Bezigon tool you used in the previous lesson. With the Pen tool, you click and release the mouse to add a corner point and drag the mouse to define the control handles of a curve point.

In this task, you will trace the sunbeam displayed in the background by creating corner points with the Pen tool. Next you will make a copy of that element and rotate it around the center of the sun. Then you will duplicate the transformation to create a sky full of sunbeams radiating out from the sun.

1] Select the Pen tool by clicking it once in the toolbox.

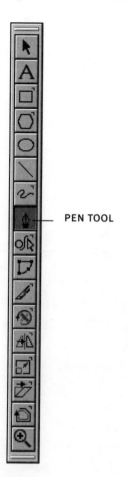

PEN TOOL

2] Position the Pen tool cursor at the center of the sun and click the mouse once. Move to the top-right corner of the sunbeam and click, and move to the bottom-right corner and click again. Now close the path by clicking once on the starting point.
Only closed paths can be filled, so it is important to close this path by clicking the starting point. You have created an empty triangular shape, which you will now fill.

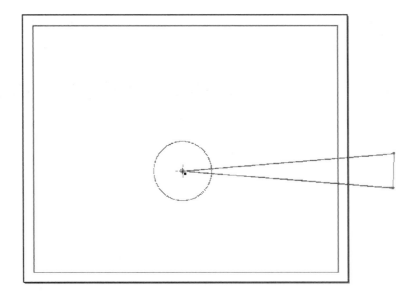

3] Display the Fill Inspector by choosing Window › Inspectors › Fill. Change the type of fill to Gradient and use the menus to change the top color to PANTONE 161-6 and the bottom color to PANTONE 1-5. Change the angle to 180 degrees.

You could also drag swatches of these colors from the Color List and drop them on the top and bottom swatches on the gradient in the Fill Inspector. Remember that you can change the angle by rotating the direction control or by typing a new value into the field just above the bottom color and pressing Enter. The angle of 180 degrees makes the gradient extend from the top color on the right to the bottom color on the left.

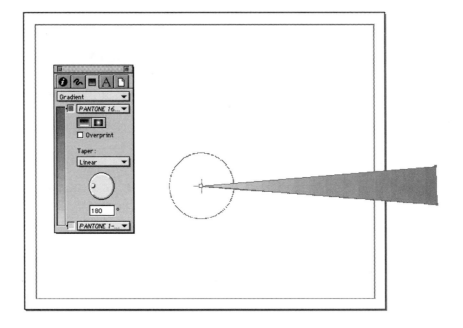

4] Click the Stroke tab in the Inspector panel group to display the Stroke Inspector. Change the type of stroke to None.

The first sunbeam is complete.

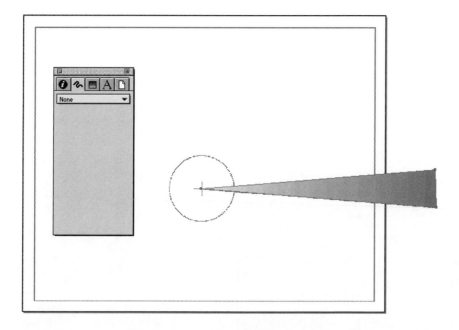

5] Press the Tab key to deselect the artwork. Then save your work.

Now you will create additional copies of this sunbeam rotating around the center of the sun.

ROTATING A COPY AND DUPLICATING THE TRANSFORMATION

You have used the transform handles to manually rotate elements into position. In this task, you will use the Transform panel to precisely control both the amount and the center of rotation.

Important: Follow these steps in this exact sequence; missing a step or clicking something else can disrupt the sequence and alter your results.

1] Select the sunbeam with the Pointer tool. Double-click the Rotation tool in the toolbox to display the Transform panel showing the rotation controls.

This panel allows you to enter specific information for transforming elements. The transformations include moving, rotating, scaling, skewing, and reflecting elements.

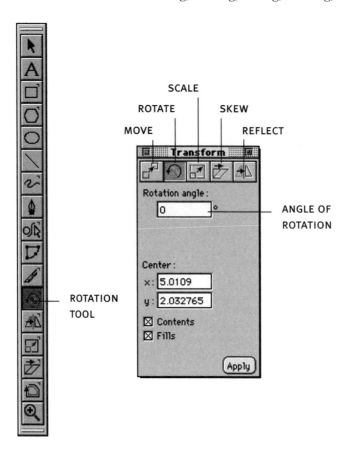

2] **With the original sunbeam selected, choose Edit › Clone (Windows Ctrl+Shift+C, Macintosh Command+=).**

The Clone command creates a duplicate of the selected item directly on top of the existing item, so no change is visible on the screen.

3] **Click the Rotation tool once and release it at the center of the circle (on the left tip of the sunbeam) to specify the center of rotation.**

This spot will now be the point the sunbeam rotates around.

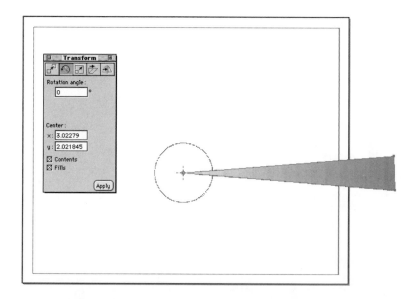

4] Enter a rotation angle of 20 degrees in the Transform panel and click Rotate (Windows) or Apply (Macintosh).

The cloned sunbeam now appears in position, rotated 20 degrees counterclockwise from the original.

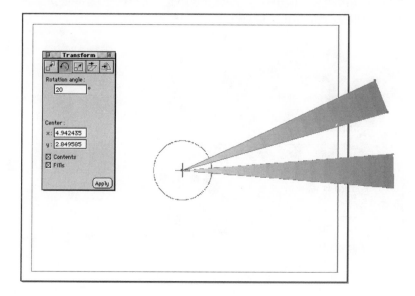

5] Choose Edit › Duplicate (Windows Ctrl+D, Macintosh Command+D).

This duplicates the cloning and transformation (rotation) of the sunbeam to create a third sunbeam.

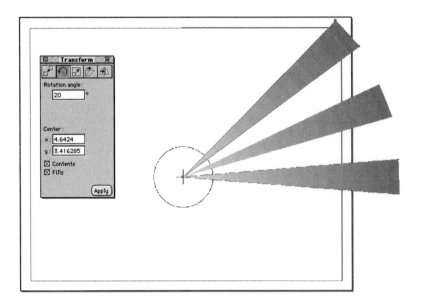

6] Repeat step 5 seven more times to complete the sunbeams.

There should now be 10 sunbeams, evenly spaced, radiating out from the center of the circle (which will become the sun in your illustration).

If you have trouble, you probably performed some steps out of order. Try deleting all the sunbeams except the first and starting again with step 2.

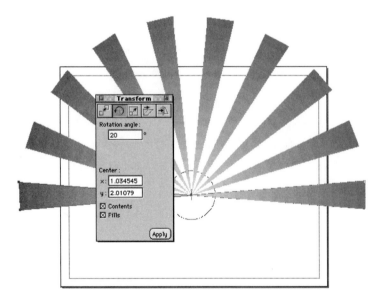

7] Close the Transform panel and save your work.

The sky is almost complete.

COMBINING ELEMENTS WITH PASTE INSIDE

Now that the sunbeams are complete, you will add the sun and use the Paste Inside feature to create **clipping paths** to limit the visible portion of the sunbeams to the area within the sky rectangle. To create a clipping path, you paste artwork inside a closed path using the Paste Inside command. Only the part of the artwork located inside the closed path will appear; the part of the artwork that extends outside of the clipping path will not be displayed or printed.

1] Select the Ellipse tool from the toolbox. Position the cursor on the center of the circle in the tracing pattern, hold down Shift to create a perfect circle and Alt (Windows) or Option (Macintosh) to draw the circle from the center, and drag downward and to the right. Release the mouse when your circle is the same size as the circle in the tracing pattern.

To ensure that the new ellipse you create remains a perfect circle, always release the mouse before you release the Shift and Alt or Option keys.

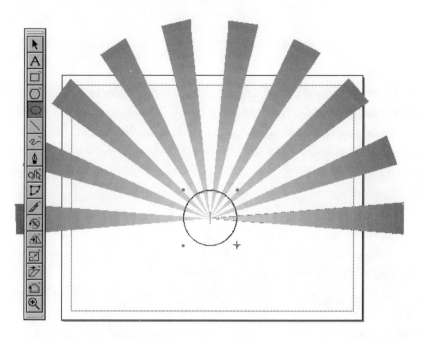

2] Fill the sun with PANTONE 1-5 and set the stroke to None. Choose Edit › Select › All to select all of the sunbeams and the sun (Windows Ctrl+A, Macintosh Command+A). Choose Modify › Group to group these elements together (Windows Ctrl+G, Macintosh Command+G).

Grouping these elements will make it easier to select all of the elements at once to work with them later.

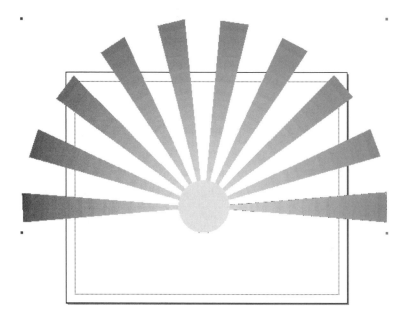

3] Display the Layers panel and click the space to the left of the Sky layer in the column where a check mark appears for the other layers.

The Sky layer should now be visible (indicated by the check mark) and should appear behind the sunbeams, since the Sky layer is below the Sun layer in the Layers panel.

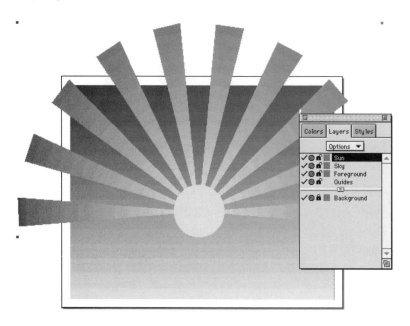

4] With the sunbeam group still selected, click the Sky layer in the Layers panel to move the sunbeam artwork to the Sky layer.

Clicking a layer name in the Layers panel moves the selected elements to that layer.

tip *You can check to see which layer any element is on by selecting the element. The layer containing the selected element will be selected in the Layers panel. If you have artwork selected on several layers at once, no layer name will be selected in the Layers panel.*

Next you will use the sky rectangle to mask the unwanted portions of the sunbeams using FreeHand's Paste Inside command.

5] With the sunbeam group selected, choose Edit › Cut. Then click the sky rectangle and choose Edit › Paste Inside.

The sunbeam artwork was in the desired position over the sky when you cut the artwork. The cut operation removed the artwork from the page. After you select the sky rectangle and choose Paste Inside, only the portion of the sunbeam artwork that appears within the edges of the sky rectangle appears on the page. This makes the sky a clipping path that hides the portions of the sunbeams that extend beyond the rectangle.

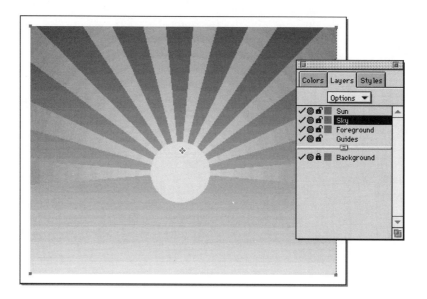

The Paste Inside feature can save a great deal of time. Instead of having to trace each sunbeam individually and trying to match the edges of the sky rectangle for each one, one sunbeam was created that extended well beyond the edge of the rectangle. All of the other sunbeams were cloned and rotated from that first one—each one extending beyond the edge of the rectangle. Paste Inside clips all the elements to the desired border in one step, saving you time in creating the elements and ensuring that the edges of all elements are perfectly aligned.

6] Save your work.

Now that the sky is complete, you will begin working on the hills.

CHANGING YOUR VIEW OF THE ARTWORK

FreeHand offers different ways for you to view artwork on your monitor, using the View menu at the bottom of the document window. Preview is the fully rendered view you have been working in; it displays the highest quality view. Fast Preview enables you to sacrifice some display quality for speed while still displaying the fills and strokes. Faster still is the Keyline mode, which displays the elements without fills and strokes. The quickest display mode is Fast Keyline, which displays only those elements that define the basic layout of your artwork.

1] Use the View menu at the bottom of the document window to change the view from Preview to Keyline.

Keyline mode enables you to clearly see all of the paths in your artwork, even if some are behind other elements.

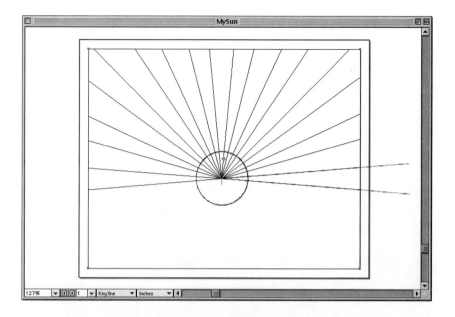

2] Use the same menu to change the view to Fast Keyline.

The elements that you pasted inside the sky rectangle are no longer displayed.

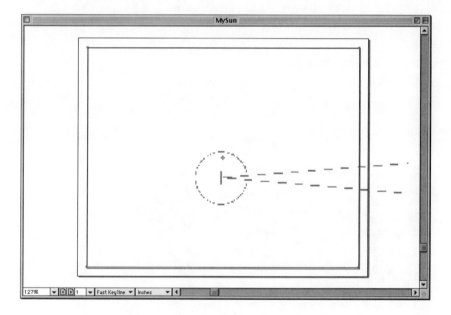

The two keyline views provide an excellent way to see through elements as you work. And although you can apply fills and strokes in the keyline views, don't forget to change back to one of the two preview modes to see the results!

3] Change the view to Fast Preview mode.

This mode provides lower quality display of fills and strokes, but with faster screen redraw than Preview mode. This lower quality is especially apparent in gradient fills, which are displayed as bands of color rather than smooth color transitions.

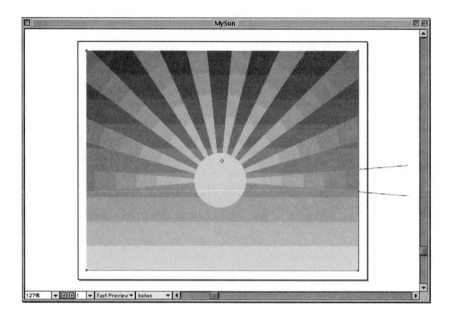

4] Change back to the Preview mode.

The speed difference between the Fast Preview and Preview modes will be more apparent as the complexity of the artwork increases.

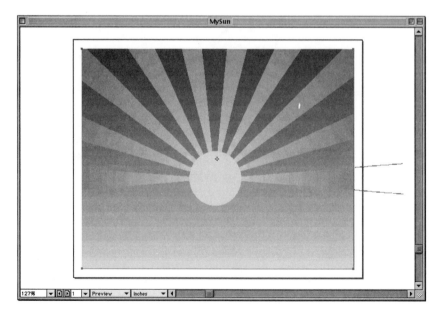

174

CREATING OTHER FOREGROUND LAYERS

You will use a different tracing pattern to create the next elements.

1] Press the Tab key to make sure that no elements are selected. Hide the Sky layer by clicking the check mark to the left of the layer name in the Layers panel. Rename the Sun layer by double-clicking the name, typing *Pattern 2*, and pressing Enter.

An advantage of using layers is you can hide layers that are not currently being used. Remember that clicking a layer name when elements are selected moves those elements to that layer. Pressing the Tab key deselects all elements so no elements will change layers when you rename this layer.

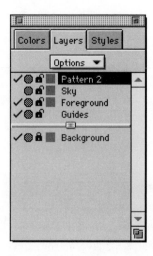

2] Create a new layer by choosing New from the Options menu in the Layers panel. Double-click the default name of the new layer, type *Hills*, and press Enter.

This will be the layer where you will create the hills artwork.

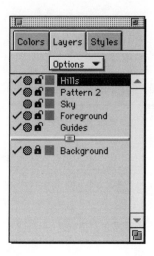

3] Point to the name of the Pattern 2 layer in the Layers panel. Hold down the mouse button, drag the layer down below the Background layer, and then release the mouse.

Moving this layer below the separator line in the Layers panel makes Pattern 2 a background layer. Any artwork you put on this layer will be visible as a tracing pattern but will not print.

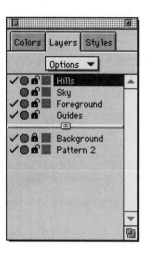

4] Hide the artwork on the Background layer by clicking the check mark to the left of that layer name in the Layers panel.

Since Background is above Pattern 2 in the Layers panel, the artwork on the Background layer will cover up the artwork you will put on the Pattern 2 layer in the next step. Hiding the Background layer will allow you to see the Pattern 2 layer.

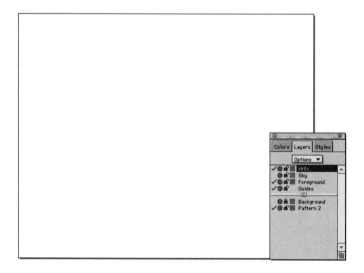

5] Choose File › Import, select Pattern2.tif from the Media folder within the Lesson4 folder, and click Open. Align the cursor with the top-left corner of the page and click the mouse to position the artwork accurately on the page.

This image extends below the bottom edge of the page.

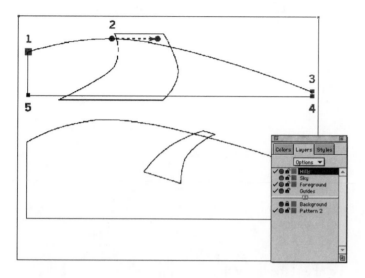

6] With this image selected, click once on the Pattern 2 layer in the Layers panel to send the artwork to that layer. Click the Lock icon to the left of the Pattern 2 layer to lock the layer and prevent accidental changes.

The Hills layer should be the active layer, ready for you to begin tracing the shapes.

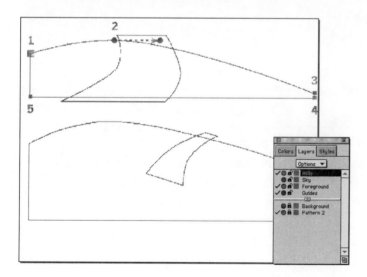

7] Save your work. You can hide the Layers panel if you wish.

CREATING CURVED PATHS WITH THE PEN TOOL

You need to create three hills for this illustration, each with its own road. You will use the Pen tool to create these features.

1] Using the Pen tool, click once on the top-left corner of the top pattern (point 1) to start the path.

This first pattern has the point positions identified. You will create this path by adding the points in order, from 1 to 5, and then clicking again on point 1 to close the path. Clicking point 1 adds a corner point in this position.

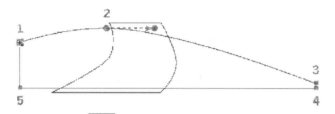

2] Position the cursor on point 2 at the top of the curve. Drag to the right to pull out the control handles until the first segment of the path matches the pattern (which will occur when the cursor is positioned over the red dot in the pattern). Then release the mouse button.

When you drag with the Pen tool, you create a curve point.

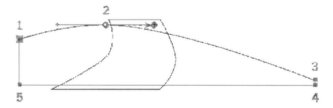

3] Click once on point 3 to add a corner point.

The top-right segment may not match the pattern exactly, but don't stop to make adjustments until you have completed and closed the path. It will be much easier to make the adjustments after all of the points have been created.

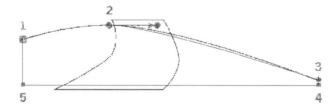

4] Hold down the Shift key and click point 4 and then point 5. Then click the original point (point 1) to close the path.

Holding down Shift when adding additional points ensures that the segment being added will be vertical, horizontal, or at a 45-degree angle to the previous point.

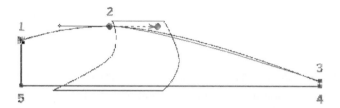

5] Using the Pointer tool, click the curve point (2) to display the control handles. Drag the right handle out farther to the right until the curve matches the pattern. Save your work.

Try to drag directly to the right to avoid changing the segment to the left of the curve point, which already matches the pattern.

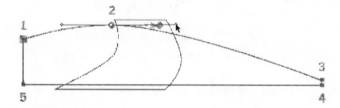

> **tip**   *If the pattern for the road is not visible, it's probably because your hill shape has a fill. If so, change the fill to None in the Fill Inspector.*

6] Press the Tab key to deselect the hill path. Trace the road that overlaps this hill shape by clicking the Pen tool at the upper-right corner of the road pattern to create a corner point.

The road will extend beyond the edges of the hill; you will trim off the excess later.

7] Add a curve point at the outermost part of the curve on the right side by holding the mouse and dragging downward to pull out control handles. Release the mouse and then trace around the rest of the pattern, adding corner and curve points as needed. Finally, click the original point to close the path.

> **tip**   *Always work around a path, and trace the entire path before making adjustments with the Pointer tool.*

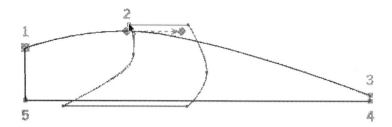

8] Display the Color List by choosing Window › Panels › Color List. Drag the swatch next to PANTONE 18-7 and drop it inside the road you just created. Drag the swatch next to None and drop it on the edge of the path to change the stroke to None.

You can also make these changes using the Fill and Stroke Inspectors.

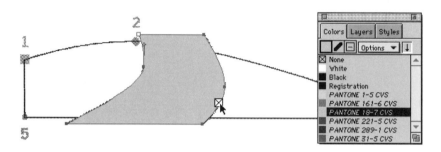

9] Press the Tab key to deselect the road. Fill the hill with PANTONE 289-1 and set the stroke to None.

Drag color swatches from the Color List or use the Fill and Stroke Inspectors to make these changes.

tip *Windows users should remember that the document window must be active for Tab to deselect elements. If the Color List is active, for instance, simply click the page or pasteboard to activate the document window.*

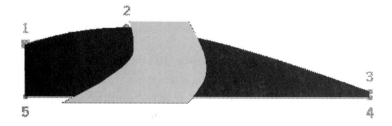

10] Save your work.

Next you will define object styles for these two elements.

DEFINING AND APPLYING OBJECT STYLES

You can record the visual characteristics of an element as an object style to make it easier to apply the same characteristics to other elements in the future. In addition, when you change a style definition, all of the elements that have been assigned that style will automatically be updated to reflect the changes.

You will create two styles for filling the hills and roads in your illustration.

1] Display the Styles panel by choosing Window › Panels › Styles.

FreeHand offers two types of styles: object and paragraph. **Object styles**, which you are using in this task, record the stroke and fill characteristics of a selected element. **Paragraph styles** record character and paragraph formatting for text. Two default styles—a Normal style for objects and a Normal style for text—are already displayed in the Styles panel.

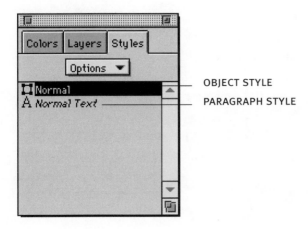

OBJECT STYLE

PARAGRAPH STYLE

In the first lesson you learned how to import a style from a library. Next you will create styles of your own.

2] Select the hill element with the Pointer tool. Choose New from the Options menu in the Styles panel to define a new style based on the fill and stroke of the selected element.

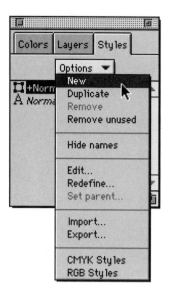

A new object style, named Style-1, appears in the Styles panel. The artwork does not visibly change, but it is now connected to this style.

3] Double-click the name Style-1, type *Hill*, and press Enter to change the name of this style.

The Hill style is defined as a basic PANTONE 289-1 fill with no stroke—the current style of the selected object.

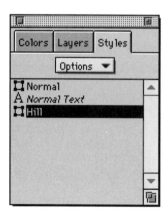

4] Select the road element with the Pointer tool and create another new style by choosing New from the Options menu in the Styles panel. Double-click the default new style name and change it to *Road*.

The Road style is defined as a basic PANTONE 18-7 fill with no stroke.

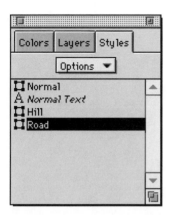

5] Save your work.

Next you will trim off the excess portion of the road to match the edges of the hill.

COMBINING ELEMENTS WITH PATH OPERATIONS

In an earlier task, you used the Paste Inside feature to make the sunbeams visible only within the sky rectangle. In this task, you will use the **Intersect** command to trim off the excess portions of the road to match the edges of the hill.

Although Paste Inside will work here as well, the Intersect command creates less complex artwork when you are dealing with an individual element that you will not need to move later. Paste Inside is useful when there are multiple elements, or when you may wish to move the artwork in the future; no matter how you arrange the elements later, the clipping path will always define the visible edges of the artwork. Intersect and the other path operations permanently clip off unwanted portions of selected elements, simplifying the document; however, your work will be much more difficult if you ever need to move these elements.

tip   *If you have multiple elements or may need to move elements later, it is usually best to use Paste Inside. Otherwise, you can use Intersect, Union, and the other path operations to easily create complex and accurate paths.*

1] Select the hill with the Pointer tool and choose Edit › Clone to make a duplicate of the hill in the same position, on top of the existing artwork. The clone of the hill is already selected, so now add the road to the selection by holding down Shift and clicking the edge of the road that is visible.

183

Do not use the Select All command, since that would select both copies of the hill.

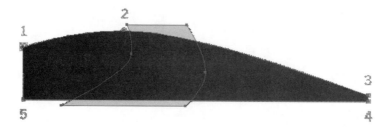

2] Choose Modify › Combine › Intersect.

The two individual shapes are replaced by the shape defined by the intersection, or overlap, of the two selected shapes: the trimmed road. You cloned the hill before creating the intersection, so the trimmed road now sits in front of the original hill.

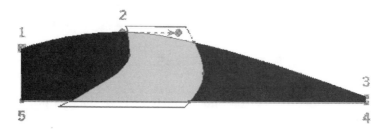

3] The trimmed road is already selected. Add the hill to the selection by Shift+clicking it with the Pointer tool. Then group the hill and road together by choosing Modify › Group.

Grouping the elements will prevent you from accidentally moving either the road or the hill without the other element.

4] Save your work.

CREATING OTHER ELEMENTS

Now you will trace the other two hills and roads.

1] Press the Tab key to make sure that no elements are selected. Click Normal in the Style panel so that the next items you create will have a black stroke and no fill.

The active style when no elements are selected determines the style that is assigned automatically to the next elements. Using Normal while tracing the shapes will make it easier to see the patterns, since Normal specifies a black stroke and no fill.

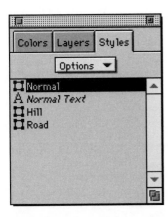

2] Use the Pen tool to trace the next hill pattern in the same manner as the first, clicking to position corner points and dragging to pull out control handles for curve points.

Remember to trace around the entire shape and to click the starting point to close the path.

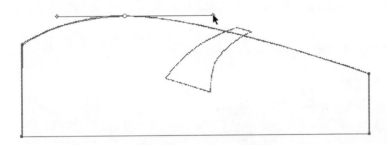

tip   *To trace the remaining elements, you can use either the Pen or Bezigon tool, as you prefer.*

3] Trace the road for this second hill.

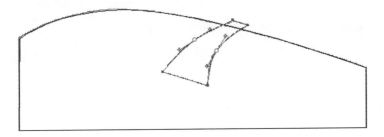

4] Apply the Road style to this element by clicking Road in the Styles panel. Select the hill element and apply the Hill style.

You can also apply a style by dragging the icon to the left of the style name in the Styles panel and dropping it on the desired object.

Next you will trim off the excess portion of the road with the Intersect command.

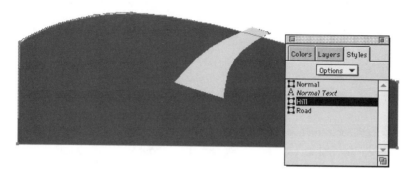

5] With the hill path selected, choose Edit › Clone. Hold down the Shift key and click a visible portion of the road to select it along with the clone of the hill. Choose Modify › Combine › Intersect.

The road is trimmed to match the edges of the hill.

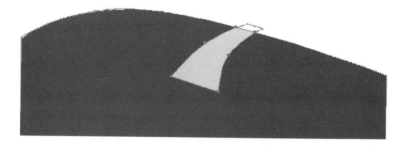

tip   *Zoom in closer if you have difficulty selecting the road and the hill at the same time.*

6] Select the hill and road and choose Modify › Group.

The second hill is now complete—only one more hill to go!

7] Repeat steps 1 through 6 for the third hill pattern and its road.

This third pattern is visible below the page, so you may need to scroll down to see it clearly.

186

8] Save your work.

ALIGNING ELEMENTS

The three groups that make up the hillsides in this illustration need to be aligned to one another so the road appears to be continuous. To align the three individual hill groups, you will select them together and use the Align panel.

1] Choose Edit › Select › All in Document to select all three hill groups.

Note that the Select All command selects only the items on the page, not those on the pasteboard. Select All in Document selects all of the elements in the document, on all pages and the pasteboard, in any unlocked and visible layers.

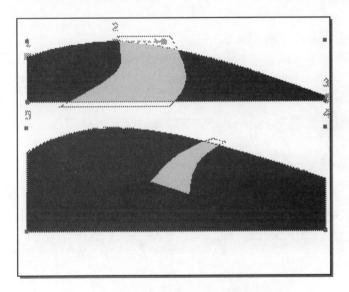

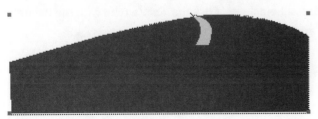

2] Choose Window > Panels > Align to display the Align panel. Click the bottom-middle square on the Align panel grid to set the panel to center the groups horizontally and align the bottom edges.

You can set the alignment by clicking the grid or by choosing from either menu at the bottom of the Align panel.

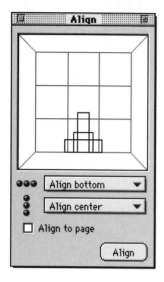

3] Click Apply (Windows) or Align (Macintosh).

All three hills are now aligned to one another, but they are stacked up in the wrong order. The road should be visible going over all of the hills.

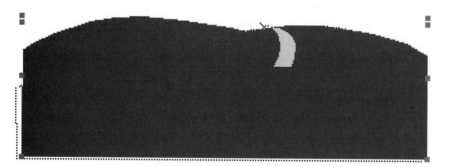

4] Press the Tab key to deselect all elements. Click the visible road with the Pointer tool to select the hill in front and choose Modify > Arrange > Send to Back.

The most distant road segment is now on the bottom of the stack, and the middle segment is in front of the others, hiding the closest segment.

5] Press the Tab key to deselect all elements and click the middle (larger) road with the Pointer tool. This element must be moved only one item back, rather than all the way to the back, so choose Modify › Arrange › Move Backward.

Send to Back and Bring to Front move selected items to the very back or front within the current layer. Move Backward and Move Forward move selected elements one item backward or forward. If more than one element is on top of the element you want to move forward, you select this command again until the element is placed correctly.

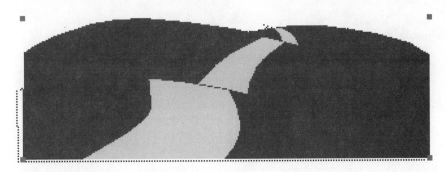

Now group the hills in their correct positions.

6] Choose Edit › Select › All in Document to select all three hill groups and then choose Modify › Group. Save your work

The hills are ready to be positioned on the page.

POSITIONING ARTWORK AND EDITING STYLES

Now turn on the Sky layer so you can see how the Hill layer looks with it and make any modifications to the styles.

1] In the Layers panel, hide the Pattern 2 layer and show the Sky layer by turning their check marks off and on, respectively. Use the Pointer tool to move the hills into position so that the bottom and sides of the hills slightly overlap the edges of the sky rectangle.

You will use the Paste Inside feature to trim these hills the same way you did with the sunbeams earlier. Before you do this, though, you will change the style definitions to change the appearance of the hills.

2] Display the Tints panel (Window › Panels › Tints). Select PANTONE 289-1 as the base color from the menu at the top. Click the 40 percent swatch to display it in the color well at the bottom of the panel and then click the Add to Color List button. In the dialog box that appears, accept the default name for this tint by clicking the Add button.

This will add 40 percent PANTONE 289-1 to the Color List.

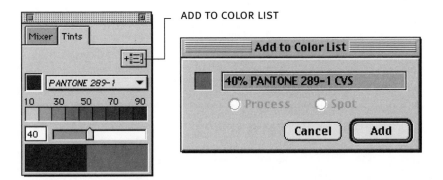

ADD TO COLOR LIST

3] Display the Styles panel (Window > Panels > Styles) and press the Tab key to make sure that no elements are selected in your document. Click the Hill style once in the panel and choose Edit from the Options menu in the Styles panel.

This displays the Edit Style dialog box, where you can change the characteristics of elements that have this style assigned.

4] Change the fill to Gradient, with PANTONE 289-1 at the top and the 40 percent tint of that color at the bottom. Then change the angle to 90 degrees and press Enter.
The fill settings appear on the left side of the dialog box. You can change the angle by entering a new value in the field just above the bottom color in the gradient strip or by rotating the angle dial just above the angle field.

191

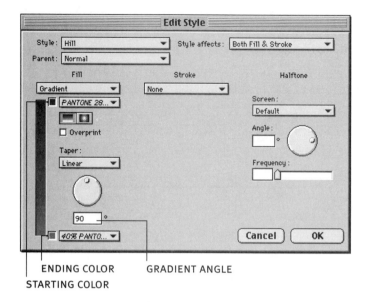

ENDING COLOR   GRADIENT ANGLE

STARTING COLOR

5] Click OK to apply the changes and return to the artwork.

Changing the style definition automatically changes the style of all elements that have this style applied.

6] Edit the Road style by selecting that style in the Styles panel and choosing Edit from the Options menu in the panel. Change the fill to Gradient, with PANTONE 18-7 at the top and PANTONE 31-5 at the bottom, with an angle of 270 degrees.

In both the hill and road elements, the gradients will flow from a lighter color on the top to a darker color at the bottom.

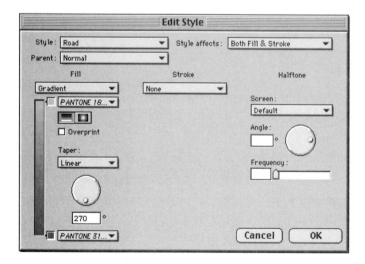

7] Click OK to see the results. Click Normal in the Style panel. Then save your work.

The hills and roads are now filled with gradient fills. Notice how the gradients give the impression of sunlight highlights on the hilltops.

tip *This is a simple demonstration of the power that object styles can offer. Imagine that you had created a state map and made all interstate highways 2 points wide and blue by defining and applying a style. If your client then decides that these highways should all be 4 points wide and red, you can simply edit the style definition to update every highway on the map.*

ADDING ELEMENTS TO THE CLIPPING PATH

You will hide the parts of the hills that extend beyond the edges of the sky rectangle by adding the hill group to the clipping path you created earlier.

1] The hills are in the correct position, so select the hill group and choose Edit › Cut.

The hills disappear from the page.

2] Select the sky rectangle and choose Edit › Paste Inside.

The hills are added to the sunbeam artwork inside the sky rectangle, and the edges of the artwork are defined by the rectangle.

The hills have been removed from the Hills layer and pasted into the Sky layer. Notice how the edges of the hills now perfectly match the edges of the sky graphic.

3] Save your work.

SCALING AND REFLECTING ARTWORK

You still need to create the trees in the illustration. The artwork for the four trees is identical, so you can create one tree and then scale and reflect copies into position.

1] Hide the Sky layer. Use the Options menu in the Layers panel to create a new layer and change the name of that layer to *Trees*. Rename the Hills layer *Pattern 3*. Move the Pattern 3 layer below the separator line to make it a background layer.
Remember that the check mark next to a layer name allows you to control the visibility of the individual layers. Also remember that you rename layers by double-clicking the layer name and entering a new one.

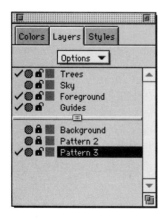

tip *In this case, you renamed the empty Hills layer to use it for a new purpose. When you no longer need a particular layer in your document, you can also use the Options > Remove command in the Layers panel to delete the selected layer.*

Now open the tracing pattern for the trees.

2] Choose File › Import, select Pattern3.tif from the Media folder within the Lesson4 folder, and click Open. Position your cursor at the top-left corner of the page and click the mouse.

The image of four trees appears on the Pattern 3 layer, because it is the active layer.

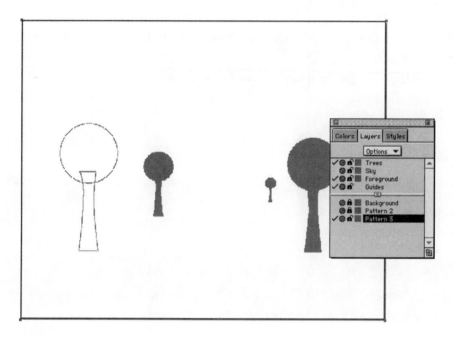

tip *If the image does not appear on the Pattern 3 layer, move it to that layer by clicking that layer in the Layers panel when the image is selected.*

3] Press the Tab key to deselect the image. Lock the Pattern 3 layer and click the Trees layer to make it the active layer. Save your work.

You are now ready to begin creating a tree.

4] Zoom in to clearly see the tree pattern on the left. Trace the tree trunk using the Pen or Bezigon tool.

Make sure to close the path so it can be filled in later.

5] Fill the tree trunk path with PANTONE 31-5, and change the stroke to None.

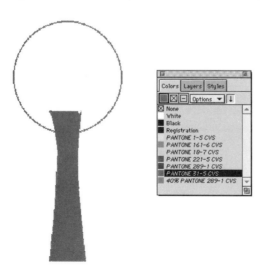

The next element to trace is a circle. You can make it easier to create a circle that will accurately match the pattern by using nonprinting ruler guides.

6] Choose View › Page Rulers to display the rulers at the top and left edges of the document window (Windows Ctrl+Alt+M, Macintosh Command+Option+M). Position your cursor on the numbers in the top ruler and drag a nonprinting ruler guide down to the top of the circle pattern. Drag a ruler guide from the left ruler and position it at the left edge of the circle pattern.

These guides will make it easier to trace the circle pattern.

7] Select the Ellipse tool and position the cursor at the intersection of the two ruler guides. Hold down the Shift key to create a perfect circle and drag downward and to the right until the circle you are drawing matches the pattern.

Use ruler guides any time you need assistance in positioning or aligning elements.

8] Using the Fill Inspector, change the type of fill to Gradient. Click Radial Fill and change the top color to PANTONE 18-7. Change the bottom color to 40% PANTONE 289-1. Then drag the PANTONE 289-1 color swatch from the Color List and drop it in the middle of the color ramp to add a third color to the gradient. Move the center point up and to the left by dragging the center point control in the Fill Inspector.

The color ramp can be used to create a gradient fill combining up to 32 colors. Your Fill Inspector settings should look similar to the ones shown here.

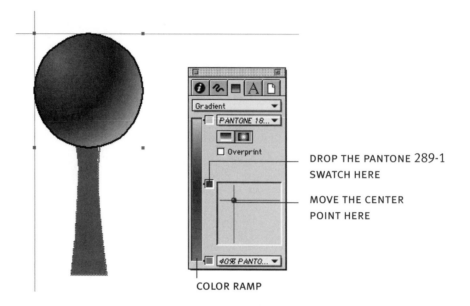

DROP THE PANTONE 289-1
SWATCH HERE

MOVE THE CENTER
POINT HERE

COLOR RAMP

9] Change the stroke around the circle to None. Then select both the circle and the trunk and group them together to complete the tree. Save your work.

The first tree is finished.

10] Choose Edit › Duplicate to create another copy of the tree. Move this tree just to the right of the second tree pattern from the left, so its trunk bottom aligns with the trunk bottom of the pattern tree.

This second tree is much too large.

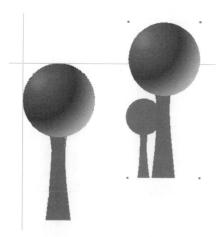

11] Hold down the Shift key and use the Pointer tool to drag the upper-right selection handle downward and to the left until the height of the tree matches the pattern. Then move the tree to position it to match the pattern.

tip   *Holding the Shift key prevents the object proportions from changing.*

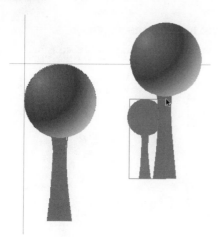

Two trees have been created, and there are only two more trees to go. However, you want the side of the trees with the lighted lower edge to face the sun, so the trees on the right must be reflections of the trees on the left.

12] Select both trees and choose Edit › Clone. Using the Reflection tool, position your cursor somewhere in the center of the page, between the center two trees. Hold down the Shift key and drag the mouse downward to reflect the trees around a vertical axis. Press the Tab key to deselect the new trees.

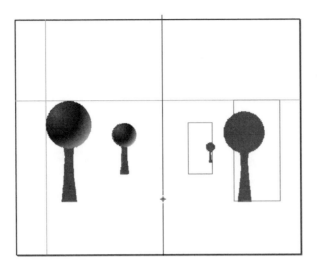

The two trees on the right now have the "lighted" lower edge on the left, facing the sun. The line that appears when you reflect an object is the reflection axis. By holding down the Shift key, you constrain the reflection axis vertically, horizontally, or to a 45-degree angle.

13] Resize and position the two trees on the right to match the pattern.
Remember to hold down Shift while resizing so you do not accidentally distort the trees.

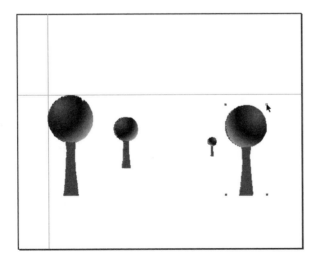

14] Display the Sky layer to see your trees in position on the rest of the artwork you have created. Save your work.

If you do not see the trees in front of your sky and hills, make sure that your layers are in the right order.

Your work in this lesson is almost complete.

IMPORTING A PICTURE FRAME

Layers make it easy to add optional elements to your documents, allowing you to show or hide the artwork as needed. Organize your documents into layers when this will make it easier to select, modify, or view the elements.

In this task, you will import a frame to surround your illustration. By placing this frame on a layer by itself, you will be able to easily view and print the artwork with or without the picture frame.

1] Create a new layer and rename it *Frame*.

The Frame layer will now be the active layer, where the artwork you are about to import will appear.

2] Import Frame.fh8 from the Media folder within the Lesson4 folder. Position your cursor at the top-left corner of the page and click.

This picture frame graphic was created to fit this page; positioning the import cursor at the top-left corner of the page imports the artwork in the correct position. Reposition the frame if necessary so it fits on the page.

3] Save your work.

OTHER LAYER PANEL CONTROLS

The Layers panel provides two more controls that may be useful to you in the future: You can change the colors of the selection boxes that appear on different layers so you can more easily identify the layer you are using, and you can use the Keyline view to see your artwork without fills or strokes.

Experiment with changing the color of selection boxes.

1] Select one of the trees on your page.

Notice that the selection boxes appear in a light blue—the same blue that appears next to the name of the Trees layer where that artwork is located. You can change these colors so the colors of the selection boxes indicate the layer on which the selected artwork is located.

2] Display the Color Mixer and create a bright red or magenta color. Drag the new color from the color well in the Mixer and drop it on the color swatch next to the Trees layer.

The selection boxes of the selected tree should now be displayed in this new color, which also appears next to Trees in the Layers panel. Items on the Trees layer now display green selection boxes when selected.

tip *One of the preference settings you specified in Lesson 1 made this feature available. If your selection boxes do not match the color of the swatch, choose File > Preferences > General and turn on the Smoother Editing option.*

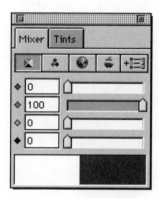
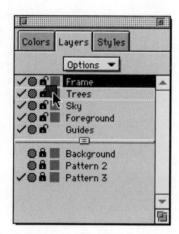

Now experiment with the Keyline view.

3] Click the small gray circle next to Trees in the Layers panel.

This changes the display of this layer from Preview to Keyline. Preview shows the printing image, whereas Keyline shows the paths without the fills and strokes. This view can be useful when you need to see the position of elements on another layer but do not want that other layer to obstruct a background image. Clicking the circle again turns the Preview for this layer back on.

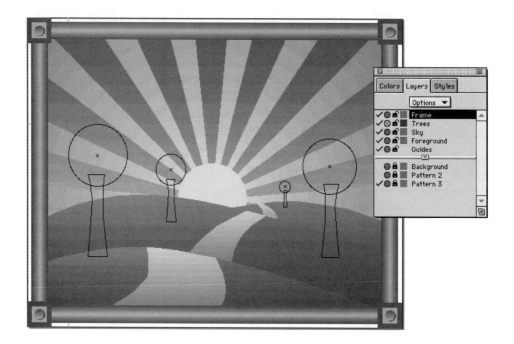

4] You do not need to save these changes, so choose File › Revert.

The Revert command restores the document to the last saved version. This command is useful only if you save frequently as you work.

EXPORTING ARTWORK FOR USE IN OTHER PROGRAMS

FreeHand 8 files are the same on both the Macintosh and Windows platforms, so no special preparation is needed to switch your files from one system to another. Simply save your file as you would normally, and you can open the file directly using FreeHand on either computer platform.

To use your FreeHand artwork in other applications, you will need to use the Export command.

1] Choose File › Export.

A dialog box appears where you can identify a location for the new file, type a name for the file, and choose a file format.

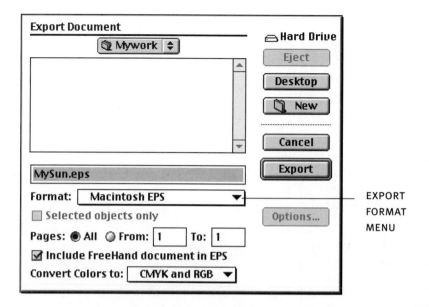

EXPORT
FORMAT
MENU

By default, FreeHand artwork is exported as an EPS, or Encapsulated PostScript, file. This is the best format to use for print production, because it delivers the same quality as the original FreeHand artwork, maintaining the high quality and resolution independence that you count on with FreeHand when the artwork is printed to a PostScript printer or output device.

The EPS format can be imported into the leading page layout applications, including QuarkXPress and Adobe PageMaker. FreeHand provides EPS formats for both platforms, so you can easily prepare artwork for both computer systems.

2] Hold down the mouse on the Format menu to see the wide range of file formats FreeHand exports.

The formats available enable you to create files ready to use in your own print, multimedia, and Internet projects. FreeHand also supports several other formats so you can prepare artwork for other specific applications.

```
   Adobe Illustrator 1.1™
   Adobe Illustrator 88™
   Adobe Illustrator® 3
   Adobe Illustrator™ 5.5
   Adobe Illustrator™ 7.x
   ASCII text
   BMP
   DCS2 EPS
   Flash 2 SWF
   FreeHand 3.1
   FreeHand 3.1 text editable
   FreeHand 4.x/5.x document
   FreeHand 7 document
   Generic EPS
   GIF
   JPEG
✓  Macintosh EPS
   MS-DOS EPS
   PDF
   Photoshop™ 3 EPS
   Photoshop™ 4 RGB EPS
   PICT
   PICT (paths)
   PICT2 (paths)
   PNG
   QuarkXPress™ EPS
   RTF text
   Targa
   TIFF
   xRes (paths)
   xRes LRG
```

For situations where you will be printing to a non-PostScript printer, the TIFF format is available. TIFF is a bitmap image format that supports both color and grayscale images at high or low resolutions, according to your specific needs.

To save a file for a multimedia project, you select Formats > BMP (Windows) or Formats > PICT (Macintosh). To use your FreeHand files in multimedia applications such as Macromedia Director and Authorware, you select the bitmap format appropriate for the platform where you are developing the multimedia project.

To prepare a graphic for use on a Web page, you choose Formats and then GIF, JPEG, or PNG. These are the most popular bitmap formats for the World Wide Web. In Lesson 9 you will have an opportunity to create Web graphics using bitmap formats and Shockwave Flash technology, which allows you to embed animated, high-resolution vector graphics in your Web pages as an alternative to the bitmap formats described here.

3] Choose GIF from the Format menu. Click Setup (Windows) or Options (Macintosh) to display specific controls for this file format. Then click More to see other options.

Although these buttons are not available for every format, you will be able to choose your own settings for the graphics you create in formats that do offer choices. For example, many of the bitmap image formats give you control over the pixel resolution of the exported image. The GIF format, for instance, offers you Transparent and Interlaced options when you are creating that type of graphic.

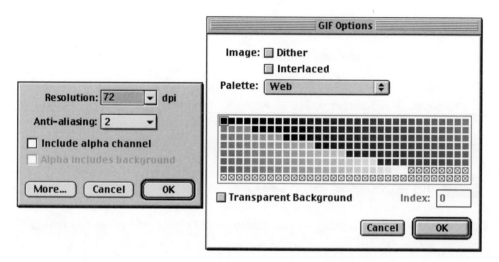

4] Click Cancel twice to return to the Export dialog box.

Several formats are available for preparing graphics for specific applications.

5] Select Formats › Photoshop 4 RGB EPS.

Adobe Photoshop users can easily transfer their FreeHand artwork to Photoshop by selecting either the Photoshop 3 or Photoshop 4 EPS format. The Photoshop EPS formats save the file differently than FreeHand's default EPS format and deliver better results when files are transferred to Photoshop.

You can also export artwork in the QuarkXPress EPS format for graphics that will be imported into QuarkXPress. There is actually no output quality difference between FreeHand's default EPS format and the QuarkXPress EPS format; however, user testing has indicated that many new users find it easier to choose the correct export format if the name of the destination application is available as an option. Thus, if you are preparing artwork for QuarkXPress, you can either select the QuarkXPress EPS format or simply export the files in FreeHand's default EPS format. The

QuarkXPress EPS format does have a color TIFF preview, making it a good choice for cross-platform work. (The Windows platform uses TIFF previews for EPS files.)

Other application-specific formats allow you to prepare artwork as files for previous versions of FreeHand, as Adobe Illustrator or Macromedia xRes files, or as PDF files for viewing in Adobe Acrobat.

6] Select Formats › EPS with TIFF preview (Windows) or Macintosh EPS (Macintosh). Choose your MyWork folder as the location in which to save this file and click Export.
This creates a new file with the specified format. By default, FreeHand also saves the FreeHand document information in the EPS file so you can open it to make changes in FreeHand at a later time.

As you can see, because FreeHand offers such a wide variety of export formats, it works equally well whether you're designing for print, multimedia, or the World Wide Web. It also enables you to use your artwork in all three of these types of projects simply by exporting the same artwork to different formats.

tip *At times, you may need to make changes to your artwork after you have exported the file. Remember that the Save command saves only the FreeHand document—it does not update the exported file. In this situation, after making the desired changes and saving the FreeHand file, choose File > Export Again to update the exported file with the changes.*

ON YOUR OWN

Experiment with these techniques in a new document by creating another sunset image. This time, select your own colors and use a circle as the clipping path that defines the outer edge of your sunset image.

WHAT YOU HAVE LEARNED

In this lesson you have:

- Practiced creating a custom-size page [*page* **152**]

- Imported tracing patterns into nonprinting background layers [*page* **154**]

- Locked tracing pattern layers so they cannot be accidentally changed [*page* **156**]

- Created and named multiple foreground and background layers to organize elements [*page* **157**]

- Learned when to use spot color and when to use process color [*page* **158**]

- Practiced importing colors into the Color List [*page* **159**]

- Activated and repositioned layers to organize your document [*page* **161**]

- Created paths with the Pen tool [*page* **162**]

- Rotated elements around a point and duplicated that transformation [*page* **165**]

- Created clipping paths with the Paste Inside command [*page* **169**]

- Experimented with the Preview and Keyline views [*page* **172**]

- Defined and modified object styles [*page* **181**]

- Trimmed artwork using the Intersect command [*page* **183**]

- Scaled objects proportionately using the Shift key [*page* **199**]

- Practiced reflecting objects around a central axis [*page* **200**]

- Imported another FreeHand document onto a new layer [*page* **201**]

- Color-coded layers so that the object selection boxes show which layer the object is on [*page* **202**]

- Exported your illustration as an EPS file [*page* **204**]

documents

multiple-page

LESSON 5

In addition to creating a wide variety of graphics and illustrations, you can use FreeHand to design and construct multiple-page documents by adding pages to your documents and flowing text from one page to the next. In fact, FreeHand allows you to create several different-size pages within the same document. For example, you could add a business card and envelope as additional custom-size pages in the letterhead document you completed in Lesson 2.

This three-page catalog was created entirely in FreeHand using the program's page layout tools, which combine the text-handling features you find in page layout programs with the graphics management features you expect from a professional-level drawing program.

Designed by Tom Faist of Datrix Media Group. Robot illustrations by Stewart McKissick.

In this lesson, you will construct a three-page mini-catalog.

If you would like to review the final result of this lesson, open Robotz.fh8 in the Complete folder within the Lesson5 folder.

WHAT YOU WILL LEARN

In this lesson you will:

- Attach text to a path
- Add pages to a document
- Import text into a layout
- Flow text from one page to another
- Format text using styles
- Wrap text around graphics
- Copy colors from imported images for use elsewhere in a document
- Print your document
- Prepare files for a commercial printer

APPROXIMATE TIME

It usually takes about 2 hours to complete this lesson.

LESSON FILES

Media Files:

Lesson5\Media\Robotz.rtf
Lesson5\Media\Spacebtz.tif
Lesson5\Media\Terrabtz.tif
Lesson5\Media\Tranzbtz.tif

Starting Files:

Lesson5\Media\Robotz.ft8 (optional)

Completed Project:

Lesson5\Media\Robotz.fh8

SPECIFYING A CUSTOM PAGE SIZE

The catalog you will be creating requires a custom page size, plus a specific amount of bleed area around the page. In addition, you will enter the printer resolution of the output device that will be used to print this document. This allows FreeHand to optimize the resolution of gradient fills for the best printed results.

1] Close any open FreeHand document windows and then choose File › New to create a new document.

A page appears within a new document window. You will change the page size and document settings to match the layout.

2] Choose Window › Inspectors › Document to display the Document Inspector. Change the Page Size menu option to Custom and type *7i* as the value for x and *5i* as the value for y. Then press Enter and click the Landscape orientation button.

Currently the measurement units for your document are set to points, so the values in these fields are displayed that way. To enter a value with a different unit of measure than that in which the value is displayed (for instance, to enter 7 inches in a field that displays values in points), simply add the unit to the measurement. For example, FreeHand understands that *7i* indicates 7 inches instead of 7 points.

When you press Enter, the values you specified will be converted to the current measurement unit. Thus, your 7-inch by 5-inch page will appear as a 504-point by 360-point page in the Document Inspector.

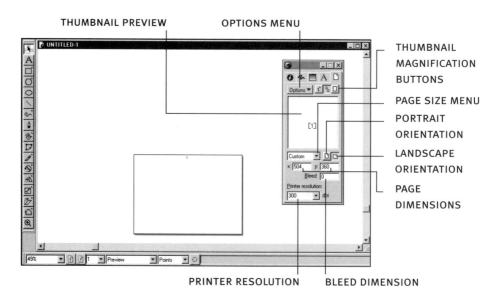

THUMBNAIL PREVIEW   OPTIONS MENU

THUMBNAIL MAGNIFICATION BUTTONS

PAGE SIZE MENU

PORTRAIT ORIENTATION

LANDSCAPE ORIENTATION

PAGE DIMENSIONS

PRINTER RESOLUTION   BLEED DIMENSION

3] Choose View › Fit to Page. Type *9* as the bleed size in the Document Inspector and press Enter.

The bleed size defines how much beyond the edge of the page FreeHand will print when this document is output. Bleed size is important when preparing artwork for a printing press. The measurement of 9 points is equal to the standard one-eighth inch bleed you specified earlier.

4] In the Document Inspector, set the printer resolution to 600.

Setting the printer resolution to match the characteristics of the printer or output device that this project will be printed on allows FreeHand to optimize color transitions—graduated fills and blends in the document—so you will get the best possible results. Set this value to the resolution of your final output device. For example, as you are creating a document, you may print it on a 300-dot-per-inch (dpi) printer, and then you may send it to a service bureau for final output at 1,270 dpi. Since the final output is what you are concerned with, you would type *1270* as the printer resolution in FreeHand for that document.

5] Close the Document Inspector and choose View › Magnification › 100%.

Working at actual size makes it easier to precisely adjust the size and position of elements.

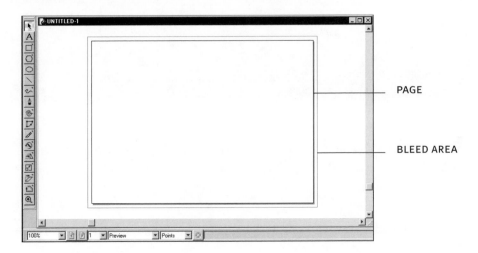

PAGE

BLEED AREA

6] Save the document as *MyToys* in your MyWork folder.

Instead of adding the two additional pages at this time, you first will first set up one page with all of the elements and guides you want to appear on every page. Then you will duplicate that page, which duplicates the elements as well, so you don't have to copy, paste, and reposition items manually.

213

CREATING GUIDES FOR A CONSISTENT LAYOUT

To position elements on your pages consistently, you will set up several nonprinting guides on the page.

1] Show the rulers by choosing View › Page Rulers and show the Info bar by choosing Window › Toolbars › Info.

The rulers must be visible for you to add ruler guides to the page. The Info bar will help you position them accurately.

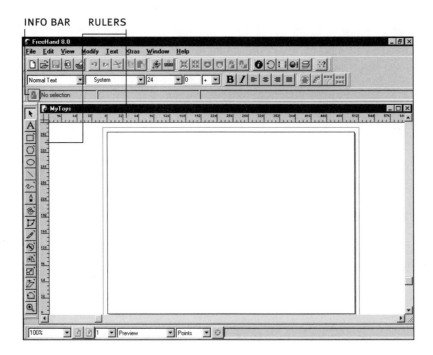

tip *The Info bar works just like the toolbox and other toolbars. If you prefer to have this displayed as a floating panel rather than a toolbar docked to the top of the screen, simply drag it toward the center of the screen.*

2] Change the unit of measure for this document to Picas using the Units menu at the bottom of the document window.

Picas and points are units of measure widely used in the graphic arts field. You already have been using points to specify type sizes and stroke widths. There are 12 points per pica and 6 picas per inch. Each inch, therefore, is equivalent to 72 points. Using this system, you can avoid having to deal with the fractional or decimal values required when working with inches.

3] Drag a ruler guide out from the center of the vertical ruler on the left side of the document window. Watch the Info bar at the top of the window and position this guide when the *x* value is 7p8 (7 picas, 8 points).

This nonprinting guide is 7 picas and 8 points out from the left edge of the page.

tip   *Make sure to drag ruler guides out from the center of the rulers. If you drag from the top-left corner of the rulers, where the vertical and horizontal rulers intersect, you will reposition the zero point on the page. If the zero point is repositioned, all of the values for the horizontal (x) and vertical (y) positions will be now measured from that new point. If this ever happens by mistake, double-click the point where the rulers intersect to reset the zero point to the lower-left corner of the page. All measurements in these lessons assume that the zero point is in this default position: the lower-left corner of the page.*

INFO BAR X VALUE

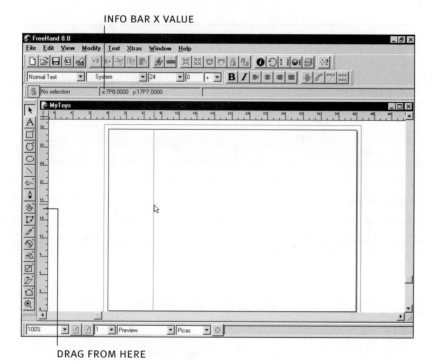

DRAG FROM HERE

4] Drag a new vertical guide out to 10p6. Now drag a ruler guide from the horizontal ruler across the top of the window down to 25p.

You can pull ruler guides from the vertical or horizontal ruler as needed.

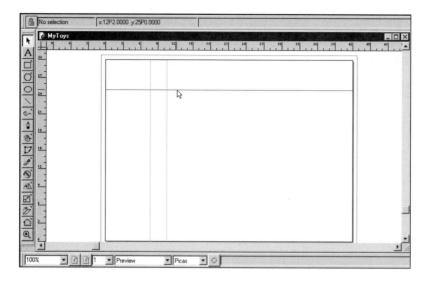

In addition to the ruler guides, any element on the page can be converted into a guide. You will next create a rectangle to indicate the position of the text block that you will create on this page and then convert that rectangle into a guide.

5] Create a rectangle anywhere on the page using the Rectangle tool. Then choose Window › Inspectors › Object to display the Object Inspector. For the *x* dimension in the Inspector, type *13p4*. Press the Tab key to select the *y* value and type *2p8*. Press Tab again to select the width value and type *25p5*. Then press Tab and type *18p0* as the height value. Press Enter.

This rectangle is now the precise size and in the correct location required for this layout.

tip *Entering specific values in the Inspectors helps you position elements with precision.*

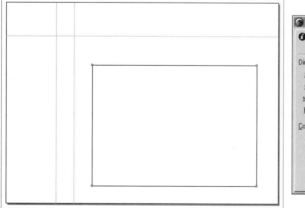

6] Click the Layers button on the main toolbar to display the Layers panel, or choose Window › Panels › Layers. With the rectangle selected on the page, click once on the name of the Guides layer to convert the selection into a guide.

If you move elements to the Guides layer, they automatically become nonprinting guides, just like the ruler guides you created earlier.

You have used foreground and background layers in previous lessons. The Guides layer is special—even though it appears above the divider in the Layers panel, elements on the Guides layer do not print. You can move this layer above or below other layers, depending on how you want the guides to appear. You can also hide and lock the Guides layer the same way you can other layers.

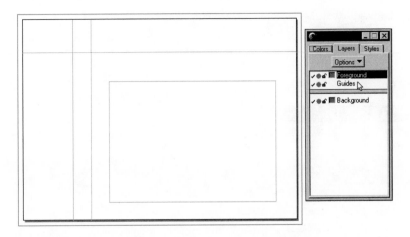

7] Create another rectangle. Position it so that *x* is 8p7 and *y* is 10p0, and set the width to 18p6 and the height to 12p4. Then convert this rectangle into a guide.

All of the guides are now in place.

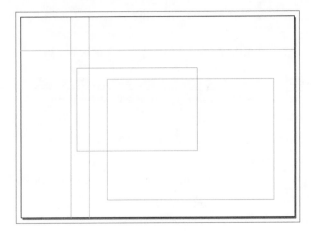

217

8] Hide the page rulers and Info bar and save the document.

You are now ready to begin assembling elements on the page.

USING THE EDIT GUIDES COMMAND

Another way to set up and manipulate guides is to use FreeHand's Edit Guides controls. In the Guides dialog box you can create new guides in precise positions, adjust the positions of existing guides, evenly distribute guides across a page, and release guides. Try it.

1] Create a new document. Choose View › Guides › Edit.

A new document window appears in front of your current document, where you can experiment with Ruler guides. The Guides dialog box displays a list of the guides on the designated page. No guides have been created for this new document, so the list is blank.

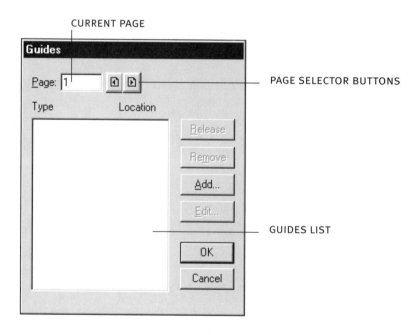

CURRENT PAGE

PAGE SELECTOR BUTTONS

GUIDES LIST

2] Click Add. Click Vertical and type *6* in the Count field, *.5i* in the First Position field, and *8i* in the Last Position field.

The First and Last Position values allow you to enter a distance in from the edge of the page where you want the first and last guides to be placed. As in all FreeHand entry fields, if you want to enter an inch value in a field that currently displays points or picas, simply add the unit after the value, such as *.5i*.

These settings will create six vertical ruler guides that are evenly spaced across the page, starting and ending 0.5 inch in from the left and right edges of the page.

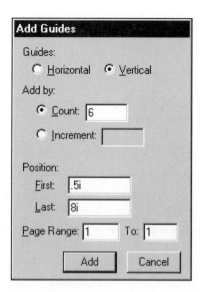

3] Click Add to return to the Guides dialog box.

All of your new guides now appear in the Guides list, which displays the type and location of each guide.

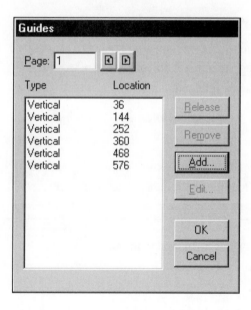

4] Click OK in the Guides dialog box to apply these changes and view your document.

FreeHand has added the six guides to the page, positioned precisely as you indicated in the dialog boxes.

5] Return to the Guides dialog box and experiment with the other options: deleting, editing, and releasing guides.

The Edit button allows you to numerically reposition each guide.

The Release button actually releases a guide from the Guides layer and changes it into a printing path on the active layer in your document. Ruler guides created by dragging out from the rulers become lines when released.

Delete will do exactly as you would expect, removing the selected guide completely from the document.

If you add a path to the Guides layer, the Guides dialog box will display the path as one of the guides in the list, and it can be modified in the same ways as any other guide.

6] Close this document and return to the MyToys document window.

You do not need to save changes to the Untitled document.

IMPORTING PANTONE PROCESS COLORS

In the previous lesson, you learned that documents that use many colors, and especially those that include photographic artwork, are usually printed with process colors. The Robotz catalog fits this description, so you will specify process colors for this document. In this task, you will import a set of process colors from a color library for accurate results.

In the first step you will create the rectangle at the left side of the page. Then you will fill the rectangle with a PANTONE color.

tip *Since most computer monitors cannot represent color exactly as it will be printed, it's best to choose your colors from a swatch book—a printed book that shows how colors from the PANTONE or other color libraries will look when printed on coated or uncoated papers. (You can purchase these swatch books from a graphic art supplier.) Then, when you have chosen the colors you want, you can specify them in FreeHand.*

1] Draw a rectangle that begins at the upper-left corner of the bleed area (off of the page) and extends over to the second vertical ruler guide and down to the bottom of the bleed area below the page.

This rectangle should extend off of the top, left side, and bottom of the page. Your rectangle should be similar to the selected one shown here extending off of the left edge of the page.

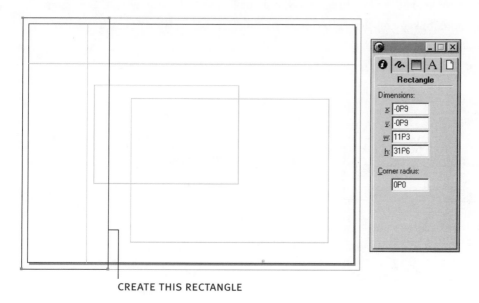

CREATE THIS RECTANGLE

2] Display the Color List by clicking the Color List button on the toolbar. Choose PANTONE Process from the Options menu at the top of the panel.

The PANTONE Process color library dialog box appears, where you will select two colors to be imported.

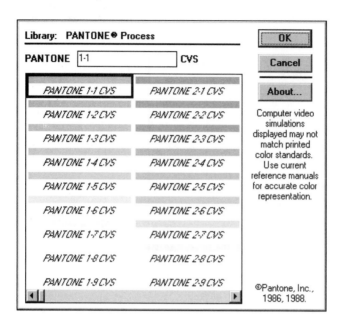

3] In the field at the top, type _140–5_. Hold down the Ctrl (Windows) or Command (Macintosh) key and click 140-6 (the color directly below the original selection). Click OK to import both colors.

The two new colors now appear at the bottom of the Color List.

4] **Select the rectangle on your page with the Pointer tool. Click the Stroke tab in the Inspector panel and set the stroke to None. Click the Fill tab and change the fill to a gradient that goes from White on the left to PANTONE 140–6 on the right.**

Notice how the color bleeds off the edge of the page.

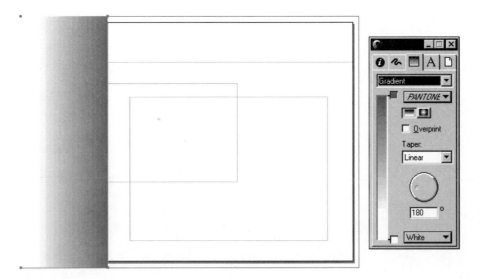

tip *When setting up a bleed, you must do two things. First you need to specify the desired bleed size in the Document Inspector. (Your commercial printer can tell you the size of bleed you need.) Then make sure all elements you create that should run off the edge of the page also extend out to or beyond the edge of the bleed.*

5] **Save the document.**

CREATING TEXT AND GRAPHIC ELEMENTS

Now you will add the other text and graphic elements that should appear on each page of the catalog.

1] **Using the Text tool, click at the top of the page and type *robotz toy company* (all lowercase). Highlight all of the text by dragging across the type with the Text tool and then use the controls in the text toolbar to change the text to 12-point News Gothic T Light.**

You could also select the text with the Pointer tool to change all of the text in the text block.

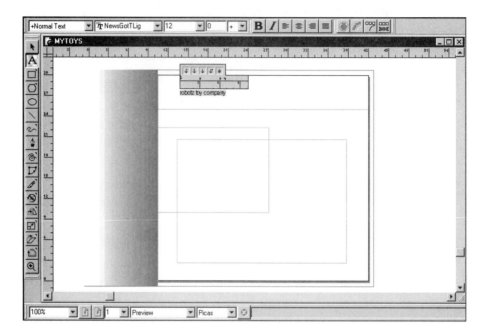

2] Now select the word _robotz_ by itself and change it to 48-point News Gothic T Bold.
To change some of the text within a text block, you must use the Text tool to select the desired characters.

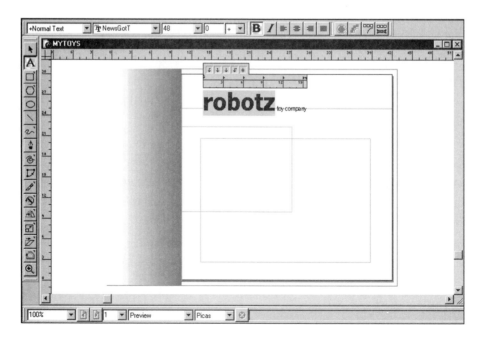

224

3] Click the text with the Pointer tool to select the text block. Position the tip of the Pointer tool cursor precisely on the bottom edge of the first character in the text. Hold down the mouse button and drag the cursor toward the ruler guide that runs across the top of the page. Release the mouse when FreeHand snaps your cursor and the baseline of the text to the ruler guide.

This demonstrates FreeHand's Snap to Guides feature. When an object you are moving or creating comes within a few pixels of a guide, FreeHand snaps the object to the guide. You can snap the edges of objects to guides, or you can position your cursor at a significant location on the object (as you did here in pointing to the bottom of the text), and FreeHand will snap the object into position when the cursor nears the guide.

The **baseline** of text is the imaginary line on which all the characters sit. For example, the lowest parts of the character *m* are touching the baseline. Some lowercase characters (such as *g* and *p*)have descenders that hang below the baseline.

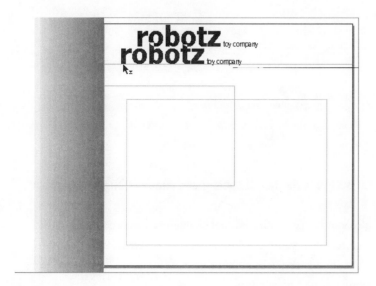

tip *Notice the snap cursor that appears as you move an element when that element is snapped to a guide. Occasionally, the snap feature can interfere when you are trying to position an element near, but not on, a guide. You can deactivate this feature by choosing View > Snap to Guides (a check mark next to this menu item indicates that the feature is turned on).*

4] Display the Text Inspector by clicking the Text tab at the top of the Inspector panel. Click the Spacing button and change the Horizontal Scale value to *130* percent.

225

Horizontal Scale adjusts the width of the characters without changing the height. Entering a value greater than 100 percent (the original font width) expands the characters. Entering a value less than 100 percent compresses the characters.

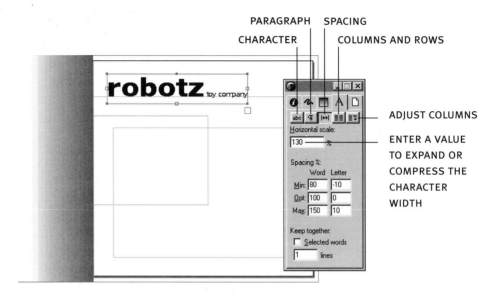

If the text did not change when you made changes in the Inspector, make sure that you press Enter to apply your changes. Also, make sure that the text block is selected with the Pointer tool so that all of the characters change.

5] Click the Character button in the Text Inspector and change Range Kerning to *12* percent.

Kerning changes the spacing between individual characters without changing the shapes of the letters. Entering a positive value increases the letterspacing; entering a negative value reduces the letterspacing. Entering zero for range kerning restores the original letterspacing defined by the font.

Notice that no font or size is identified in the Inspector. When the Text Inspector (and text toolbar) do not display a font or size for a selected block of text, the text block contains more than one font or size.

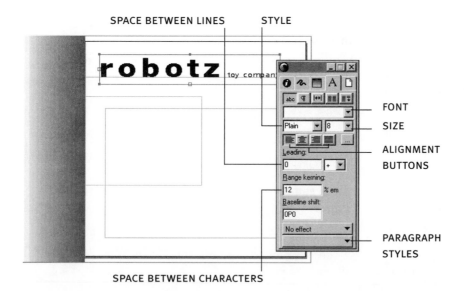

SPACE BETWEEN LINES   STYLE

FONT

SIZE

ALIGNMENT
BUTTONS

PARAGRAPH
STYLES

SPACE BETWEEN CHARACTERS

6] To slide the text left or right without moving it up or down off of the ruler guide, start to move the text block with the Pointer tool. Then hold down the Shift key as you continue to move left or right, and position the text so that the first two letters are over the filled rectangle on the left.

Holding down Shift constrains the movement to horizontal, vertical, or 45-degree angles, depending on the direction your mouse travels the farthest.

7] Change the first two letters to white by selecting them with the Text tool and then dragging the White color swatch from the Color List onto the selected characters.

Always select text with the Text tool when you want to change some of the characters in the text block without changing others.

The text is now complete.

8] Click the Pointer tool on an empty part of the page to deselect all elements. Then save your work.

Now you will add a rectangle below the text. To view the ruler guides that you placed on the left part of the page, you will first change the view so you can see the artwork without the fills and strokes.

9] Use the View menu at the bottom of the document window to change the view from Preview to Keyline. Draw a wide, short rectangle just beneath the text that begins at the left ruler guide at the far left of the page and extends almost to the right edge of the page.

The Keyline view allows you to see through the rectangle to find the ruler guide.

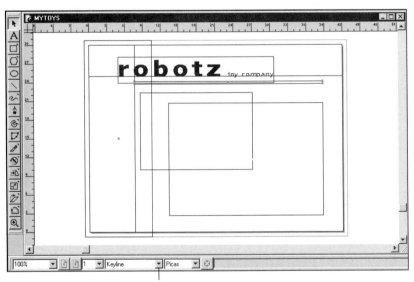

CHANGE VIEW FROM PREVIEW TO KEYLINE

10] Fill this rectangle with a gradient that goes from PANTONE 140–6 on the left to White on the right and set the stroke to None. Change the view from Keyline back to Preview so you can see the filled artwork.

Don't forget to turn Preview back on when you want to see the fills and strokes.

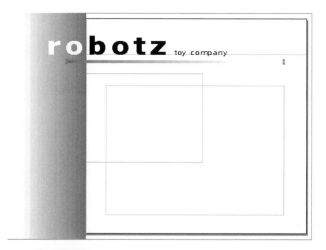

Next you will create a duplicate of this element and position it at the bottom of the page.

11] Choose Edit › Clone to create a copy of this rectangle directly on top of the original. Begin to move this copy downward with the Pointer tool and hold down the Shift key after you start to move the object. Position the rectangle just above the bottom of the page.

Again, holding down Shift constrains the movement of the element.

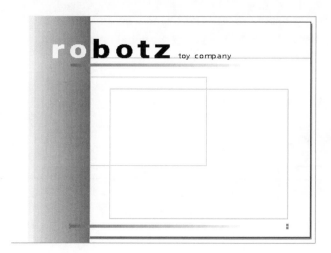

12] Save the document.

There is just one more element to add before you duplicate the page.

ATTACHING TEXT TO PATHS

In this task you will attach text to a spiral path, so it follows the path as it circles outward from the center. Text in FreeHand can be attached to open or closed paths.

1] Choose Window › Xtras › Xtra Tools to display the Xtra Tools panel.

This panel contains additional drawing, manipulation, and special-effect tools. Xtras are plug-in software extensions that enhance FreeHand's capabilities. Each Xtra adds a specific feature or group of features; Xtras providing additional tools are located in the Xtra Tools panel. A wide variety of Xtras are included with FreeHand and are installed when you install the program.

2] Double-click the Spiral tool to set preferences for this tool before you use it to create a path. Click the Loose Spiral button to select the spiral type, specify _3_ rotations, click the Clockwise Direction button, and click OK.

Remember that all tools displaying a small mark at the upper-right corner have preferences you can set by double-clicking the tool.

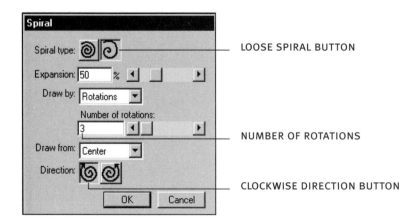

LOOSE SPIRAL BUTTON

NUMBER OF ROTATIONS

CLOCKWISE DIRECTION BUTTON

3] Position the cursor on the page, hold down the mouse button, and drag upward to draw a spiral.

Release the mouse when the size and orientation of the spiral is similar to the example shown here.

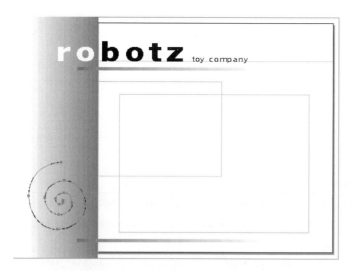

4] Choose Text › Attach to Path to enter text along this path. Change the type size to 9 points and the font to News Gothic T Medium.

A blinking insertion point appears near the center of the spiral.

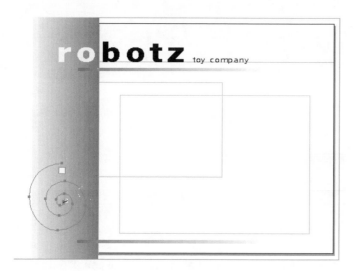

5] Type *the robotz toy company pledges to always deliver quality, safety, and value in each of its toys.* Select the word *robotz* by itself with the Text tool and change it to News Gothic T Bold.

The words wrap around the spiral as you enter the text directly on the path.

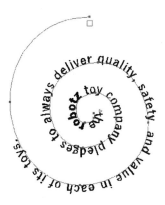

6] Click the spiral text with the Pointer tool. Drag the small triangle at the center of the spiral to reposition the start of the text out from the center to make the text easier to read. Type _12_ in the Range Kerning field in the Text Inspector to extend the text to fill the spiral.

Make sure that the text all fits on the spiral. If the Link box at the outside end of the spiral is filled with a dot, there is an overflow—some of the text does not fit and is not displayed. If a dot appears, reduce the Range Kerning and Horizontal Scale values as needed so the entire sentence appears. Remember that Range Kerning increases or decreases the space between letters, and Horizontal Scale changes the width of the letters themselves.

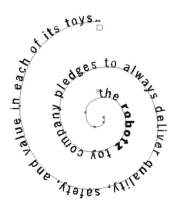

7] Display the Color List and click the Fill Selector at the top of the panel. Select PANTONE 140–5 to change the fill of the text characters.

Alternatively, you can drag the swatch for PANTONE 140–5 and drop it on the spiral text, but you may want to zoom in to see the text more clearly before attempting to drop a color on it.

Remember: If something goes wrong—for instance, if color fills the spiral instead of the text—you can choose Edit > Undo (Windows Ctrl+Z, Macintosh Command+Z) and try again.

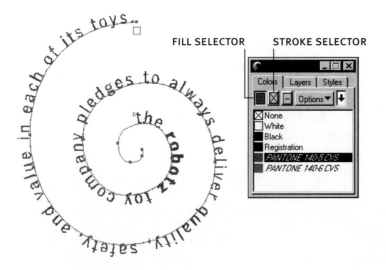

FILL SELECTOR   STROKE SELECTOR

8] Use the Pointer tool to move the spiral into position near the bottom of the rectangle. Save the document.

tip *Change to the Keyline view to make sure that the entire spiral text element is positioned on the page. Then return to Preview mode to continue.*

The common elements for all pages are now in place.

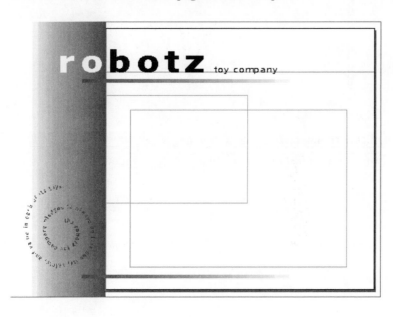

233

DUPLICATING PAGES IN A DOCUMENT

The basic design you just created will serve as a master for all the pages of the catalog. You will now create two additional pages that look just like the one you have been working on.

1] Display the Document Inspector and choose Duplicate from the Options menu at the top of the panel. This creates a second page just like the first.

The Document Inspector now displays two numbered icons, or **thumbnails**, that represent document pages on the pasteboard.

FreeHand supports multiple-page documents—it even allows you to add pages with different dimensions and orientations as needed for your specific projects. In this case, you want the three pages identical to the one you just created.

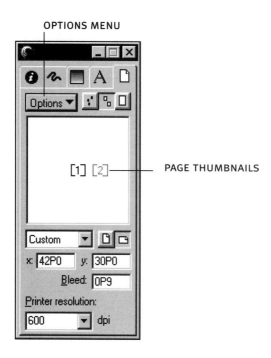

OPTIONS MENU

PAGE THUMBNAILS

2] Repeat the Duplicate command to create a third page.

The Document Inspector now displays three numbered page thumbnails on the pasteboard.

3] Click the right Thumbnail Magnification button to see one page displayed in the page thumbnail preview window in the Document Inspector. Then click the middle Thumbnail Magnification button to see several page thumbnails in the preview window (which displays all three of the pages in this document).

The left Thumbnail Magnification button will display tiny thumbnails showing where the pages are positioned on the pasteboard.

This display shows you how the pages are arranged on the pasteboard. If the new pages appear to the right of page 1 in the Inspector, that is where they are located in the document window.

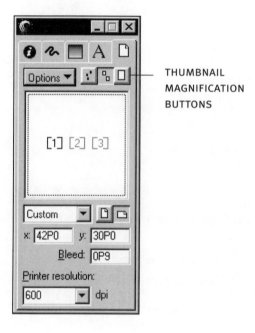

THUMBNAIL
MAGNIFICATION
BUTTONS

4] Double-click the thumbnail for page 2 in the Document Inspector.

The Inspector indicates the active page with a black outline and page number. The number of the current page is also displayed at the bottom of the window in the Page Selector field.

235

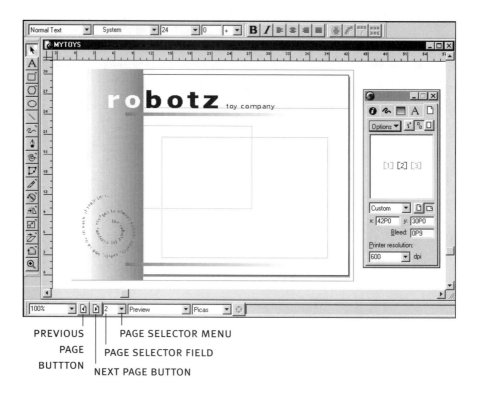

PREVIOUS PAGE BUTTTON

PAGE SELECTOR MENU

PAGE SELECTOR FIELD

NEXT PAGE BUTTON

5] Change to page 1 by selecting it from the Page Selector menu at the bottom of the Document window.

You can also change pages by clicking the Previous Page and Next Page buttons. As you can see, you can change pages in several different ways.

6] Save your work.

Make sure that the Page Selector field and Document Inspector thumbnails indicate that you are on page 1 before you continue.

IMPORTING TEXT AND LINKING TEXT BLOCKS

The text for this project has already been entered into a word processor and saved as a Rich Text Format (RTF) file. FreeHand can import RTF files, which retain text formatting characteristics, and ASCII text files, which do not retain any formatting.

In this task, you will import the text into your layout, starting on page 1. Then you will continue the text on the other two pages by linking text blocks together, allowing the text to flow from one text block to another.

The text will flow into text blocks that duplicate the size and position of the large rectangular guide you positioned on the page earlier.

1] Choose File › Import, locate Robotz.rtf in the Media folder within the Lesson5 folder, and click Open. Position the import cursor at the upper-left corner of the large rectangular guide, drag down to the bottom-right corner of this rectangle, and then release the mouse.

Formatted text flows into this text block. RTF files contain both text and formatting.

The text will not look like the finished layout yet—some of the text is not formatted properly, and this page contains more text than you need for page 1.

Notice that there is a dot in the Link box, the small square near the bottom corner of the text block. This indicates an overflow: There is more text than will fit within the current text box.

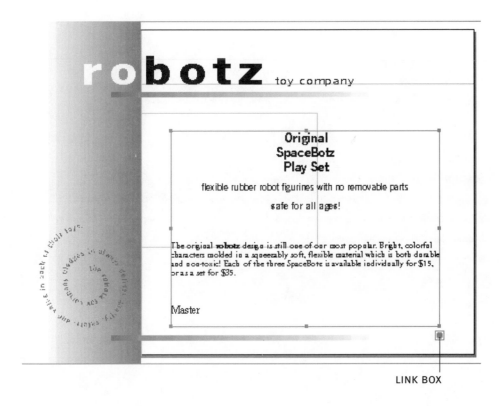

LINK BOX

Before you can flow the remaining text onto the other pages, you must first create a text block for the text to flow into on each of those pages.

2] Change to page 2. Use the Text tool to create a text block the same size and position as the large rectangular guide. Then change to page 3 and create a new text block in the same position on this page. Save your work.

Now each page has a text container, so you are ready to link the text blocks together.

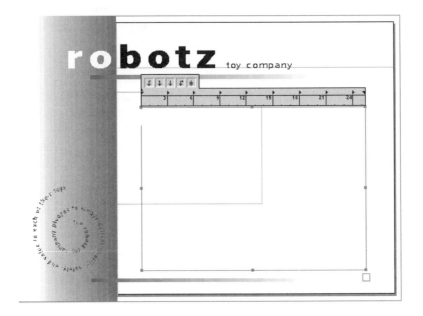

3] Choose View › Fit All. Close any panels that interfere with your view of the pages (except the toolbox).

This reduces the view so you can see all of the pages within your document. This will help in the next step, where you will link the text block on page 1 to the text blocks on the other two pages.

 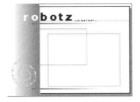 

4] Select the text block on page 1 with the Pointer tool to see the Link box with its dot indicating an overflow. Point to the Link box and drag a link line to the inside of the empty text block on page 2.

238

The text will flow into the text block on page 2, and the Link box for this text block will also indicate an overflow.

5] Repeat this process for page 3 by dragging a link line from the Link box on page 2 into the empty text block on page 3.

The text is now linked across all three pages. All of the text fits.

6] Select the text block on page 1 and choose View › Magnification › 100%.
FreeHand centers the selected elements on the screen when you change the magnification, so you now see the text block on page 1.

7] Save your work.

DEFINING PARAGRAPH STYLES

In the previous lesson, you used object styles to apply preset fill and stroke attributes to multiple objects. Paragraph styles can provide similar benefits for text.

1] Choose Window › Panels › Styles to display the Styles panel. Use the Text tool to select the title at the beginning of the text ("Original SpaceBotz Play Set").

This was imported as 16-point News Gothic T Demi. Now create a style based on the selected text.

2] Choose New from the Options menu at the top of the Styles panel.

A new paragraph style named Style-1 appears in the panel. Paragraph styles can record text formatting information, including font, size, alignment, color, and leading, that you can apply to paragraphs elsewhere in the document.

3] Double-click Style-1. Type a new name, *Title*, and press Enter.

The style has automatically picked up the formatting of the selected text, and that text now is linked to the Title style.

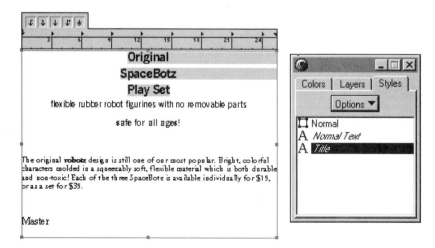

240

4] Using the Text tool, double-click the word *flexible* in the second paragraph to select that word. Create another new style and name it *Subhead 1*.

Styles apply to entire paragraphs. Selecting just a portion of a paragraph when creating a style records the characteristics of that text and assigns that new style to the entire paragraph to which the selected text belongs.

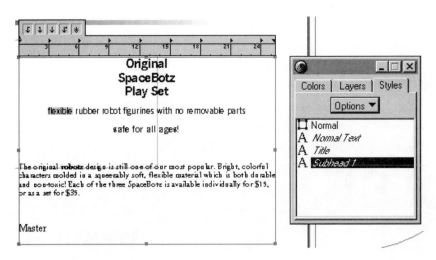

5] Use the Text tool to select all of the text in the third paragraph ("safe for all ages!"). Change the color of this text to PANTONE 140-6. Then create a new style and name it *Subhead 2*.

Paragraph styles also record the color of the text.

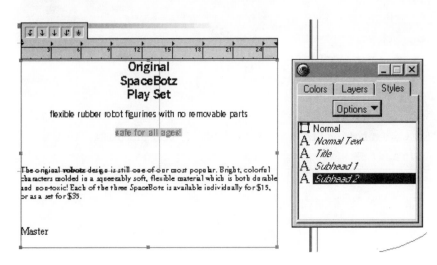

The last remaining new style you need is for the description. However, suppose you select the word *original* in the first line of the description paragraph. This text is 10-point URW Garamond Regular—but the word *robotz* and the two prices in this description are the demi version of the same font. Styles apply to entire paragraphs, so you will create a style for the Regular text and then manually apply the demi weight of the font to just those words within the paragraph that require it.

6] Select the description paragraph and display the Text Inspector. Choose the equal sign from the Leading Options menu and specify a leading of *14* points to specify a fixed leading. Then create a new style and name it *Body*.

When you create a new style, the characteristics of the style are set to match those of the first character selected. Assigning this new style to the paragraph eliminated the boldfacing used for some of the words in the paragraph.

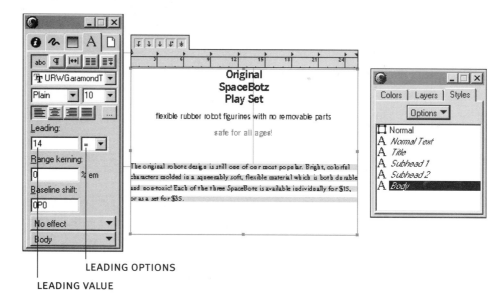

LEADING OPTIONS

LEADING VALUE

7] Select the word *robotz* and change it to bold type. Repeat this process for the two prices, $15 and $35.

Local formatting of individual characters within a paragraph must be performed manually, one selection at a time—there is no way to select separate portions of the text at the same time. When local formatting has been applied to selected text, the Styles panel displays a plus sign next to the style name, to indicate that this text no longer exactly matches the style characteristics.

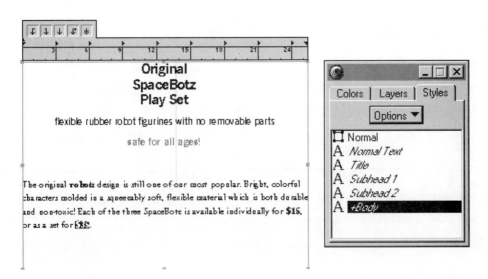

8] Save your work.
The four styles you need have been defined, so now you can apply them throughout the remaining text.

USING THE TEXT EDITOR

In addition to directly editing the text on the page, you can also open text in FreeHand's Text Editor. This enables you to edit an entire text block and apply formatting and paragraph styles without having to change from page to page.

1] Click the Spacebotz text block with the Pointer tool and choose Text › Editor to open the Text Editor window. Adjust the size and position of the Text Editor so you can also see the Styles panel.
The Text Editor displays the contents of the selected text block (and all linked text blocks) in a word processor view. This enables you to edit and apply formatting to this entire text block without changing pages.

The Text Editor displays the text in the actual font and type size unless you turn on the 12 Point Black option, which changes the display to 12-point black text. (This option is especially useful when editing white or light-colored text.)

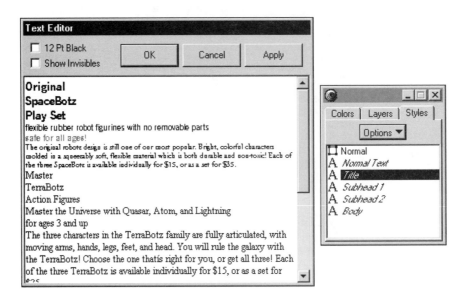

2] Turn on Show Invisibles by clicking its check box at the top of the Text Editor window.

FreeHand now displays all of the nonprinting characters in your text, making it easy to see where spaces, returns, and tabs are entered. Paragraph marks indicate returns. The small dots that appear between words indicate spaces. Tabs are displayed as small right-pointing arrows; this text block does not contain any tabs.

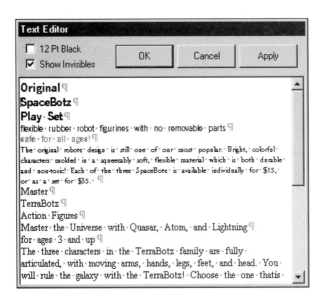

244

tip   *You can see the invisible (nonprinting) items only within the Text Editor window. Leaving this option on in the Text Editor has no effect on the display of text on the pages or on the printing of your documents.*

3] Scroll down in the Text Editor window and select the name of the second toy described in the text, "Master TerraBotz Action Figures." Click Title once in the Styles panel to apply the Title formatting.

The font, size, and alignment of the Title paragraph style are applied to the paragraph containing the selected text.

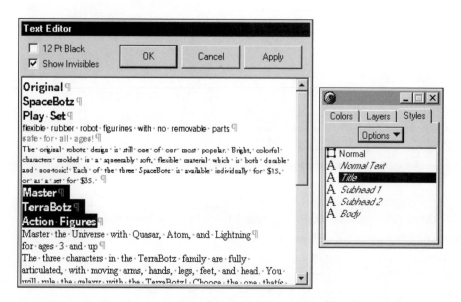

Styles apply to entire paragraphs, even though you may have selected only one word within the paragraph.

4] Select one word of the next paragraph ("Master the Universe...") and apply the Subhead 1 style. Select a word in the following paragraph ("for ages 3 and up") and apply the Subhead 2 style. Then select a word in the description paragraph and apply the Body style.

As you work through the rest of the text applying styles in the Text Editor, you don't have to worry about changing pages.

5] Apply local formatting by changing the word *robotz* and the prices to bold type wherever they appear in the description.

The TerraBotz description has two prices that should be set to URW Garamond Demi.

6] Select a word in the name of the last toy ("New TransBotz Action Figure") and apply the Title style. Repeat steps 4 and 5 to format the remaining text.

The TransBotz description has *robotz* in the first and fourth lines and a price at the end which should be changed to URW Garamond Demi.

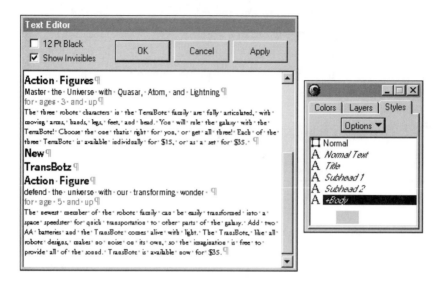

7] Click OK to close the Text Editor window. Switch to page 2 and then to page 3 to see the formatted text on all of the pages.

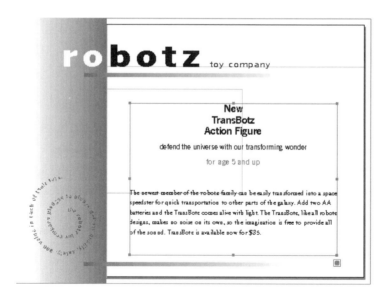

The text is completely formatted, but it will not fit the pages properly until you add the graphics.

8] Select the Pointer tool and click an empty part of the pasteboard to deselect all elements. Return to page 1.

> **tip** *You have used the Tab key to deselect elements as you work. Be careful not to press the Tab key when text blocks are being edited, or FreeHand will enter a Tab character in the text instead of deselecting the element.*

Before you finish with the text, it is a good idea to check the spelling.

9] Choose Text › Spelling to display the Spelling window. Click Start and review each suspected error.

Several suspected "errors" will be identified for your review. In this document, you will be asked about possible capitalization errors where this layout uses a lowercase character to start the header text or spiral text. In addition, FreeHand's dictionary will not recognize the company name "robotz" and will present it as a possible error. When the capitalization or spelling displayed for your review is correct (such as the name "robotz" in this project), click Ignore to skip this occurrence or click Ignore All to skip all occurrences of the suspected error. If a misspelling is found, FreeHand will suggest possible alternatives to choose from. Select the correct spelling and then click Change to correct this instance or click Change All to automatically correct every occurrence of this error in the document.

Remember that, like the spell check features in other applications, the Spelling feature will help you identify obvious errors. It is not, however, a substitute for careful proofreading of your work.

SUGGESTED SPELLING

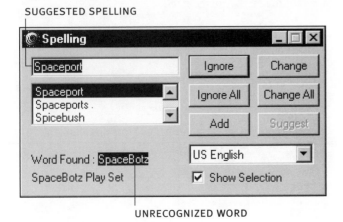

UNRECOGNIZED WORD

10] When FreeHand indicates that it is finished checking the document, close the Spelling window and save your work.

IMPORTING IMAGES

Next you will import the illustrations for this catalog.

1] Change to the Keyline view.

This allows you to see the small rectangular guide on the page, which indicates where the image should be positioned.

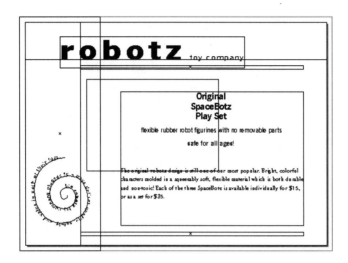

2] Choose File › Import, locate spacebtz.tif in the Media folder within the Lesson5 folder, and click Open. Position the import cursor at the upper-left corner of the small rectangular guide and click once to place the graphic on the page.

The graphic is displayed in the Keyline view as a rectangle with an X inside it. You have to change to Preview mode to see the image itself.

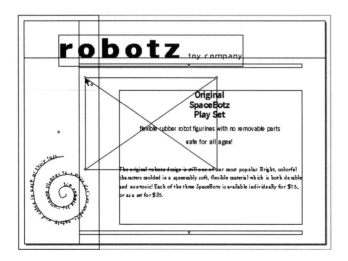

248

When importing graphics, always just click to put the image on the page, rather than dragging the import cursor as you do to define a text area when importing text. Clicking once will put the image on the page with its original size and proportions. If you drag the cursor, you will distort the graphic to fit between the points on the page where you start and stop dragging.

3] Change to Preview mode so you can see the image as it appears on the page.

The image appears on the page, overlapping the text.

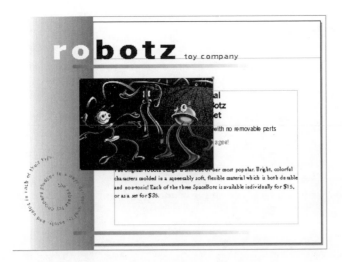

4] Switch to page 2 and repeat steps 1 through 3 to import the terrabtz.tif image.

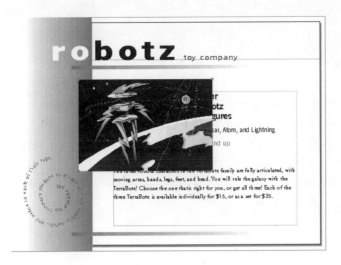

249

5] Repeat steps 1 through 3 to position the tranzbtz.tif image on page 3.

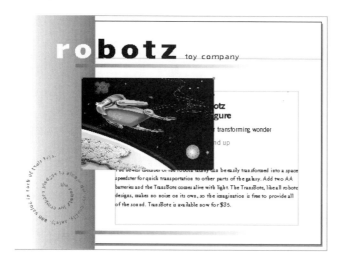

All three images are in the correct position on their respective pages. However, the images overlap the text on all three pages, and the text does not fit on the correct pages throughout the document. You will fix this in the next task.

6] Return to page 1 and save your work.

WRAPPING TEXT AROUND GRAPHICS

FreeHand can easily run text around graphics. You will use this capability to fit the images into the layout without overlapping the text.

1] Select the image on page 1 and choose Text › Run Around Selection. Assign text wrapping to the selected image by clicking the button at the top right of the dialog box. Specify a space of 6 points along the right and bottom edges of the image.
Since your document is set to measure in picas, the values in this dialog box are displayed as *0p0*, which represents zero picas and zero points. You must type *6pt* to specify 6 points. (Alternatively, you could type *0p6*, which represents zero picas and 6 points.) If you just type *6* with no units, FreeHand will set the **standoff**, or space between the text and the graphic, to 6 picas (6 picas equals 1 inch).

The left and top standoff values can remain at zero, since text will not be touching the image along those edges in this layout.

CLICK TO REMOVE TEXT WRAPPING FROM A SELECTED OBJECT

CLICK TO ASSIGN TEXT WRAPPING
FROM A SELECTED OBJECT

2] Click OK in the Run Around Selection dialog box.

The text now flows around the graphic, with a small space between the graphic and the text along the image's right and bottom edges.

If your text stays about an inch away from the right and bottom edges of the graphic, go back to the Run Around Selection dialog box and type *0p6* (that is, 6 points instead of 6 picas).

If the text does not wrap around the image at all, choose Modify > Arrange > Bring to Front—graphics must be in front of text for this feature to work.

The text should wrap around the image, and the entire description should fit on this page. (The description on each page ends with the words *for $35.*)

No text below this paragraph should appear on page 1. If text does appear below this point, you will need to adjust the size of this text block. (If the text fits properly on this page, skip to step 4.)

3] If the name of the next toy appears at the bottom of page 1, use the Pointer tool to drag the bottom-corner handle of the text block up slightly so the next toy's name no longer fits in this block.

You must drag a *corner* handle to make this adjustment. Dragging the bottom-middle handle of the text block adjusts the leading for the text block, but will not change the amount of text that the block contains.

When you make this text block shorter, the text that no longer appears in the block is automatically pushed to the top of the text block on the next page, where it belongs.

Once the text on this page fits as it should, you are ready to go to the next page.

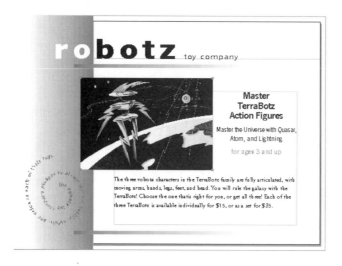

4] Repeat steps 1 through 3 for pages 2 and 3.

The text should now flow around the graphic on each page as desired.

5] Return to page 1 and save your work.

There is one last task remaining before you complete your work on this layout.

ADDING COLORS FROM BITMAP IMAGES TO THE COLOR LIST

Another exciting Xtra tool allows you to copy a color from any element in the document, including colors within a bitmap image. You can then use that color elsewhere within your document.

1] Display the Xtra Tools panel by choosing Window › Xtras › Xtra Tools. Select the Eyedropper tool. Then display the Color List.

You will pick up a color from the robot illustration on this page and use that color for the name of this toy. This will tie the text and illustration together nicely.

2] Position the tool over a bright blue color in the image and drag the color swatch into the Color List.

Your color is added to the list, so you can use it for other elements in your document. It is defined in this list by its CMYK values since the image is a CMYK TIFF file.

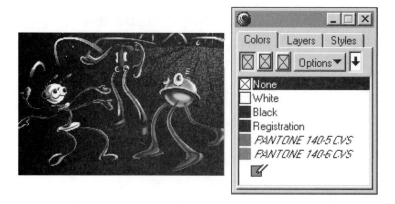

3] With the Text tool, select the name of the toy on page 1, "SpaceBotz." Drag the color swatch for your new color from the Color List and drop it on the selected text. Switch back to the Pointer tool to see the results.

That individual word now appears in the color that you picked up from the image.

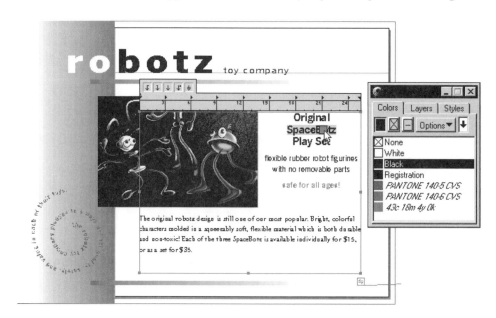

4] Go to page 2 and add a bright red color from the page 2 image to the Color List. Apply that color to the name on this page, "TerraBotz." Repeat this process for page 3, applying a color of your choice from the image on page 3 to the name "TransBotz."

The three new colors are displayed in the Color List.

5] Return to page 1 and save your work.

The layout is now complete.

PRINTING YOUR DOCUMENT

Now it is time to print your work. FreeHand is designed to take full advantage of PostScript printers and high-resolution output devices, which are the standard for desktop publishing and the graphic arts community. However, FreeHand can print to other types of printers as well. If you are printing to a non-PostScript printer, the options displayed in the Print dialog box will vary depending upon the type of printer selected.

If your system is configured to print to a PostScript printer or a high-resolution output device, FreeHand offers several special capabilities when it comes time to print. The steps in this task illustrate the options available for PostScript printers.

1] Choose File > Print to display the Print dialog box.

If your system is not configured to print to a PostScript output device, the dialog box will be different than the example shown here.

A variety of controls enables you to set the most common printing options within this dialog box. The Print Setting menu provides quick access to preset or custom print setup configurations.

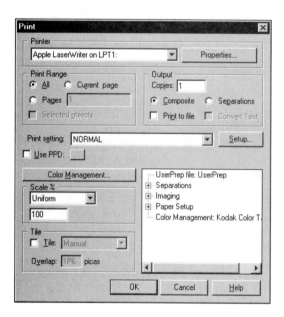

2] Click the Setup button to display the Print Setup dialog box.

Print Setup enables you to customize settings for this print job or specify print settings you can use for future print jobs. The preview window on the left shows how the document will print on the page with the current settings. At the right, three tabbed panels allow control over printing separations, imaging options, and paper size and orientation. At the top left, the name of the current Print Setting file is displayed.

You can save your print settings in a settings file that then becomes available from a menu in the Print dialog box. You record custom settings by clicking the Save Settings button at the top left of the Print Setup dialog box.

The Print Setup dialog box has three tabbed sections. The first one you see, Separations, controls how your printer will print the colors in your document—as a composite print, with all the colors printing on the same page, or as separations, with each color printing on a different sheet (this is the setting used by printers to create separate printing plates for each color). A commercial printer can advise you how to use the other settings in this dialog box when you need output for a printing press.

tip *Print settings can also be shared easily with other users. Each of the settings files are saved in a folder called PrintSet installed with FreeHand. Simply copy the specific settings files into the PrintSet folder on another workstation to make them available on that system.*

SAVE
SETTINGS
BUTTON

CONTROLS FOR ADDING LABELS
AND MARKS, SPECIFYING HOW
PAGES SHOULD BE PRINTED, AND
PRINTING INVISIBLE LAYERS

CONTROLS FOR
PAPER SIZE AND
ORIENTATION

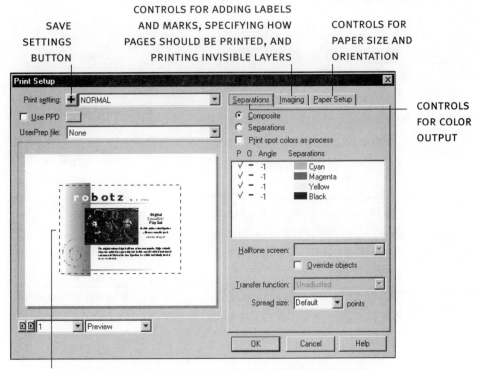

CONTROLS
FOR COLOR
OUTPUT

PREVIEW OF THE DOCUMENT PRINTED WITH CURRENT SETTINGS

3] Click the Imaging tab at the top of the dialog box and click Crop Marks to turn on that option.

Crop marks indicate the edges of your page. (They will print only if your document's page size is smaller than the paper size, as it is here.)

Imaging also contains an option that allows you to choose whether to print invisible (hidden) layers. There are no hidden layers in this document, so in this case it does not make any difference whether this option is selected or not.

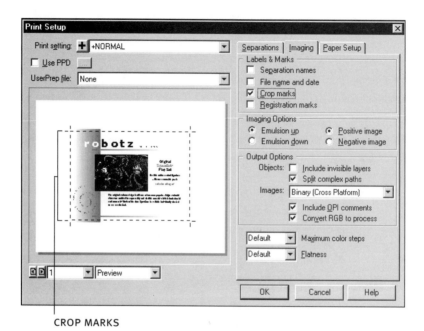

CROP MARKS

4] Click the Paper Setup tab.

Here you can select the paper size and orientation for output. The Automatic Orientation default setting tells FreeHand to automatically determine the optimum orientation based on the size of the pages in your document, the output device, and the paper size identified.

5] To select from among other paper sizes that your specific printer may offer, click the Use PPD button at the upper left of the dialog box and select the PostScript printer description file for your printer.

These PPDs, or PostScript printer descriptions, contain optimized print settings for specific PostScript printers. You will achieve the best printing results when you use PPD information, and FreeHand will be able to support the full range of features and paper sizes your printer offers.

258

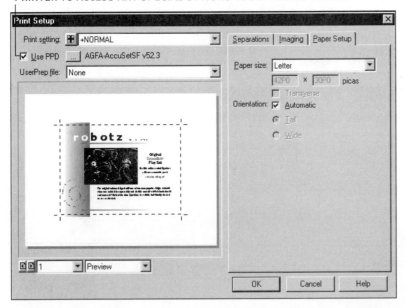

6] Click OK to return to the Print dialog box. If you want to print at this time, click the Print button. If not, click Cancel.

Remember that this is a multiple-page document, so you have the choice of printing the entire document or just specific pages.

7] Save your work.

You have now completed the three-page catalog.

COLLECTING FILES FOR OUTPUT

The TIFF images you imported into the robotz catalog were imported as linked graphics by default, which means that a preview image was imported for you to work with in your document. When you print the document, FreeHand sends the high-resolution information from the individual disk files for each image. That means that the images must remain with the FreeHand document.

When sending your completed documents to a service bureau or commercial printer for high-resolution output, you must also include any linked graphics so they can be output at high resolution as well.

FreeHand offers two features to help you prevent problems when printing or transferring files: Links and Collect for Output.

259

1] Choose Edit › Links to display the Links window.

The Links window lists the three TIFF images you imported, and it shows that they are CMYK TIFF files, their sizes, and the pages where the graphics are located.

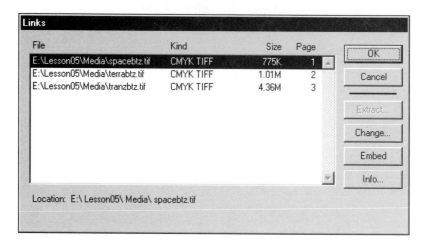

The buttons on the right side of this window provide direct control over the images in your document. Info provides more detailed information about the selected graphic. Change enables you to substitute another graphic for the one currently in place. Select the desired graphic and click Embed if you want the selected graphic to be completely contained within the FreeHand document. Embedded graphics are not linked to disk files, so you can achieve high-resolution printing without supplying the original disk files for the embedded images. This can make it easier to transfer FreeHand files without having to worry about auxiliary images.

Embedded graphics do have their drawbacks, however. Embedding many high-resolution images will dramatically increase the size of your FreeHand document and may slow down FreeHand's performance (though you may be able to counteract that drawback somewhat by switching to the Fast Preview mode). When an embedded image is selected, the Extract button is available so you can export the image as a linked file on a disk.

Linked files have one other advantage as well. If the original image is modified after it has been imported as a linked image, FreeHand will automatically update the image in your FreeHand document.

2] Click Cancel to return to the document window without making changes. Then choose File › Collect for Output.

This feature is designed to collect all of the elements required to send this document to your service bureau or commercial printer for output. The first thing you will see initially is an alert reminding you that fonts are copyrighted works, and you should check your font license before sending copies of your fonts to your output service.

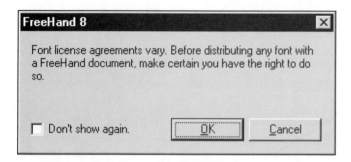

3] Click OK in the font license alert box.

The Document Report window appears. This enables you to specify what information you want collected in a report on this document.

4] Accept the default settings and click Report.

A Save dialog box appears, asking for a location for all of the files needed to output this FreeHand document and requesting a name for the report that summarizes the document characteristics. Typically, you would select the disk or cartridge you want to send to the printer.

Collect for Output will save the text file report and copy the FreeHand document, all linked images, the fonts used in the document, and the active printer description files to the selected folder or disk volume.

Since you will probably not send this document to a service bureau for high-resolution printing, you do not need to actually complete this process at this time.

5] Click Cancel to return to the document window without collecting the files for output.

ON YOUR OWN

Do you have any multiple-page projects you can use FreeHand for? Remember that a FreeHand document can contain different-size pages, so it is perfect for that letterhead, business card, and envelope project you have in mind.

Develop your own multiple-page project, or open the letterhead you created in Lesson 2 and create a business card and envelope to accompany the letterhead.

To create custom page sizes for these items, it may help to remember that a standard business card is 3.5 by 2 inches, and a business size (number 10) envelope is 4.125 by 9.5 inches.

WHAT YOU HAVE LEARNED

In this lesson you have:

- Specified document measurements in alternative units [*page* **212**]

- Set the printer resolution for gradient fills [*page* **213**]

- Created custom, nonprinting guides for a document layout [*page* **214**]

- Practiced importing PANTONE process colors [*page* **221**]

- Used Snap to Guides to position elements exactly [*page* **225**]

- Used FreeHand's kerning and scaling controls to manipulate text [*page* **226**]

- Attached and repositioned text on a path [*page* **230**]

- Duplicated pages in a document [*page* **234**]

- Imported RTF text into your layout [*page* **236**]

- Linked text from one text block to another [*page* **238**]

- Formatted text with paragraph styles [*page* **240**]

- Used the Text Editor to format text [*page* **243**]

- Practiced importing bitmap images [*page* **248**]

- Applied the Run Around Selection feature to graphics [*page* **250**]

- Copied colors from imported images with the Eyedropper tool [*page* **253**]

- Made adjustments to the Printer Setup settings for PostScript printing [*page* **256**]

- Explored how to use the Links window with linked and embedded images [*page* **259**]

- Learned how to prepare files for a commercial printer with Collect for Output [*page* **261**]

complex artwork

creating more

LESSON 6

FreeHand provides many advanced features that enable you to produce rich illustrations such as the artwork for Lighthouse Publishing that you will create in this lesson. In creating this drawing, you will import files, including a 3D image, from different sources and work with graphics on multiple foreground layers. You will use one of FreeHand's special effects—transparency—and blend multiple shapes.

If you would like to review the final result of this lesson, open Beacon2.fh8 in the Complete folder within the Lesson6 folder.

To create the logo for Lighthouse Publishing, you will trace a graphic you import from another program and add a three-dimensional graphic. You will also use transparency effects, multiple layers, and blends to achieve the final result.

Designed by Julia Sifers of Glasgow & Associates and Craig Faist and Tom Faist of Datrix Media Group.

WHAT YOU WILL LEARN

In this lesson you will:

- Import graphics created in other programs

- Trace an imported graphic

- Work with multiple foreground layers

- Create blends between multiple shapes

- Use a transparent fill

APPROXIMATE TIME

It usually takes about 2 hours to complete this lesson.

LESSON FILES

Media Files:

Lesson6\Media\Sky.jpg

Lesson6\Media\Beacon1.fh8

Starting Files:

Lesson6\Start\Water.ft8

Lesson6\Start\Ground.ft8

Completed Project:

Lesson6\Complete\Beacon2.fh8

CREATING A NEW CUSTOM-SIZE DOCUMENT

You will begin working on the artwork for the lighthouse illustration in a new document. You'll need to create a special page size for this project.

1] Create a new document by choosing File › New (Windows Ctrl+N, Macintosh Command+N).

A blank page appears, which you will now adjust so that the page size matches the size you need for this illustration.

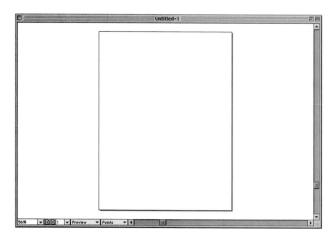

2] Change the unit of measure to Inches using the Units menu at the bottom of the screen. Choose Window › Inspectors › Document to display the Document Inspector.

The Document Inspector shows the current page dimensions and orientation.

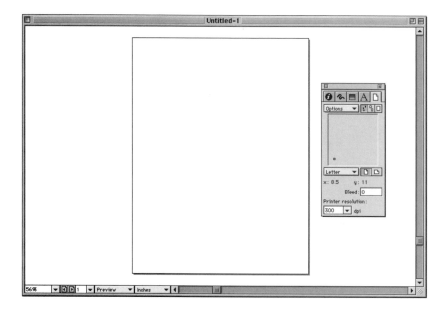

3] In the Document Inspector, change the page size from Letter to Custom, enter the dimensions _7.25_ by _6_ inches, and click the Landscape Orientation icon.

Your page is now the correct size, but it appears small in the document window.

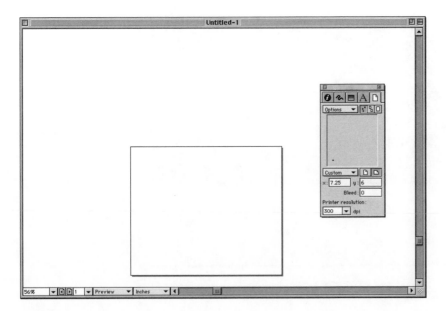

tip   _Remember to press Enter to apply your changes after typing values in a panel._

4] Close the Document Inspector and choose View › Fit to Page (Windows Ctrl+ Shift+W, Macintosh Command+Shift+W). Save the document as _MyBeacon_ in your MyWork folder.

The page is now ready for you to begin the illustration.

IMPORTING AND TRACING AN IMAGE

In this section you will import a JPEG image of the sky created in Adobe Photoshop as a tracing pattern. JPEG (one of the many graphic formats FreeHand can import) is a file format for compressing bitmap images so they take up less room on the disk while retaining nearly the same image quality as an uncompressed file.

You have already learned to trace patterns manually with the Bezigon and Pen tools. Here, you will use the Autotrace tool to do it automatically.

1] Choose File › Import (Windows Ctrl+R, Macintosh Command+R). Select Sky.jpg in the Media folder within the Lesson6 folder and click Open. Position the cursor on the page and click the mouse.

267

The sky image appears on the page. You will position it next.

2] To position the sky image accurately, display the Object Inspector. Enter an _x_ dimension of _0.25_ inch and a _y_ dimension of _2.35_ inches.

This will position the artwork so there is a 0.25-inch border on the left and right sides of this image. The _x_ and _y_ coordinates define the position of the lower-left corner of the selected object.

tip   *When you import a JPEG file into FreeHand, it is converted to a TIFF image. That is why the Object Inspector states that an RGB TIFF file is currently selected.*

3] Deselect the sky image by either using the Tab key on the keyboard or clicking with the Pointer tool in any empty area of the page.

You must not have anything selected when you create a new layer in the next step, or you may accidentally move the selected artwork to the new layer.

4] Create a new layer by choosing New from the Options menu in the Layers panel. Double-click the name for the new layer, Layer-1, and type *Sky* as the new name for this layer. Press Enter to complete the name change.

The Sky layer is a foreground (printing) layer since it appears above the separator line in the Layers panel. This new layer is now the active layer, so the artwork you will create next will be added to this layer.

5] Select the Autotrace tool in the toolbox. To change the settings for this tool, double-click the tool. Verify that the Autotrace tool has the settings pictured here. (These are the default settings for the tool.)

The default settings for the Autotrace tool provide good results when tracing bitmap and vector graphics. You will apply the Autotrace tool to the sky image to create editable shapes that look like that image.

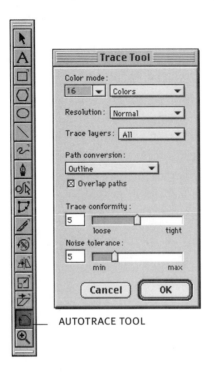

AUTOTRACE TOOL

tip *For information on options for this tool, consult the FreeHand User Guide that is included with the FreeHand 8 software.*

6] Use the Autotrace tool crosshair cursor to drag a selection marquee around the sky image.

The part of the image you select—in this case, the entire image—will be traced when you release the mouse. (It may take a few moments for the tracing process to be completed.) The result is a series of paths that traced the shapes in the image, dividing it into 16 colors (as specified by the Color Mode setting in the tool's Preferences dialog box). These new paths appear on the Sky layer since it was the active layer when you used this tool.

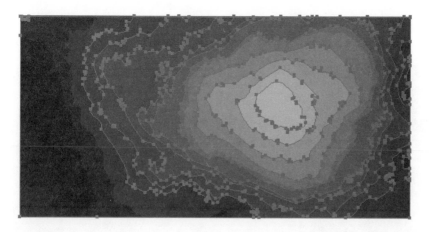

tip *It is helpful to use multiple layers when using the Autotrace tool. Place the image to be traced on a layer by itself and then select a different layer when using the Autotrace tool. This will place the results of the Autotrace tool on a separate layer. You will now be able to easily access both the original image and the editable shapes. (To delete the original image, you simply delete the layer that contains the original image.)*

7] With the results of the Autotrace tool still selected, choose Modify › Group.
This combines all the resulting shapes into one single grouped element. You can now more easily use the sky image shapes in your drawing.

271

8] Deselect the grouped element by pressing the Tab key. To remove the original sky image and the layer it's on, select the Foreground layer in the Layers panel and choose Remove from the Options menu in the Layers panel. Then click OK in the dialog box that appears warning that this layer contains data.

This will remove the original sky image and the layer named Foreground from the illustration since they are no longer needed.

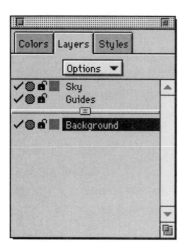

tip   *Always make sure that no artwork is selected before you click a different layer name in the Layers panel. Otherwise, you will accidentally move selected artwork to the layer you click.*

9] Save your work.

ADDING A 3D IMAGE AND A TRANSPARENCY EFFECT

Now you will import another image: a lighthouse that was created in Macromedia Extreme 3D. You will then add the beam of light and create a transparency effect using the beam and text.

1] Create a new layer by choosing New from the Options menu in the Layers panel. Double-click the name for the new layer, Layer-1, and type *Beam* as the new name for this layer. Press Enter to complete the name change.

This will create the layer that will contain the beam of light.

272

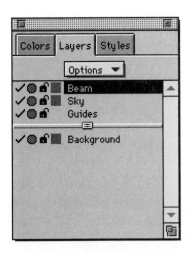

2] To import the lighthouse graphic, choose File › Import. Select Beacon1.fh8 in the Media folder within the Lesson6 folder and click Open. Position the cursor anywhere on the page and click the mouse.

The three-dimensional lighthouse graphic you just imported was created in Extreme 3D and pasted inside a path in FreeHand to remove the background. The path and image were then grouped together and imported as a group into your document. This will be a printing element in your illustration. Along with the graphic, a layer named Foreground was imported.

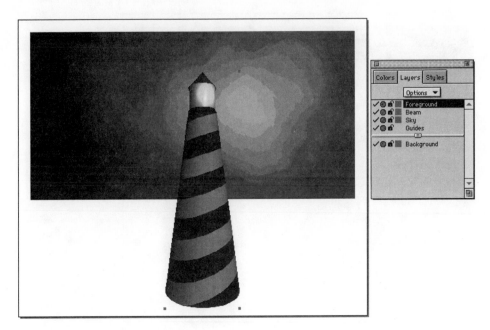

273

3] Double-click the Foreground layer name and type *Lighthouse* to rename this layer. Press Enter to complete the name change.

The layer the lighthouse graphic is on is now named Lighthouse.

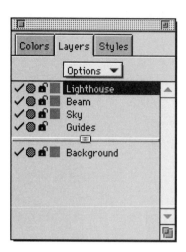

4] To position the lighthouse image accurately, display the Object Inspector. Set the *x* dimension to *5* inches and the *y* dimension to *1.1* inches.

The placement of the lighthouse is important because the beam of light that will be created depends on the position of this graphic.

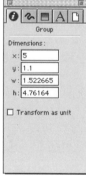

5] Press Tab to deselect all elements and then click the Beam layer. Using the Bezigon or Pen tool, draw the beam of light as shown in the following illustration. All points used will be corner points. Make sure that the resulting closed path goes into the lighthouse light and continues off the page at the left. Then apply a white fill and no stroke to this path.

The actual placement of points is not critical; the picture shows the approximate placement.

The width of the resulting beam of light can vary; its dimensions are not critical. What is important is that this be a closed shape, and that it is well into the lighthouse and continues off of the page; otherwise, the transparency effect you will be creating will not be convincing.

6] Make sure that the beam of light is still selected. In the Fill Inspector, change the fill type from Basic to Lens and set the lens fill to Transparent. Click OK if an alert box appears explaining that spot colors viewed through a lens fill are converted to process colors.

The light beam is now filled with a 50% transparent fill, allowing the sky to show through the beam. FreeHand must convert spot colors viewed through a lens fill to process colors. However, no spot colors exist in the current document.

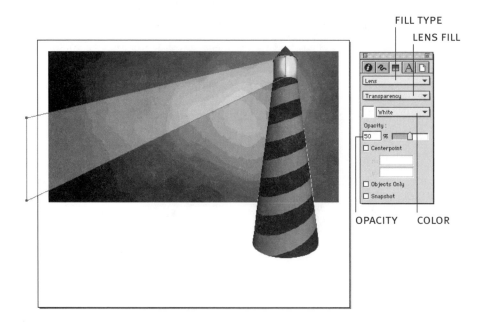

7] Change the fill transparency to 40% and save the document.

The Beam layer should be in front of the Sky layer and behind the Lighthouse layer.

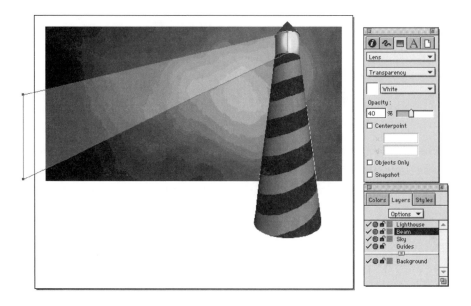

8] Using the Text tool, type _Lighthouse Publishing_. Press Enter after the word _Light-house_. Still using the Text tool, select all of the text. Using the controls on the text toolbar near the top of the screen, change the font to URWGaramondTMed with a size of 76 points, a fixed leading of 66 points, and center alignment.

This places the type on the Beam layer, in front of the beam of light. Exact positioning of this text will be done later.

tip _To set a fixed leading value, choose the equal sign on the Leading Options menu on the text toolbar and then enter the desired leading value._

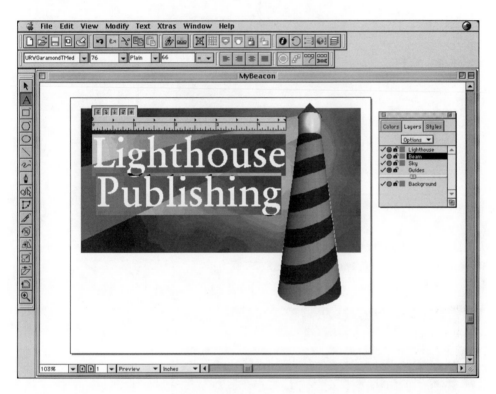

9] Using the Color Mixer, click the CMYK button and create a color that is 100 percent yellow and 0 percent cyan, magenta, and black. Add this color to the Color List. With the text still selected with the Text tool, change the fill color for the text to this 100 percent yellow.

277

On the screen, the text appears to be blue and not yellow. Why? This is because you have the text highlighted with the Text tool. Once you deselect the text, it will become yellow as the Color List indicates.

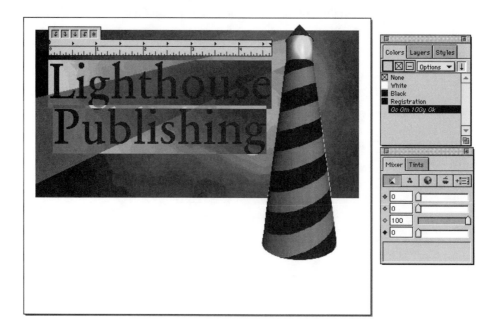

10] Using the Pointer tool, position the text so it is roughly centered between the left edge of the sky and the lighthouse.

Exact positioning is not critical, but the following illustration shows what you're aiming for.

278

11] With the text still selected, choose Modify › Arrange › Send to Back.

This moves the type behind the light beam, because both are on the same layer. The Arrange commands move artwork in front of or behind other elements on the same layer. Now the transparent beam of light overlaps the text as well as the sky, allowing both text and sky to show through the beam.

12] Save your work.

Your drawing should now look like the following illustration.

BLENDING MULTIPLE SHAPES

Your next task is to create the water needed for the illustration. Using a template for assistance, you will blend three shapes.

1] Open the document Water.ft8 in the Start folder within the Lesson6 folder.

The Water.ft8 document has the three shapes in the background that you will need to trace. You will then blend these three shapes together to create the water.

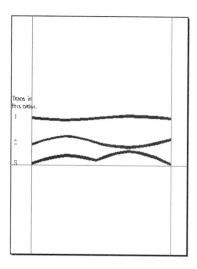

2] With the Zoom tool, zoom in on the left side of the page.

It is important that you trace the closed shapes in the order indicated.

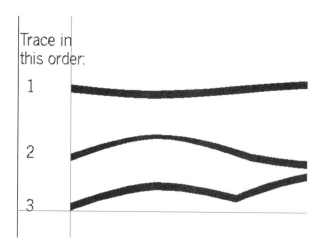

3] Using either the Bezigon or Pen tool, trace around each of the wavy shapes in the specified order, from top to bottom.

Make sure that you end up with three separate closed shapes. You can verify that a shape is closed by checking the information displayed in the Object Inspector. If you get stuck, refer to the illustration for the placement of points.

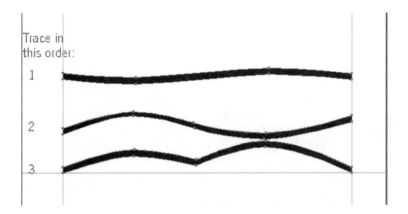

4] In the Color Mixer, click the CMYK button. You will create two colors that will be added to the Color List. In the Color Mixer, enter the values to create a color that is 80 percent cyan, 70 percent magenta, 0 percent yellow, and 40 percent black. Add this color to the Color List. Then enter the values to create a color that is 90 percent cyan, 80 percent magenta, 50 percent yellow, and 60 percent black. Add this color to the Color List as well.

Two shades of blue have now been added to the Color List.

CREATING MORE COMPLEX ARTWORK

5] With the Pointer tool, select the top two closed shapes and fill them with 80c70m0y40k. Change the stroke to None.

6] With the Pointer tool, select the bottom closed shape and fill it with 90c80m50y60k. Change the stroke to None.

Now blend the three shapes.

7] With the Pointer tool, select all three closed shapes. Choose Modify › Combine › Blend.

This creates a blend from all three closed shapes. You can also find the Blend command by choosing Xtras > Create > Blend.

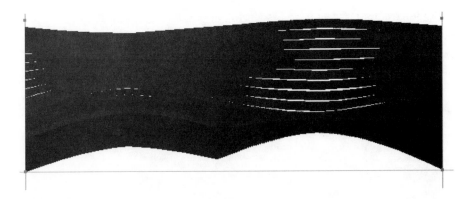

8] In the Object Inspector, change the number of steps for the blend to *20*, and press Enter.

By increasing the number of steps, you create a smooth, continuous blend.

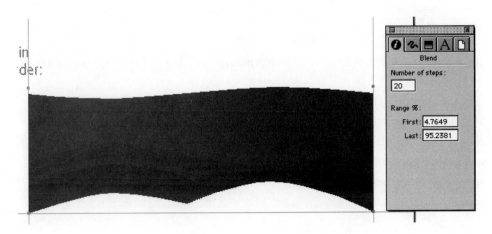

Now copy the blend to your document.

9] With the blend selected, choose Edit › Copy. Switch to the MyBeacon document by choosing Window › MyBeacon and then choose Edit › Paste.

This copies your completed water blend from the template to the lighthouse illustration. Notice that it also pasted the Foreground layer as the top layer in the Layers panel.

10] Return to the template by choosing Window › Untitled-2. Close this document without saving it.

11] In the MyBeacon document, use the Pointer tool to position the water so it is flush with the left and right edges of the sky. Make sure the top of the water covers the bottom of the sky so that no gap exists between the two. Zoom in to verify your placement.

If you need to nudge the water, remember to use the arrow keys on the keyboard.

12] In the Layers panel, double-click the layer named Foreground. Type *Water* as the new name for this layer and press Enter to complete the name change. Reorder the layers so the Water layer is below the Beam layer.

To reorder the layers, drag a layer name in the Layers panel and drop it above or below another layer name.

tip *Giving your layers descriptive names helps during the organization and editing of an illustration.*

13] Save your work.

Your illustration should now look like the one shown here.

CREATING MORE COMPLEX ARTWORK

BLENDING SHAPES TO CREATE A REFLECTION

To create the reflection that the lighthouse casts on the water, you will blend two ovals.

1] Press the Tab key to deselect all elements and then select the Lighthouse layer in the Layers panel. With the Ellipse tool, draw a narrow oval at the base of the lighthouse.

Make sure that the width of the oval does not exceed the width of the base of the lighthouse. The height of the oval should be fairly small.

2] In the Color Mixer, click the Tint button. Add 10 percent of the color 0c0m100y0k to the Color List. With the oval selected, change its fill color to 10% 0c0m100y0k and set the stroke to None.

286

3] Using the Ellipse tool, draw another extremely small oval in the upper-left portion of the water.

This second oval should be smaller than the first one. Make sure that this second oval does not overlap into the sky area or off the left edge of the water.

4] Using the Color List, change the fill color of the second oval to 80c70m0y40k and set the stroke to None.

The second oval is now the same color as the water that is beneath it.

5] Using the Pointer tool, select both of the ovals. Choose Modify › Combine › Blend. In the Object Inspector, change the number of steps for the blend to *16*.

Because you chose the water color for the second oval, the resulting blend gradually fades away.

If it becomes difficult to see or select the two ellipses, change to the Keyline view to make the selection and create the blend. Then switch back to the Preview mode.

6] Create a new layer by choosing Options › New in the Layers panel. With the oval blend still selected, double-click the name of the new layer, Layer-1, and type *Reflection* as the new name for this layer. Press Enter to complete the name change.
This also puts the oval blend on the Reflection layer. Remember: If an element is selected when you rename a layer, you will not only rename the layer, but you will also move the selected element to that layer.

7] Reorder the layers so that the Reflection layer is below the Beam layer and above the Water layer.
This will appropriately place the reflection behind the lighthouse and on top of the water.

8] Save your work.

USING A TEMPLATE TO ADD A SHAPE

You still need to create the ground in front of the lighthouse. You will use a template to help you create this shape.

1] Open the Ground.ft8 template in the Start folder within the Lesson6 folder.

In the background of this template is the shape you need to create the ground for the illustration.

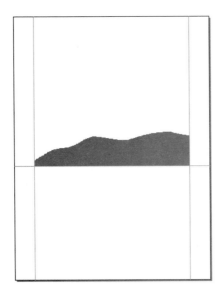

2] Using the Zoom tool, zoom in on the ground shape. Using the Bezigon or Pen tool, trace the shape.

Make sure that you end up with a closed shape so it can be filled later. If you get stuck, refer to the illustration for the placement of points. When you are finished tracing, use the Object Inspector to verify that you indeed have a closed shape.

3] In the Color Mixer, click the CMYK button. You will create two colors that will be added to the Color List. In the Color Mixer, enter the values to create a color that is 30 percent cyan, 70 percent magenta, 90 percent yellow, and 90 percent black and then add this color to the Color List. Then enter the values to create a color that is 50 percent cyan, 70 percent magenta, 80 percent yellow, and 30 percent black and add this color to the Color List as well.

This adds two shades of brown to the Color List.

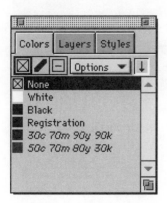

4] With the ground shape selected, display the Fill Inspector. Change the fill type from Basic to Gradient. Set the top color to 50c70m80y30k and the bottom color to 30c70m90y90k. Set the control angle to 270 degrees and set the stroke to None.

This fills the ground shape with a gradient that shades from brown at the top to darker brown at the bottom.

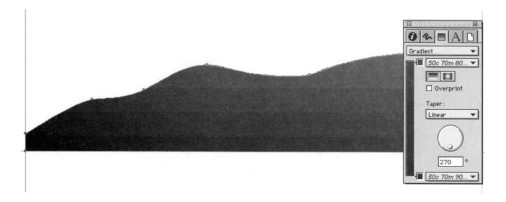

5] With the ground shape still selected, display the Object Inspector.

To position the ground shape accurately, you need to use coordinates. However, when you have a path selected as you do now, the Object Inspector does not display the coordinates of the shape.

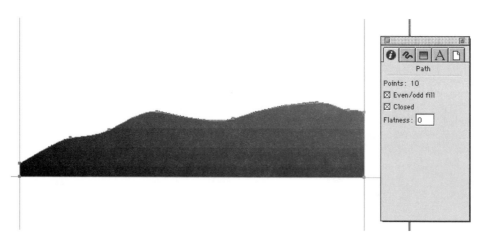

6] Choose Modify › Group.

Notice that now the Object Inspector indicates that you have a grouped element selected, and therefore, the coordinates for this shape are now available.

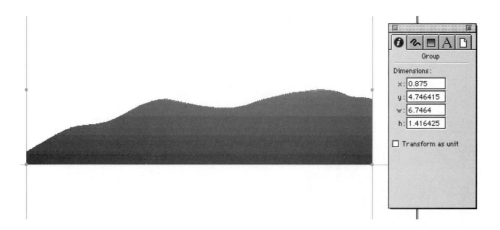

7] With the ground shape selected, choose Edit › Copy. Switch to the MyBeacon document by choosing Window › MyBeacon and then choose Edit › Paste.

This copies your completed ground shape from the template to the lighthouse illustration. Notice that this operation also pasted the Foreground layer as the top layer in the Layers panel.

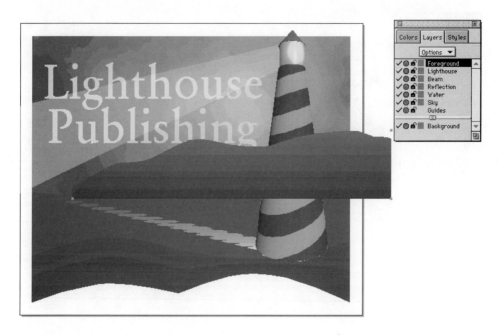

8] In the Layers panel, double-click the Foreground layer. Type *Ground* as the new name for this layer and then press Enter to complete the name change.

The Ground layer should be the topmost layer in the document. If it isn't, press the Tab key to deselect all elements and then drag the Ground layer to the top of the Layers panel list.

tip   *To quickly identify which layer contains a particular element in your illustration, hide the layers one at a time and watch to see which layer is hidden when the element disappears.*

9] Return to the template by choosing Window › Untitled-3. Close this document without saving it.

10] In the Object Inspector, set the *x* and *y* dimensions both to *0.25* inch.

This positions the bottom-left corner of the ground so it is 0.25 inch from the left side of the page and 0.25 inch from the bottom of the page.

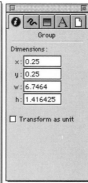

11] Save your work.

The lighthouse illustration looks terrific. Who would guess you imported two graphics, used two templates, and blended a variety of elements to create it?

295

ON YOUR OWN

Explore the Transparent lens fill in a new document by creating a color wheel similar to the one shown here. Apply different colors, such as cyan, magenta, and yellow, to each circle and then experiment with different transparency values to achieve a variety of results.

WHAT YOU HAVE LEARNED

In this lesson you have:

- Imported a JPEG image [*page* **267**]

- Traced an image using the Autotrace tool [*page* **269**]

- Placed artwork on multiple foreground layers [*page* **269**]

- Imported a three-dimensional graphic [*page* **272**]

- Applied a Transparent lens fill [*page* **275**]

- Created a blend between two shapes and another among three shapes [*page* **280**]

- Practiced combining artwork from different documents with Copy and Paste [*page* **283**]

techniques
advanced

LESSON 7

The Aquarium sign you will create in this lesson provides an opportunity for you to apply the illustration skills you have learned in previous lessons and explore new techniques that will enable you to produce more sophisticated results. You will complete a fish illustration using gradient fills, blends, compound paths, and Paste Inside. Using FreeHand's Graphic Hose Xtra tool, you will combine your fish with others to create a school of fish, and using the Envelope Xtra, you will change the shape of a text object to achieve a visually interesting effect. You will then use Transparency, Lighten, and Magnify lens fills to achieve the final result.

This Aquarium sign was created using a composite path, a blend of multiple paths, lens fills, the Graphic Hose Xtra tool, and the Envelope Xtra. You will learn how to apply these tools in this lesson.

Illustration by Steve Botts, layout by Tom Faist.

If you would like to review the final result of this lesson, open Aquarium.fh8 in the Complete folder within the Lesson7 folder.

WHAT YOU WILL LEARN

In this lesson you will:

- Create a composite path
- Apply gradient fills
- Name a view
- Create a blend of three elements
- Paste elements inside a path
- Paint graphics onto the page
- Distort the shape of an object
- Use lens fills to enhance an illustration

APPROXIMATE TIME

It usually takes about 1 hour to complete this lesson.

LESSON FILES

Media Files:

Lesson7\Media\3-Fish.ft8

Starting Files:

Lesson7\Start\1-Fish.ft8

Lesson7\Start\2-Fish.ft8

Lesson7\Start\Aquarium.ft8

Completed Project:

Lesson7\Complete\Aquarium.fh8

Lesson7\Complete\1-Fish.fh8

CREATING A COMPOSITE PATH

Some of the paths you will need for this fish have been prepared in advance, so you will begin by opening a template containing these paths.

One of the ways you can combine elements is by creating a **composite path**, which is a single element made up of several paths. When two overlapping paths are combined into a composite path, the overlapping areas become an opening in the composite path.

1] Close any open documents. Then open 1-Fish.ft8 in the Start folder within the Lesson7 folder.

This template contains several paths and colors that you will use to create the first fish.

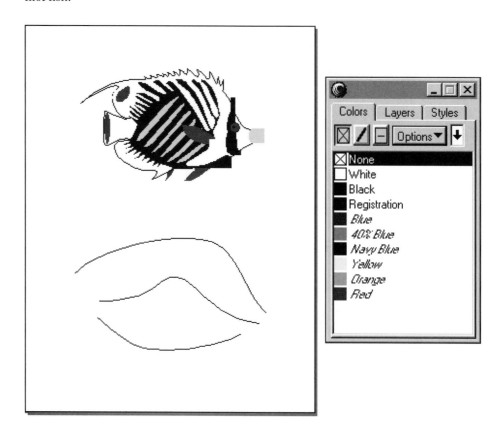

2] Zoom in on the body of the fish at the top of the page.

Inside the body of the fish is a large, irregular element filled with black. In front of this are six yellow paths that are roughly elliptical in shape.

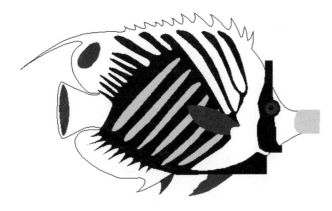

These yellow shapes should actually become openings, or holes, in the larger shape. You will create these openings by combining the shapes into a composite path.

3] Select all six elliptical shapes and the larger irregular shape.

Remember that to select all of these items at the same time, you first select one of the elliptical shapes and then hold down Shift while you click each of the other elliptical shapes and then the larger shape. (Make sure that you do not select the red fin!)

> **tip**   *Remember that FreeHand does not allow you to select shapes within a selected element's boundaries. Therefore, you must always select the largest shape last.*

4] Choose Modify › Join to combine these shapes.

Holes now appear where the yellow paths overlapped the larger black element. When paths are joined together they are combined into the same path—called a composite path—where overlapping shapes become holes in the surrounding path.

Now the path can be selected only by clicking the solid parts of the shape. The holes are empty and cannot be selected or filled with color.

When you join shapes, the resulting composite path is moved to the front of the elements on the current layer, which is why this black shape now appears in front of the red fin on the side of the fish.

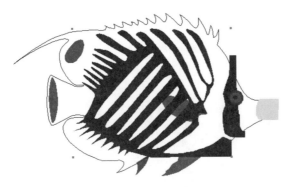

5] Deselect all elements. Then save your work as a FreeHand document named *NewFish*.

Next you will add gradient fills to enhance the illustration.

APPLYING GRADIENT FILLS

In previous lessons you applied gradient fills using the Fill Inspector. FreeHand also lets you apply gradient fills directly, by dragging and dropping colors from the Color List.

1] Display the Color List. Begin to drag the Blue color swatch and then press Control so the swatch you are dragging changes from a square to a diamond. Then drop the swatch on any solid area in the top part of the composite path.

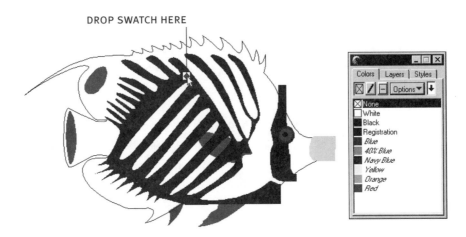

The composite path is now filled with a gradient fill that goes from blue on the top to black on the bottom.

When you press Control and then drop a swatch onto a shape, FreeHand applies a graduated fill that changes from the original color to the new color. The direction of the gradient is determined by the location of the cursor on the shape when you drop the swatch. If you had dropped the swatch on the bottom of the composite path, the gradient fill would go from black on the top to blue on the bottom.

2] Drag the Red swatch from the color list and then hold down Control and drop the swatch on the bottom of the black stripe near the eye of the fish.

Because you dropped the swatch at the bottom of this shape, this element is now filled with a graduated fill that changes from black on the top to red at the bottom.

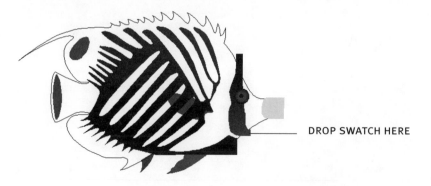

DROP SWATCH HERE

3] Drag the Yellow swatch from the Color List and hold down Alt (Windows) or Option (Macintosh) to display a circular swatch. Drop this swatch on the middle of the red shape above the tail of the fish.

Holding Alt (Windows) or Option (Macintosh) when dropping a color swatch on an object applies a radial fill. This shape is now filled with a radial fill that radiates from yellow at the spot where you dropped the swatch outward to red, the original color of this element.

DROP SWATCH HERE

Next you will apply gradient fills to the two red fins. However, the fin on the side of the fish is behind the large composite path, making it difficult to drop a swatch on this fin. You will first select this fin and bring it to the front.

4] Click once on the red fin on the side of the fish. If you instead select the composite path that is in front of the fin, hold Control and click the right mouse button (Windows) or Control (Macintosh) and click the fin again to select it.
Holding Control enables you to select items that are behind other elements on the page.

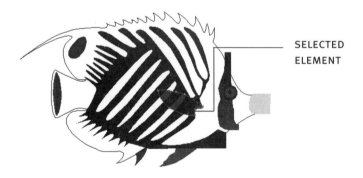

SELECTED ELEMENT

tip *To select through a stack of elements, simply hold down Control and click the right mouse button (Windows) or Control (Macintosh) and then keep clicking until the desired element is selected.*

5] Choose Modify › Arrange › Bring to Front (Windows Ctrl+F, Macintosh Command+F).

Now you can easily drop a color swatch on this element to create a graduated fill.

6] Press Tab to deselect all elements. Using Control, drop the Orange color swatch in the lower-left part of each red fin to apply graduated fills to both fins.

The fins should now be filled with graduated fills changing from red at the upper right to orange at the lower left.

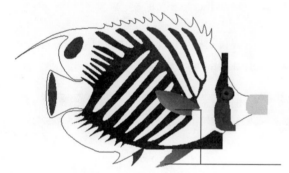

DROP SWATCH HERE

In addition to holding down Control for graduated fills and Alt (Windows) or Option (Macintosh) for radial fills, there is one other modifier key you can use when dragging and dropping colors on elements. If you hold down Ctrl+Shift (Windows) or Command (Macintosh) when dragging a color swatch, the swatch will appear as an outlined square to indicate that only the stroke will be affected. Dropping this type of swatch on an element changes the stroke of the element without changing the fill.

tip   *Remember to start dragging the color swatch before holding down Control or other fill modifier keys.*

7] Save your work.

DEFINING A NAMED VIEW

FreeHand enables you to name any view you may need to return to as you work on your illustration. Before scrolling to work with paths on another part of this page, you will make it easy to return to this view of the fish by naming the view.

1] Choose View > Custom > New. Type *Fish* as the name for this view and click OK.

You will now be able to return to this view easily by selecting a menu command.

2] Scroll down to see the three paths on the lower part of this page. Create another new custom view named *Paths*.

Now you have two custom views defined in this document.

3] Choose View > Custom > Fish to return to your view of the fish. Then use the menu in the lower-left corner of the screen to select the Paths view.

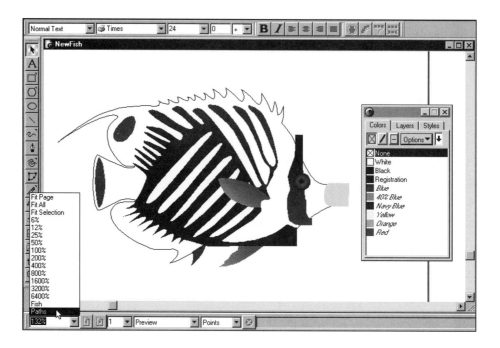

Once you name a view, you can immediately return to that view of the document by selecting it from the menu. As you work, save time later by naming any view that you may want to use again.

4] Save your work.

Next you will use the three paths to create shading for the body of the fish.

BLENDING SHAPES TO CREATE SHADING

The body of your fish should be filled with orange on top, white in the middle, and blue on the bottom. Although it would be easy to create a graduated fill with these colors, the gradient would not follow the contours of the fish. Instead, you will create a blend of three elements to create more realistic shading for this fish.

The three paths you see on the page were created to match the contours of the fish. You will use these paths to create a blend that will provide the shading you want for the body of the fish.

1] Select the three paths by first clicking one and then holding down Shift while clicking the other two.

Since there are other elements on this page, you must select the three paths directly. Remember that Select All would select all of the elements on this page, including the fish.

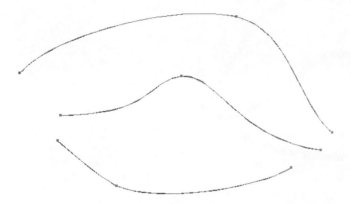

Although you can create a blend of these three open paths, it is often better to create a blend of closed shapes because the new intermediate shapes created by the blend can vary in thickness to create a smoother blend.

2] Choose Xtras › Path Operations › Expand Stroke and change the width to 10 points.

Expand Stroke converts these open paths to closed shapes based on the settings you choose in the Expand Stroke dialog box.

3] Click the middle Cap button to specify rounded ends (or caps) on the shapes. Then click OK.

The three open paths are now closed paths, each 10 points wide, with rounded ends.

4] Deselect all of the elements. Then fill the top shape with Orange, the middle shape with White, and the bottom shape with Blue.

You can no longer see the middle shape because it is filled with white and has no stroke.

5] Switch to the Keyline view so you can see all three elements.

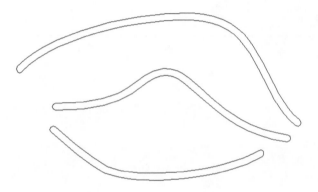

Next you will create a blend of these three elements.

6] Select the three curved shapes and choose Modify › Combine › Blend.
The Blend command creates intermediate shapes that change in shape and color
to form a smooth transition between the original shapes.

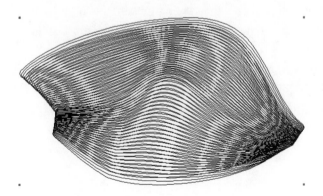

7] Change to the Preview mode to see the results.

Blending elements also groups the results together. This group should now appear as a single shape with a smooth transition of color that follows the contours of the original paths.

If you notice any gaps between the shapes in your blend, increase the number of steps in this blend in the Object Inspector.

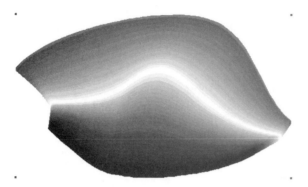

8] Save your work.

Next you will put all of the elements together to complete the fish.

CREATING A CLIPPING PATH

Many of the elements that you have created for this fish actually extend beyond the body of the fish, including the blend, composite path, and stripe. In this task, you will position these elements and paste them inside the body of the fish.

First you must move the blend into position on the body.

1] With the blend still selected, choose Edit > Cut.

This removes the blend from the page and puts it on the pasteboard. Next you will return to the view of the fish by selecting the view you named earlier in this lesson.

2] Change to the Fish view by choosing View > Custom > Fish. Then choose Edit > Paste.

The blend appears in front of the body of the fish, but it may not be positioned properly. Pasted elements are always positioned in the center of the screen.

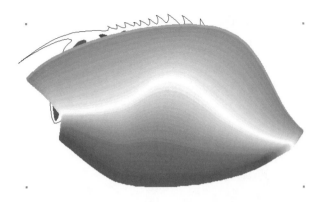

**3] Move the blend so that it covers the body of the fish and then choose Modify ›
Arrange › Send to Back.**

Next you will select all of the elements that you want trimmed to the edge of
the body.

**4] Deselect all elements. Then select the yellow block on the mouth, the stripe
behind the eye, the composite path, and the blend.**
These four elements extend beyond the edge of the body, but you do not want them
to do so in the finished illustration.

311

5] Choose Edit › Cut. Then select the body of the fish and choose Edit › Paste Inside.

The body is now a clipping path, defining the visible portion of those elements you pasted inside of it.

6] Change the stroke around the body to None in the Stroke Inspector.

Although there is a modifier key to change the stroke only, it does not always work as expected if a path has elements pasted inside of it, as with the body of the fish.

Now group the fish elements into a single object.

7] Choose Edit › Select › All (Windows Ctrl+A, Macintosh Command+A). Then choose Modify › Group (Windows Ctrl+G, Macintosh Command+G).

The fish is now complete.

8] Save your work.

Next you will combine your fish with others to create a school of fish.

THE GRAPHIC HOSE TOOL

One of the Xtra tools FreeHand includes is the Graphic Hose, which enables you to paint or spray elements on your document page for quick illustration. Each hose can contain up to 10 objects, such as groups, blends, text, EPS graphics, and TIFF images.

You will create a new hose containing your fish and a few others and then use this tool to paint the school of fish in the Aquarium sign.

1] With your fish still selected, choose Edit › Copy. Then close your NewFish document and open 3-Fish.ft8 in the Media folder within the Lesson7 folder.

This template contains three fish, each slightly different from the others.

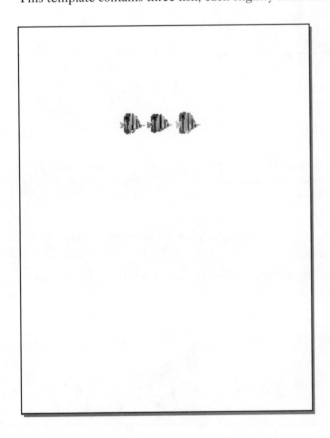

2] Choose Edit › Paste to add your fish to this page.

Your fish is much larger than the other three fish.

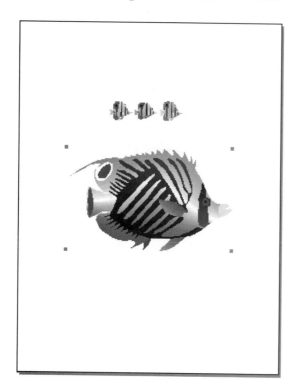

3] Hold down Shift and reduce the size of your fish so it is approximately the same size as the others in this document.

Holding down Shift while you drag a selection box keeps the artwork in proportion as you adjust its size.

4] Save this illustration as a FreeHand document named *4-Fish*. Change the view so you can again see the entire page.

Next you will create a new graphic hose.

5] Choose Window › Xtras › Xtra Tools.

The Xtra Tools panel appears.

tip *Earlier in these lessons you used the Mirror, Spiral, and Eyedropper tools. When you have time you should experiment with the other Xtra tools. The Arc tool can be used to create different types of arcs. 3D Rotation enables you to rotate an element in space, introducing the illusion of depth in your artwork. Bend and Roughen enable you to distort a selected path without manipulating points and control handles. Smudge, Shadow, and Fisheye Lens provide special effects you can apply to any selected paths. The Chart tool enables you to create detailed charts and graphs to illustrate numeric data. For more information on these tools, consult the online help system or the FreeHand User Guide included with the FreeHand 8 software.*

315

6] Choose the Graphic Hose tool from the Xtra Tools panel. Point to an empty part of the page and drag around the empty parts of this page and pasteboard to spray colorful shapes onto the document.

The Graphic Hose sprays shapes as you drag the cursor around the document window. The speed and direction that you drag the tool affects the way objects are placed. Using the left and right cursor keys increases or decreases the spacing as you spray hose objects. Using the up and down cursor keys increases or decreases the scale factor as you spray hose objects.

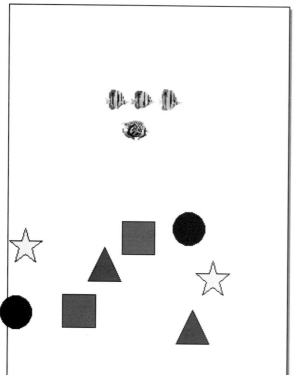

The Aquarium sign would look better with a school of fish instead of a school of shapes, so you will create a new hose containing the four fish in this document.

7] Double-click the Graphic Hose tool in the Xtra Tools panel to display the options for this tool.

At the top of this panel are two buttons: Hose and Options. Hose is currently selected The Hose menu indicates that the current hose is Shapes, and the Contents menu at the bottom of the panel lists the objects in this hose. This hose contains four objects; selecting any object from the Contents menu displays that object in the preview window.

DISPLAYS OPTIONS FOR SELECTING A HOSE, CREATING
A NEW HOSE, OR MODIFYING OBJECTS IN A HOSE

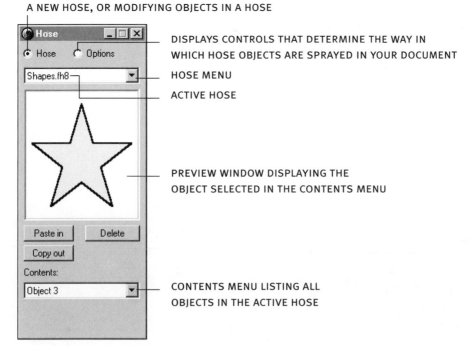

DISPLAYS CONTROLS THAT DETERMINE THE WAY IN
WHICH HOSE OBJECTS ARE SPRAYED IN YOUR DOCUMENT

HOSE MENU

ACTIVE HOSE

PREVIEW WINDOW DISPLAYING THE
OBJECT SELECTED IN THE CONTENTS MENU

CONTENTS MENU LISTING ALL
OBJECTS IN THE ACTIVE HOSE

**8] Choose New from the Hose menu at the top of the panel, type *Fish* as the name
for this new hose, and click Save.**

Your new Fish hose does not contain any elements yet.

9] Switch to the Pointer tool and select a yellow fish in your document and choose Edit › Copy. Then click the Paste In button on the Graphic Hose panel to add this object to the Fish hose.

This fish becomes Object 1 in the Fish hose.

10] Copy a different yellow fish and click Paste In to add it to the current hose. Repeat this step for the last remaining yellow fish and then copy your fish and add it to the current hose in the same way.

The Fish hose now contains four objects.

Your new Graphic Hose is ready to use.

318

ADDING ELEMENTS TO AN EXISTING LAYOUT

The Aquarium sign has already been started for you. In this task you will open a template and add a school of fish using the Graphic Hose tool.

1] Open Aquarium.ft8 in the Start folder within the Lesson7 folder.

This template already has several elements and layers in place.

You will first add a school of fish with the Graphic Hose.

2] Display the Layers panel by clicking its button on the main toolbar or choosing Window › Panels › Layers.

The artwork in this document is arranged on several layers. Make sure that the Foreground layer is active, so the first fish you add will be sprayed on the Foreground layer.

3] Double-click the Graphic Hose tool in the Xtra Tools panel. Click the Options button at the top of the Hose panel. For Scale, select Uniform and 75, and for Rotate, select Random and specify 10 degrees.

This enables the Graphic Hose to create slightly smaller fish (fish that are 75 percent of the size of the original fish) and to randomly rotate the fish up to 10 degrees from the original position as you spray objects onto the page.

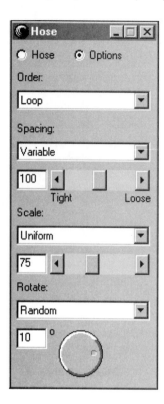

4] Close the Hose panel. Then use the tool to spray fish on the top and left side of the page, as shown here.

Your document will not match the samples shown here exactly, since the position of the elements added with the Graphic Hose will depend upon the speed and direction that you drag the tool on the page.

Some of the fish are added behind the word *Aquarium*, because that element is on the Type layer that is in front of the Foreground layer where you are adding the fish.

5] Choose the Pointer tool and click an empty part of the pasteboard to deselect all elements. Save the document as *MySign*.

You are finished with the Foreground layer for now.

6] Activate and display the Waves layer by clicking once on the name of the layer and then clicking to the left of the layer name where a check mark is missing.

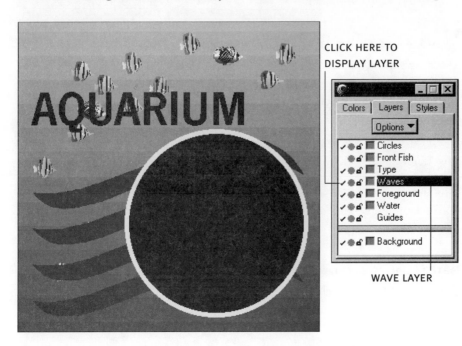

CLICK HERE TO
DISPLAY LAYER

WAVE LAYER

In the next step you will make the elements in the Waves layer transparent.

7] Using the Pointer tool, select the four wavy blue shapes. Using the Fill Inspector, select a Transparency lens fill with an opacity of 50 percent.

Adding these transparent shapes creates an illusion of depth in your illustration, as any fish behind the waves appear to be farther away.

tip   *You can use this technique to add depth to your own artwork. Try creating shapes with various opacity settings to create the illusion of several distances within your illustrations.*

8] Lock the Waves layer by clicking the Lock icon to the left of the layer name in the Layers panel.

Remember that locking a layer prevents you from accidentally making changes to the artwork on that layer as you work on other parts of the illustration.

To make this illusion more realistic, you can move some of the fish so they are positioned completely behind the waves. If none of your fish need to be moved, skip to step 10.

9] Use the Pointer tool to move any fish that are partially behind the waves to position them completely behind the wave shapes. Resize the objects if necessary.

322

Even though these elements were sprayed in this document using the Graphic Hose, they are copies of the original fish illustrations and can be moved, scaled, and edited just like any other FreeHand graphic.

10] Lock the Foreground layer and save your work.

USING THE ENVELOPE XTRA

In previous lessons you learned how to modify a path by adjusting the positions of points and control handles. However, you cannot make those adjustments to groups of objects in the same way. To change the shape of a group of objects, you can use the Envelope Xtra, included with FreeHand. The Envelope Xtra enables you to distort an object or group of objects by altering its outer boundary.

The word *Aquarium* appears across the top of the sign layout. To add pizzazz, you will distort the shape of this word, making it appear to swim though the water with the school of fish.

1] Activate the Type layer by clicking its name in the Layers panel.

This layer contains *Aquarium*, the word you want to change.

You want to distort this type and assign a Lighten lens fill. Since FreeHand cannot apply these effects to text, you must first convert the text to paths. The word *Aquarium* has already been converted to paths for you.

323

tip *If you select the word* Aquarium *with the Pointer tool and look in the Object Inspector, it will be listed as a group instead of as text.*

2] Select the word *Aquarium* with the Pointer tool and choose Xtras › Distort › Envelope.

The Envelope window appears, displaying points and control handles surrounding the selected object.

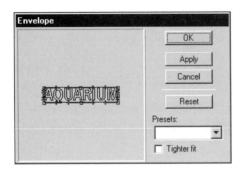

tip *You will be making several changes in this window, so resist the temptation to press Enter after each step. If you do press Enter or click OK before you have completed the adjustments, be sure to choose Undo before returning to the Envelope window. Otherwise, you will find it very difficult to achieve the desired results. If things do go wrong, choose File > Revert and start this task again.*

3] Select Peak Right from the Presets menu at the lower right of the Envelope window. Then click Apply.

The type is now distorted to fit the shape shown in the Envelope preview window.

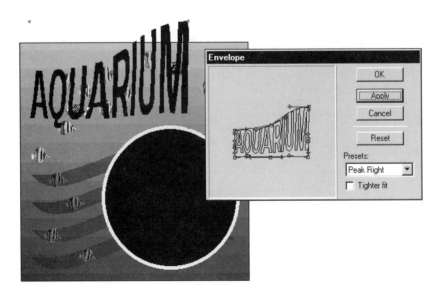

324

tip *Windows users may have to scroll down the list of Presets to find Peak Right.*

4] In the Envelope preview window, drag the point at the lower right (the point at the bottom right of the *M*) up toward the middle-right point (the middle point on the right side of the *M*). Then drag the middle point on the right side up to approximately center it between the top and bottom points on that side. Adjust the middle points and handles to create an envelope similar to the one shown here. Click Apply after each set of changes to see the results on the page.

Try to keep the points above the letters aligned over the points below the letters to avoid angling the letters excessively. Don't worry if your type does not match the samples shown here exactly. It should bend up and increase in size on the right side. When finished and positioned on the page, it should appear to wrap above the circles at the lower right of the page.

If you have trouble, click Reset to return to the original shape and then try again. When you are happy with the appearance of the type, continue with the next step.

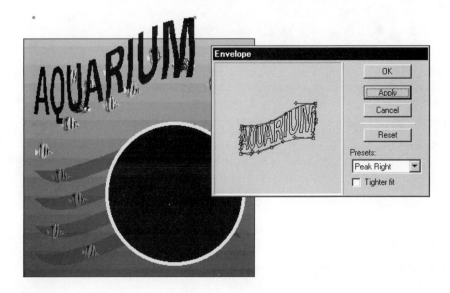

tip *If you would like to apply the same envelope distortion to other elements later, choose Save from the Presets menu and give your envelope a name. Then you can select this envelope from the Presets menu whenever you want to create the same distortion again.*

5] Click OK in the Envelope window to complete the distortion.

The type ends too high up on the page; you need to reposition it.

6] Use the Pointer tool to move the type down to position it on the page as shown here.

7] Save your work.

APPLYING LENS FILLS

You can use different lens fills to enhance your illustration. Choose from Transparency, Magnify, Invert, Lighten, Darken, and Monochrome lens fills to achieve different results.

note *A lens fill, like a real lens, does not actually change the properties of the objects under it. Instead, duplicate objects are created inside the lens. Remember that using lens fills, especially on top of each other, can quickly add hundreds of objects to a document, greatly increasing both file size and print time. If it takes an excessively long time to display the results of these fills on the screen, you may want to change to the Fast Preview mode.*

1] Display the Fill Inspector. With the Aquarium type still selected, change to a lens fill.

The default lens fill is Transparency.

2] Change the type of lens fill to Lighten and set the percentage to 60.

The elements behind the type now appear lighter. By adjusting the percentage, you can vary the effect from no lightening (0 percent) to completely white (100 percent).

3] Lock the Type layer and save your work.

Now you will apply lens fills to the circles at the bottom right of the page.

4] Select the yellow circle that encompasses the smaller, black circle and apply the Lighten lens fill with a percentage of 60, the same settings you applied to the type.

Now apply a Magnify fill to the black circle.

5] Deselect all elements. Then select the black circle and change to the Magnify lens fill.

The elements directly behind the circle now appear twice their original size, as indicated by the 2x that appears by default in the Fill Inspector.

You will use this lens to magnify one of the fish on the page, but first you need to spray a few more fish on the page—in front of the waves and Aquarium type.

6] Save your work.

ADDING FINAL TOUCHES

The final steps in creating this sign will be to spray a few more fish on the page with the Graphic Hose and then adjust the Magnify lens fill to enlarge one of your fish.

1] Deselect all of the elements on the page. Activate the Front Fish layer by clicking its name in the Layers panel.

This layer is in front of the waves and the type, so the fish you add to this layer will appear in front of those elements.

2] Choose the Graphic Hose tool from the Xtra Tools panel. Make sure the Fish hose is selected.

The Fish hose should already be selected, unless you have experimented with other hoses since painting the fish earlier in this lesson.

3] Paint some additional fish in front of the type and waves, as shown here. Then choose the Pointer tool from the toolbox.

After you have added the fish to your document, you can use the Pointer tool to reposition any fish, if you desire.

In this illustration, only the new fish are visible to make it easier for you to see where to put your fish. Remember that your artwork does not need to match these samples exactly.

4] Lock the Front Fish layer and save your work.

Next you will adjust the fill inside the smaller of the two circles.

5] Select the smaller of the two circles by clicking inside it with the Pointer tool, and make sure the Fill Inspector is visible.

The controls in the Fill Inspector will enable you to adjust the Magnify lens fill in this circle.

6] Display the centerpoint by clicking the Centerpoint box in the Fill Inspector.
A centerpoint handle appears in the center of the circle. The position of this handle
determines the elements that the circle will magnify.

CENTERPOINT
HANDLE

7] Drag the centerpoint handle and position it on the front part of one of your fish.
The circle will now display a magnified view of that fish and the surrounding area.

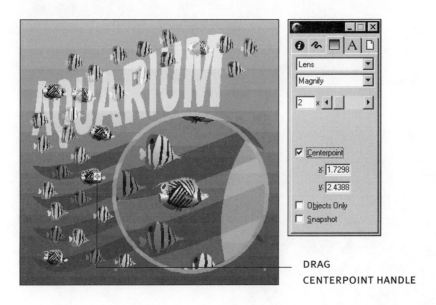

DRAG
CENTERPOINT HANDLE

**8] In the Fill Inspector, type *8* as the magnification factor and press Enter. Adjust
the centerpoint position as needed to display just the front part of your fish.**

The fish is now enlarged to eight times its original size inside the circle. FreeHand may take a while to display this enlargement. If drawing the screen takes too long, you may wish to change to the Fast Preview mode.

There are two other lens fill options in the Fill Inspector that you will not need to use in this illustration. Objects Only applies the lens effect to objects, but not empty areas, under the lens or centerpoint. Snapshot captures the current contents of the lens, so you can move the lens element anywhere in the document without changing the lens contents. The Centerpoint, Objects Only, and Snapshot options are available for each of the six types of lens fills.

9] Save your work.

Congratulations, you have completed this complex illustration!

ON YOUR OWN

Practice the techniques you learned in this lesson by creating another fish using a template named 2-Fish.ft8, which is located in the Start folder within the Lesson7 folder. This template contains an image of a fish on a locked background layer. Trace the fish and all elements and apply fills and effects as desired.

WHAT YOU HAVE LEARNED

In this lesson you have:

- Created a composite path with the Join command [*page* **300**]
- Applied gradient fills and used modifier keys to set the gradient direction [*page* **302**]
- Defined a named view [*page* **306**]
- Created a blend of three elements [*page* **307**]
- Created a clipping path with Paste Inside [*page* **310**]
- Created and used a Graphic Hose to spray objects onto the page [*page* **313**]
- Distorted the shape of an object using the Envelope Xtra [*page* **323**]
- Used Transparency, Lighten, and Magnify lens fills to enhance your illustration [*page* **326**]
- Repositioned the centerpoint of a lens fill [*page* **331**]

for shading

blending shapes

LESSON 8

In this lesson you will complete a robot illustration for a postcard by applying skills you learned in previous lessons to add the fills and shading needed to finish the robot. You will create blends, use Paste Inside, apply gradient and lens fills, and import an image to create an illustration that looks three-dimensional. At the end of this lesson, you will learn how to customize FreeHand's toolbars and keyboard shortcuts.

This robot illustration demonstrates how you can blend shapes and apply fills to add distinctive shading effects to your artwork, making the finished piece look three-dimensional.

Designed by Stewart McKissick.

If you would like to review the final result of this lesson, open FlexBotz.fh8 in the
Complete folder within the Lesson8 folder.

WHAT YOU WILL LEARN

In this lesson you will:

- Create blends for shading

- Paste blends inside paths

- Move copies of artwork into different documents

- Apply gradient fills

- Apply a lens fill

- Create a custom page size

- Import an image

- Customize your working environment

APPROXIMATE TIME

It usually takes about 1 hour and 30
minutes to complete this lesson.

LESSON FILES

Media Files:

Lesson8\Media\Planet.tif

Starting Files:

Lesson8\Start\Outline.ft8

Lesson8\Start\Parts.ft8

Lesson8\Start\FlexBtz2.ft8

Completed Project:

Lesson8\Complete\FlexBotz.fh8

Lesson8\Complete\Postcard.fh8

BLENDING SHAPES FOR SHADING

GETTING STARTED

The paths required in this robot illustration have already been created for you and saved in two template files.

1] Open the document named Outline.ft8 in the Start folder within the Lesson8 folder.

Since Outline.ft8 is a template, FreeHand opens an untitled copy of the file, which contains the robot figure.

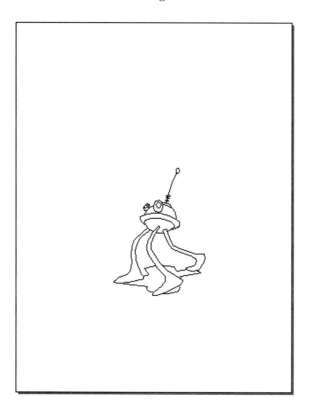

tip *Remember that opening a template opens an untitled copy of the template, instead of the template itself. This prevents you from accidentally altering the template. Any document can be saved as a template by selecting FreeHand Template as the file format instead of the default setting, FreeHand Document, in the Save As dialog box.*

2] Save this document as *FlexBotz* in your MyWork folder.

3] Open the template named Parts.ft8 in the Start folder within the Lesson8 folder.

This template contains body part shapes that will be used to create shading for your robot.

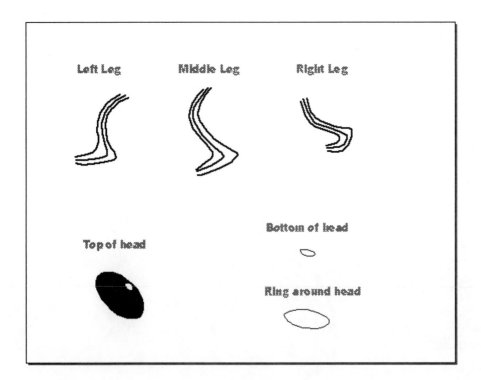

4] Save this document as *MyParts* in your MyWork folder.

CREATING BLENDS

You will be blending the body part shapes to create three-dimensional shading for the robot's legs and body.

1] Zoom in on the Left Leg element and display the Color List panel.

The colors you need were also saved in the template, so they already exist in your document.

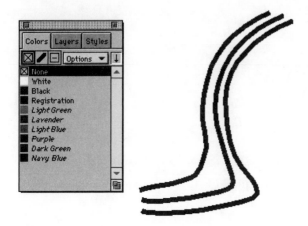

tip This document includes a predefined custom view for each part you will be working on. These views are available from the View > Custom menu and from the Magnification menu at the bottom left of the document window. Instead of manually zooming or scrolling to the different parts in this document, you can select the appropriate named view.

2] Using the Pointer tool, select the middle path of the Left Leg element and change the stroke color to Lavender.

Remember that you can change the stroke color by clicking the Current Stroke Color button at the top of the Color List and then clicking the desired color name in the Color List.

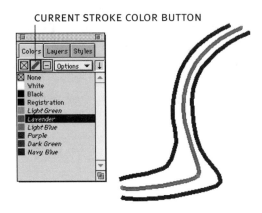

3] Select the two outer paths of the Left Leg element with the Pointer tool and change the stroke color to Purple.

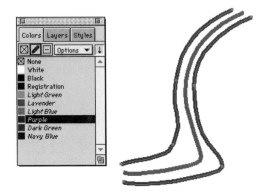

4] Select all three of the Left Leg paths and choose Modify › Combine › Blend.

This creates a blend of the three selected paths. There may be some gaps between the steps in this blend; you will eliminate these in the next step.

5] Change the number of steps in the blend to 15 in the Object Inspector.

Changing the number of steps between paths to 15 smoothes out the blend and eliminates any gaps.

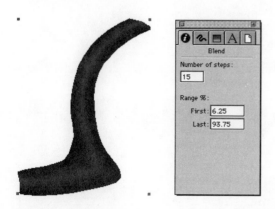

6] Change your view so you can see the Middle Leg paths.

You will now repeat the same procedure for the Middle Leg element.

7] Using the Pointer tool, select the middle path of the Middle Leg element and change the stroke color to Lavender. Select the two outer paths with the Pointer tool and change the stroke color to Purple. Select all three of the Middle Leg paths and choose Modify › Combine › Blend. Then change the number of steps in the blend to 15 in the Object Inspector.

8] Adjust the view to see the Right Leg paths.

9] Select the middle path of the Right Leg element and change the stroke color to Lavender. Select the two outer paths and change the stroke color to Purple. Create a blend of the three Right Leg paths. Then change the number of steps in the blend to 15.

10] Zoom out to see the entire page. Then save your work.

The three leg blends are ready to be used in the robot illustration.

PASTING BLENDS INSIDE PATHS TO CREATE THREE-DIMENSIONAL SHADING

Although you could fill the legs of your robot with graduated fills, the colors would not follow the contours of the legs. Instead, you blended shapes together to create three-dimensional shading that does follow the contours of the legs. In this task you will add these blends to the robot by combining them with the paths for each leg using the Paste Inside feature.

1] Select all three blended leg shapes.

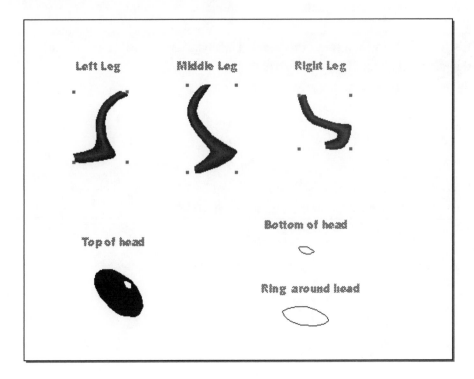

2] Choose Edit › Copy.

You will be pasting the blends into the robot document.

3] Choose Window › FlexBotz to switch to that document and bring it to the front. Then choose Edit › Paste to add the three blends to this document.

Remember that all of the open documents are listed at the bottom of the Window menu so you can easily switch from one to another.

You will reposition the blends in the following steps.

4] Deselect all items. Then select the Middle Leg blend and move this blend into position directly in front of the robot's middle leg.

The blend should completely cover the path for that leg.

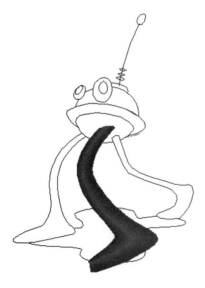

342

Now you will cut the blend and paste it inside the leg path.

5] Cut the blend. Then paste it inside the leg path with Paste Inside. Change the stroke width to 0.5 point.

The lightest part of the blend should be roughly in the middle of the foot, and the blend should completely fill the leg path. If either is not the case, drag the Paste Inside control handle to reposition the blend.

6] Repeat steps 4 and 5 for the left leg and then the right leg.

Now all three legs are complete.

7] Save your work.

CREATING SHADING FOR THE TOP OF A SPHERE

The head of this robot is a sphere with a ring around the middle. To add realistic shading, you will create a separate blend for both the top and bottom portions of the sphere.

1] Return to the MyParts document by selecting it from the Window menu. Zoom in on the top of the head elements.

These two ellipses will be used to create shading for the top portion of the robot's head.

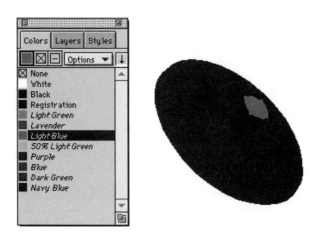

2] Using the Pointer tool, select the small oval. Change the fill to Light Blue and make sure that the stroke is set to None.

This will become the highlighted area of the top of the head.

3] Select the large oval and change the fill to Navy Blue. Make sure that the stroke is set to None.

This will be used to create the darker areas of the top of the head.

344

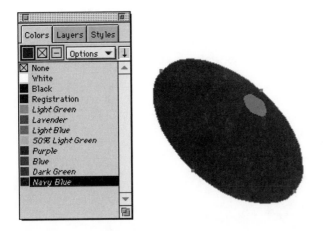

Now you will blend these two shapes together.

tip *When creating a blend of two closed shapes, make sure that the stroke for each shape is set to None. Otherwise, each of the intermediate shapes will have a stroke, which will disrupt the smooth change of color desired.*

4] Create a blend of the two ellipses. Then change the number of steps in the blend to 30 in the Object Inspector to create a smoother color transition.

This blend is ready to be added to the robot illustration.

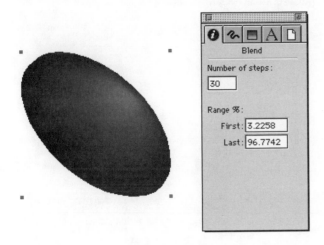

tip *If you have difficulty selecting both ellipses, be sure you select the smaller shape first, then hold Shift and click the larger one.*

5] Save your work.

Now you will add this blend to the robot.

6] Copy the blend. Then switch to the FlexBotz document and paste the blend.

Before you move this blend into position, you will change the fill and stroke for the path itself. If you need to, move the blend out of your way temporarily.

7] Select the path that defines the top of the head. Change the fill to Navy Blue and set the stroke to None.

Changing the fill to match the darkest color of the blend is a precaution. Occasionally, when you paste a shape inside a path that has no stroke, a bit of the fill color for the path is visible on the screen around the pasted object.

8] Move the blended ellipses into position on the top of the head, as shown here.

9] Cut the blend and use Paste Inside to paste it inside the path for the top of the head.

The highlight should appear on the upper-right part of the head. Drag the Paste Inside control handle to reposition the blend if necessary.

The top of the head was originally behind the eyes in this illustration. Pasting the blend inside this path does not change its current position on the page, which is why the top of the head remains behind the eyes.

10] Save your work.

CREATING SHADING FOR THE BOTTOM OF A SPHERE

Now you will create the bottom head element.

1] Return to the MyParts document and change the view to see the bottom of the head element. Select this shape using the Pointer tool and then change the fill to Light Blue and the stroke to None.

You will use this shape to create the highlighted area for the bottom of the head.

2] Save your work.

Now you will paste this shape in the robot document.

3] Copy the light blue head shape. Then switch to the FlexBotz document and choose Paste.

You will use this shape as the highlight for the lower part of the robot's spherical head. You will move this shape into position in the next step.

4] Change to the Fast Keyline mode using the menu at the bottom of the document window.

A shape located on the background layer is now visible on the bottom of the head to help you position the highlight shape correctly.

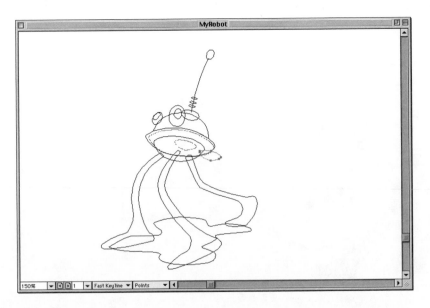

5] Move the highlight element into position on top of the gray background element.

Remember that you move an element by pointing to the middle and dragging with the Pointer tool.

tip *You may find it helpful when repositioning shapes to click and hold the selection until the cursor changes to a four-direction arrow. Then when you drag, you will see the actual shape moving instead of a rectangular bounding box.*

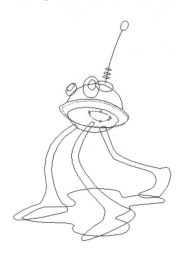

349

6] Change back to the Preview mode and select the path that defines the bottom portion of the head. Change the fill to Navy Blue and set the stroke to None.

This defines the characteristics of the darker areas for the lower head element.

7] Create a blend of the highlight element and the bottom head path. Then change the number of steps in the Object Inspector to 16.

These shapes created the shading effect for the bottom of the head. However, because the blend is a new element on the page, it is automatically placed in front of the other elements, covering the tops of the legs.

8] Select the middle and right legs and choose Modify › Arrange › Bring to Front. Then save your work.

The legs and two head sphere elements are complete.

CREATING SHADING FOR A CYLINDRICAL RING

Next you will add the appearance of a ring going around the head.

1] Return to the MyParts document and change your view to see the path for the ring around the head.

2] Using the Fill Inspector, apply a gradient that begins and ends with Dark Green. Drag the Light Green swatch from the Color List and drop it just above the middle of the color ramp in the Fill Inspector, as shown here. Change the angle of the gradient to 344 degrees and set the stroke to None.

You will use this shape to add dimension to the ring surrounding the head.

3] Copy the ellipse. Then switch to the FlexBotz document and choose Paste.

4] Zoom in on the head using the Zoom tool. Then change the view mode to Fast Keyline.

You can now see the background elements, including a gray elliptical shape near the ring ellipse to help you position the pasted ellipse accurately.

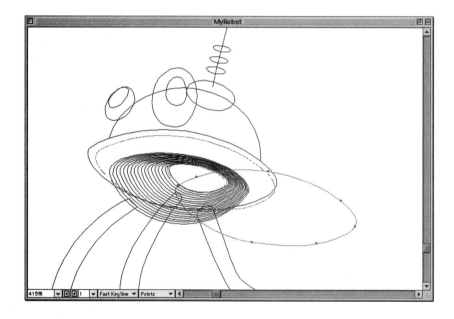

5] Using the Pointer tool, position the ring ellipse on top of the background ellipse.

The ring ellipse filled with gradient color should extend a bit below the bottom (back) edge of the ring.

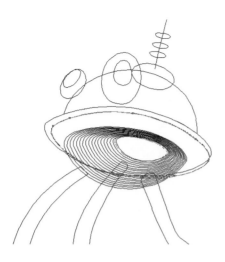

6] Return to the Preview mode. Select the path that defines the ring shape.

The path is currently filled with white and has a black stroke.

7] Apply a gradient fill that begins and ends with Light Green. Using the Color Mixer, create the color 17c2m26y0k. Add this color to the middle of the gradient on the color ramp as shown here. Then change the angle to 339 degrees and set the stroke to None.

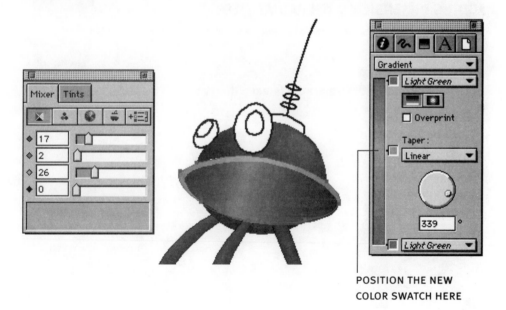

POSITION THE NEW
COLOR SWATCH HERE

You will now complete the robot's ring by combining the two ellipses.

8] Cut the dark green ellipse and paste it inside the light green ellipse.

The head and ring are now complete.

9] Save your work.

You are finished with your MyParts document, so it does not need to remain open.

10] Switch to the MyParts document and close it.

You will continue your work on the FlexBotz document.

ADDING DIMENSION WITH RADIAL FILLS

The robot's eyes will be shaded using radial fills, which will make them look three-dimensional.

1] Using the Pointer tool, select the larger path for both of the eyes.

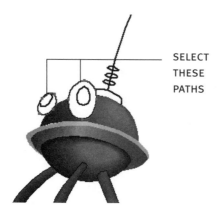

SELECT
THESE
PATHS

The outer shapes use the same fill, so you can apply the fill to both paths at the same time.

2] Using the Fill Inspector, change the type of fill to Gradient. Then click the Radial Fill button. Set White as the starting color (at the bottom of the panel) and set the ending color to Light Blue. Add another White swatch in the middle of the color ramp by dragging the White swatch at the bottom and dropping it approximately one-third of the way up the color ramp.

Using white for two of the three swatches along the color ramp in this gradient will make the white parts of the eyes appear larger than if white was used only once.

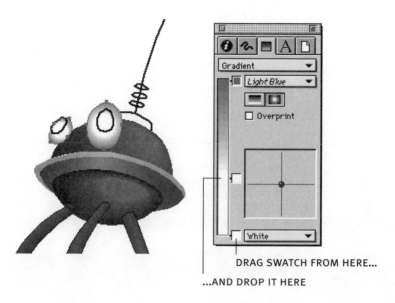

DRAG SWATCH FROM HERE...

...AND DROP IT HERE

3] Move the centerpoint of the radial gradient up and to the right as shown here and change the stroke width to 0.5 point.

The outer paths of the eyes are complete.

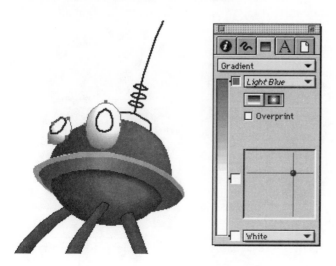

355

Since the desired shading for the eyes could be achieved using a radial gradient, you did not need to create clipping paths by pasting blends inside the paths. Radial and graduated fills are less complex than blends and clipping paths and will usually print faster. Create blends and clipping paths when a radial or graduated fill cannot achieve the desired shading, such as when you need to create a highlight shape that is not circular.

4] Select the smaller path for each eye. Change the stroke to None and then apply a radial gradient fill. Select White as the starting color and Blue as the ending color of the gradient. Drag and drop the Blue color swatch on the middle of the color ramp. Using the blue for two of the three swatches in this gradient makes the transition between white and blue take place over a shorter distance and fills the remaining portion of the paths with solid blue.

5] Move the centerpoint of the radial gradient up slightly and to the right as shown here.

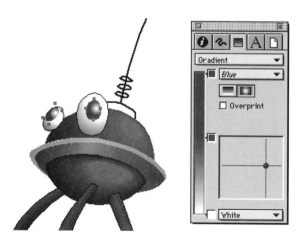

You are almost finished with the eyes.

6] Deselect all elements. Then select just the smaller path of the eye on your left. In the Fill Inspector, move the middle Blue swatch down slightly on the color ramp and move the centerpoint slightly up and to the right.

This subtle change makes the highlight in the eye that is farther away appear smaller, which adds a realistic touch to the illustration. Adjusting the position of the centerpoint makes the eyes appear to be looking in different directions.

The eyes are now complete.

7] Deselect all elements and save your work.

COMPLETING THE FIGURE

You will complete the antenna by applying basic and gradient fills.

1] Zoom out, if necessary, so you can see the entire antenna.

The antenna consists of six shapes.

357

2] Select the long path extending the length of the antenna. Change the stroke color to Purple.

The width of this line should already be set to 1 point.

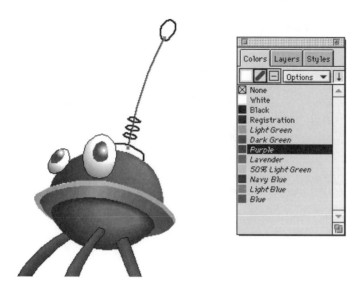

3] Select the three small oval shapes. Change the fill color to Lavender and the stroke to None.

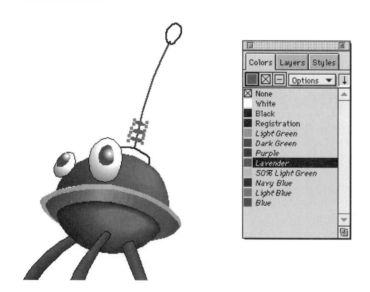

4] Select the ellipse at the top of the antenna and change the stroke to None. Apply a radial gradient fill, with Dark Green as the starting color and 50% Light Green as the ending color. Move the centerpoint up and to the right as shown here.

5] Select the element at the base of the antenna and change the stroke to None. Apply a linear gradient fill, with Purple as the starting color and Lavender as the ending color. Then change the angle of the gradient to 250 degrees.

The antenna is now complete.

6] Save your work.

CREATING A REALISTIC SHADOW

The shadow will be filled with a lens fill.

1] Zoom out so you can see the entire robot.

2] Select the shadow shape and change the stroke to None. Using the Fill Inspector, apply a lens fill. Change the type of lens fill from Transparency to Darken and set the percentage to 35.

For a Darken lens fill, a value of 0 percent would not darken the background element at all, and a value of 100 percent would make the element completely black. You will see the full effect of this fill later when you add an image behind the shadow.

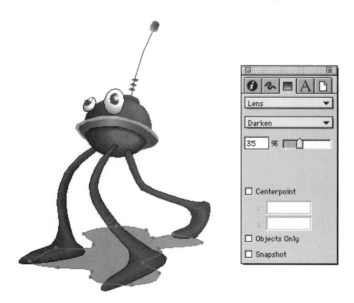

3] Save your work.

CREATING THE FINISHED DOCUMENT

Your robot illustration is so nice that you want to send it to your friends as a postcard. You need to create a new document and specify a custom page size for your postcard. You will then add the completed robot to this new document. For a finishing touch, you will import a TIFF file created in Photoshop as a background image for your robot.

1] Select all of the elements on the page and group them together.

This will make it easier to move and manipulate the robot as one object.

2] Copy this group. Then create a new document and choose Paste.

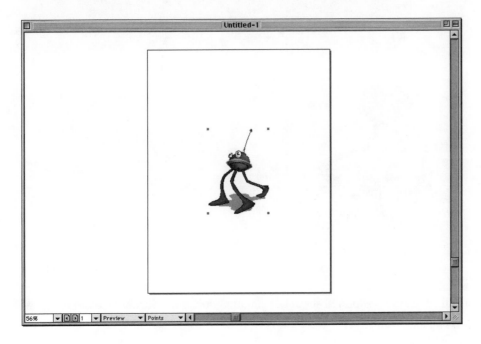

3] Save this document as *Postcard* in your MyWork folder.

4] Using the Document Inspector, change the page size to 4 inches by 5 inches.
Remember to change the unit of measurement to Inches in the menu at the bottom of the document window. Then choose Custom from the list of page sizes in the Document Inspector to enter new dimensions for the page.

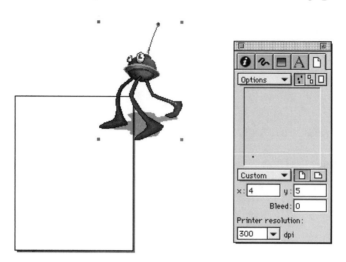

5] Move the robot so it is visually centered on the page. Then choose View › Fit to Page.

You will adjust the position of the robot one final time once the background image is in place.

6] Choose File › Import. Then select the Planet.tif graphic located in the Media folder within the Lesson8 folder. Click near the top of the page to position the image on the page.

The imported image now covers the robot artwork.

7] With the imported graphic still selected, choose Modify › Arrange › Send to Back.

Now the robot appears in front of the background image. Notice how the Darken lens fill in the shadow actually darkens the texture of the image behind it.

The next step will position the graphic and robot so they are centered on the page.

8] Select both the imported background graphic and the robot. Display the Align panel by choosing Window › Panels › Align. Click the center of the preview grid to change both the vertical and horizontal alignment settings to Align Center. Turn on Align to Page and click Apply (Windows) or Align (Macintosh).

The robot and background image are now centered on the page.

9] Save your work.

Congratulations—your robot postcard is now complete!

CUSTOMIZING FREEHAND'S TOOLBARS AND SHORTCUTS

FreeHand allows you to customize its toolbars by adding, deleting, or repositioning items. You can also define your own keyboard shortcuts or use the keyboard shortcuts from other applications.

1] Choose File › Customize › Shortcuts. Open the Keyboard Shortcuts Setting menu to see a list of available shortcut sets.

FreeHand lets you choose the keyboard shortcut sets from other popular programs to make it easier for you to switch from one program to another as you work.

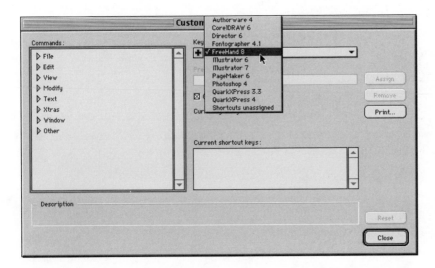

FreeHand also lets you assign keyboard shortcuts to any command. You first select the command from the list on the left, and then you click the Press New Shortcut Key box and type the shortcut you want to assign to that command. Go to Conflict on Assign is turned on by default, so FreeHand will not allow you to assign the same shortcut to different commands.

CLICK HERE TO TYPE IN NEW SHORTCUT

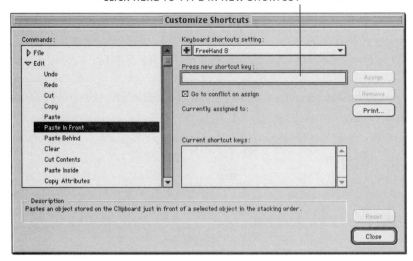

tip   *If you make any inadvertent changes in this dialog box, click the Reset button in the lower-right corner before you close it.*

Now look at how you can customize the toolbars.

2] Close the Customize Shortcuts dialog box and choose File > Customize > Toolbars.

This dialog box enables you to add or delete commands on the toolbars. On the left is a list of FreeHand commands. You can click the triangle to the left of a command name to view the commands in that command group. On the right are several buttons that represent different specific commands. The button display changes according to the command selected on the left.

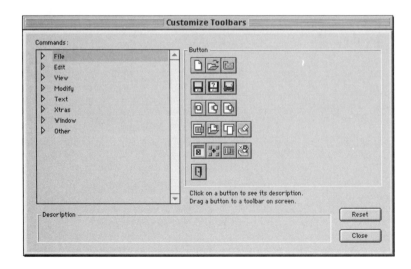

366

LESSON 8

To see how easy it is to customize your toolbars, you will add the Blend command to the main toolbar, so that feature is available at the click of a button.

3] In the Commands list, click the triangle next to Modify to expand that group and see the commands on the Modify menu. Scroll down the list to Combine and click its triangle to view the various Combine commands. Click Blend to select this command.

A heavy line now appears around the Blend button on the right of the dialog box.

BLEND BUTTON

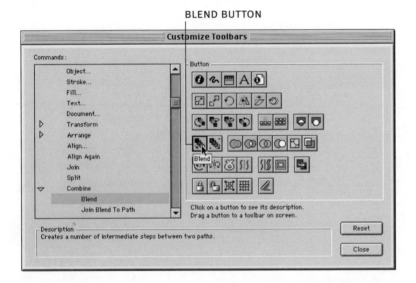

4] Drag the Blend button icon from the right side of the dialog box and drop it where you would like it positioned on the main toolbar.

If you drop a button on top of an existing button, your new button will appear directly to the right of that button. In this example, the Blend button was dropped on top of the Split button so it appears to the right of Split and before Lock.

367

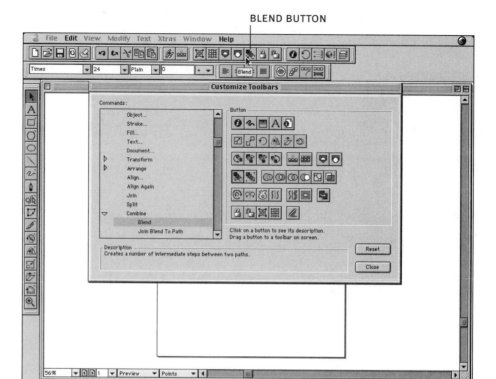

5] If you do not want to apply the change you just made, click Reset. Otherwise, click Close.

Customizable shortcuts and toolbars enable you to fine-tune your working environment, helping you take advantage of the power FreeHand provides in the manner that best suits your own working style and needs.

ON YOUR OWN

Practice the techniques you used in this lesson by adding shading effects to another robot. Open FlexBotz2.ft8, a template you will find in the Start folder within the Lesson8 folder. This document contains the outline shapes for another robot. As with the robot you just completed, you will need to add fills, strokes, and shading to give this new robot three-dimensional qualities. Experiment with blends, Paste Inside, and gradient and lens fills as you create a new illustration.

WHAT YOU HAVE LEARNED

In this lesson you have:

- Created blends to add three-dimensional shading effects [*page* **337**]
- Practiced creating clipping paths with the Paste Inside feature [*page* **341**]
- Practiced copying and pasting artwork between documents [*page* **342**]
- Created shading effects using linear and radial gradient fills [*page* **351**]
- Created a realistic shadow using a Darken lens fill [*page* **360**]
- Practiced creating a custom page size [*page* **362**]
- Imported a Photoshop TIFF document as a background image [*page* **363**]
- Customized FreeHand's keyboard shortcuts and toolbars [*page* **365**]

for the web

designing

LESSON 9

In addition to creating illustrations and layouts for your print and multimedia projects, you can also use FreeHand to extend your creativity to the World Wide Web. You can easily convert artwork into the two most popular types of images for Web pages, GIF and JPEG, or export still images and animations as **Shockwave Flash** files.

Shockwave Flash is a Macromedia technology for creating and delivering compact, scaleable, high-resolution graphics with small file sizes. Used together, FreeHand and Flash provide a high-impact way to communicate your ideas by enhancing standard Web page content with dynamic graphics.

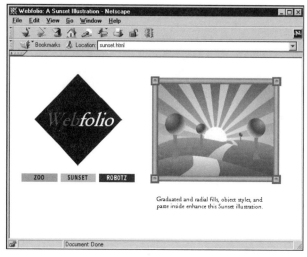

Graduated and radial fills, object styles, and paste inside enhance this Sunset illustration.

FreeHand enables you to create and export graphics, like the ones shown here, for Web pages in both GIF and JPEG formats. You can also export high-resolution still and animated vector artwork from FreeHand in Shockwave Flash format. Using the Insta.html Xtra for FreeHand, you can also export your FreeHand documents as HTML Web pages.

Designed by Craig Faist and Tom Faist.

In this lesson, you will learn how to use FreeHand to create GIF, JPEG, and Flash graphics and will view examples of each of these on Web pages. You will also see how you can publish and view FreeHand documents as HTML pages on the Web, without having to create an HTML Web page manually.

The best way to start your study of Web graphics is by creating examples of the different types of graphics in a Web browser—so that's how you'll begin here. Note that you will need a Shockwave-enabled browser to see these examples.

WHAT YOU WILL LEARN

In this lesson you will:

- Learn what a browser is and why you need one
- Learn about graphic formats used in Web pages
- Convert FreeHand artwork into Web page graphics
- Create Shockwave Flash graphics in FreeHand
- Learn how to join a blend to a path
- Learn how to use FreeHand to create Web pages

APPROXIMATE TIME

It usually takes about 1 hour to complete this lesson.

LESSON FILES

Starting Files:

Lesson9\Start\Fish.ft8
Lesson9\Start\Robot.ft8
Lesson9\Start\Flower.ft8
Lesson9\Start\Webfolio.ft8

Media Files:

Lesson9\Media\Creature.htm
Lesson9\Media\Flower.swf

Completed Project:

Lesson9\Complete\Fish.gif
Lesson9\Complete\Robot.jpg
Lesson9\Complete\Flower.swf
Lesson9\Complete\Folio\webfolio.html

OBTAINING THE BROWSER SOFTWARE AND
SHOCKWAVE FLASH PLUG-IN

A **Web browser** is software that is used to navigate around the World Wide Web and view files published there. Netscape Navigator and Microsoft Internet Explorer are two popular browsers. Each will automatically display HTML pages, along with GIF and JPEG graphics. To display Flash graphics that are embedded in Web pages, you need to download and install the Shockwave Flash plug-in.

1] If you don't already have a Web browser, download one now.

Both Netscape Navigator and Microsoft Internet Explorer are available for downloading from the Web. To download Netscape Navigator, go to http://www.netscape.com. To download Internet Explorer, go to http://www.microsoft.com.

You will not be able to view the Web graphics and HTML pages in this lesson if you do not have the software installed on your computer. You will, however, be able to learn how to use FreeHand to create Web graphics and Web pages even if you cannot view the results in a browser.

2] If you don't already have the Shockwave Flash plug-in for your browser, install the files from the CD-ROM now.

You will not be able to view the Shockwave Flash graphics in this lesson if you do not have the plug-in for your browser installed.

The most up-to-date versions of the Shockwave Flash plug-in can always be downloaded for free from Macromedia's Web site (http://www.macromedia.com). Other useful information can also be found at that site, including additional tips and techniques and suggestions for troubleshooting.

VIEWING DIFFERENT TYPES OF WEB GRAPHICS

To better understand the different types of graphics used in Web pages, you first will look at a sample document in a Web browser. If you do not have a browser, simply read these steps to learn about the different file formats.

1] Quit any other applications that may be open. Drag the Creature.htm document located in the Media folder within the Lesson9 folder and drop it on the icon for your Web browser.

This launches your browser and opens this Web page containing examples of two standard types of Web graphics, which you will learn how to create later in this lesson.

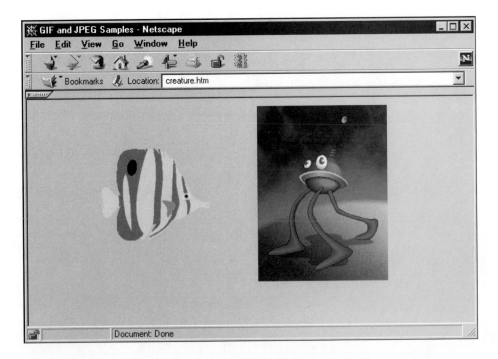

The fish on the left side of the page is a **GIF file**. GIF, or Graphic Interchange Format, is excellent for saving graphics with solid areas of color, like this fish. It also supports transparency, so the area surrounding the fish allows the background color of the Web page to show through. Because GIF files are limited to 256 or fewer colors, they are not well suited to large images with many varied colors, such as photographs or graphics that use FreeHand gradients. With that type of artwork, you will notice bands of color in the image, or you will see speckles of color throughout the image, called dithering.

The robot illustration on the right is a **JPEG file** (pronounced *jay-peg*). JPEG is a compression format designed by the Joint Photographic Experts Group for reducing the file size of continuous-tone images such as photographs and artwork containing gradient fills. JPEG compression may cause unwanted speckles or artifacts in areas of solid colors, so it is not as effective as GIF for small icons or other graphics with solid colors.

2] Close the Creature window. Then drag the Flower.swf document located in the Media folder within the Lesson9 folder and drop it on the icon for your Web browser.

This Web page contains a Shockwave Flash animation that was created in FreeHand.

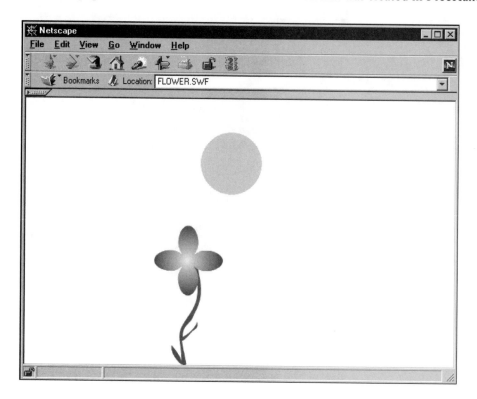

Shockwave Flash graphics are saved in vector format—just like the paths and objects in FreeHand, but unlike the GIF and JPEG formats, which create pixel images. This vector format has the advantages of small file size, quick downloading, and scaleability; images can be scaled and zoomed in a Web browser without reducing the quality of the artwork.

tip *To view a Flash graphic in a Netscape browser on the Macintosh, first open the Netscape application. Then drag the icon for the Flash graphic and drop it on an open browser window. If you do not have a Web browser with the Shockwave Flash plug-in, simply double-click the Flower.swf file located in the Media folder within the Lesson9 folder. The animation will open in the Flash Player application that is included with FreeHand. Choose Play from the Play menu to view the animation.*

3] Quit the browser application (and the Flash Player, if necessary).

In the next tasks, you will learn how to create the three types of Web graphics.

CREATING GIF AND JPEG FILES

Once you have created a graphic and scaled it to the size you want it to appear on a Web page, you must export the file in an appropriate file format.

1] In FreeHand, open Fish.ft8, located in the Start folder within the Lesson9 folder.

This fish, which you worked with in an earlier lesson, is a small graphic made up of solid-color shapes. The GIF format is well suited to this type of artwork, so you will export it as a GIF file.

tip *When creating GIF graphics, you may want to choose one of the 216 standard Web colors to prevent dithering in areas that should be filled with a solid color. These are the colors that the Windows and Macintosh platforms have in common and are often referred to as* Web Safe *colors. FreeHand includes a Web Safe color library so you can easily select from this specialized color palette; you can access this color library from the Options menu at the top of the Color List. The shapes in the fish artwork were filled with colors from the Web Safe color library.*

2] Choose File › Export and select GIF from the Format menu. Then click Setup (Windows) or Options (Macintosh) and turn on Include Alpha Channel.

You can use an **alpha channel** to record transparency within an image. Turning this option on enables you to save the fish without a white background around it. Leave the other options in this dialog box at their default settings, as they appear here.

3] Click More to display additional options. Then turn on the Transparent Background option.

Remember that GIF files are limited to 256 or fewer colors. In this dialog box you can specify what color palette, or collection of colors, you want to use for this graphic. Since this fish was created with colors from the Web Safe color library, the Web palette is a good choice here.

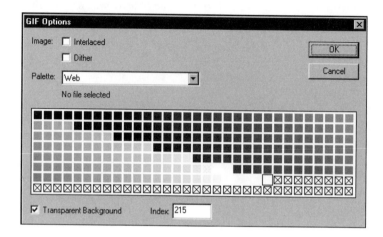

The Dither option in this dialog box is used only when you are exporting artwork containing much wider color variations than in this fish. This option sprinkles different color pixels throughout the image in an attempt to fool your eye into seeing more colors than actually appear. However, dithering also adds a speckled appearance to the image and is not necessary for graphics that utilize large areas of solid color.

The Interlaced option is useful for large files that download slowly, because it enables the image to appear on the Web page in a rough form while it is being downloaded and then slowly improve in quality until the download is complete. This option is not necessary for small graphics such as this fish.

4] Click OK in both dialog boxes to close them. Export this graphic as *Fish.gif* to your MyWork folder.

Web browsers are very particular about the names of HTML documents and graphics. To ensure correct display, you must always use .GIF as the last characters of the file name for GIF images.

tip *In Windows, FreeHand automatically adds the correct file type extensions when you export or save files in any format. On the Macintosh, however, it is up to you to make sure file names end with the correct extension when working with GIF, JPEG, or Flash files.*

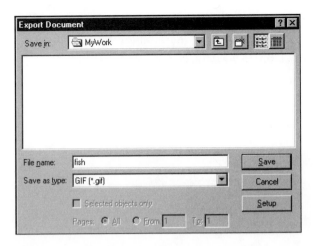

It is always a good idea to check your new graphic in a browser to make sure it looks like it should. Alternatively, you can import the GIF file into a new FreeHand document to check its appearance without having to leave the FreeHand application.

5] Close the open documents and open Robot.ft8, also located in the Start folder within the Lesson9 folder.

The FreeHand artwork and background image in this illustration contains a wide variety of colors, so you will want to export it as a JPEG file.

tip   *Experiment on your own graphics with various image quality settings to determine how much compression you can apply to a specific image before you significantly alter the appearance. You may find that for some images you can use a very low image quality setting without a great deal of visible image degradation. Smaller file sizes mean quicker download times, so you want to find a comfortable balance between image quality and file size.*

377

6] Choose File › Export and select JPEG from the Format menu. Click Setup (Windows) or Options (Macintosh) and don't change the default settings in the dialog box that appears. Then click More to view the image quality setting.

The higher the image quality setting in this dialog box, the larger the graphic will be. Setting a lower image quality will increase the compression and result in smaller file sizes.

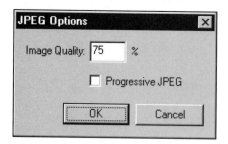

7] Click OK in both dialog boxes to close them without making any changes. Then export this graphic as *Robot.jpg* to your MyWork folder.

Web browsers require that JPEG files have .JPG as the last characters of the file name. If you try to view a graphic in a Web browser and it does not appear as you expected, check to see if the file type extension at the end of the file name is correct.

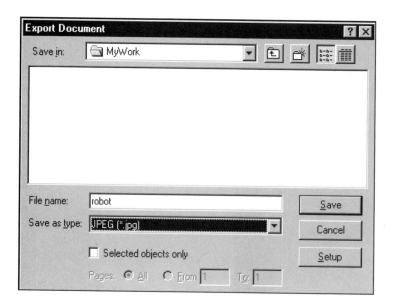

Now that you understand how to export graphics in the standard Web formats, you will learn how to create high-resolution Flash graphics.

8] Close all open documents without saving changes.

Do not quit the FreeHand application.

CREATING ANIMATED FLASH GRAPHICS WITH FREEHAND

Macromedia Flash is an application designed to create compact, scaleable, high-resolution graphics with small file sizes that can be downloaded quickly on the Internet. It provides tools to create both still images and animations and enhance these graphics with other features, including sound and interactivity.

FreeHand can export graphics as Shockwave Flash files, so you can take full advantage of the tools and features FreeHand provides for creating graphics, illustrations, and layouts. (Shockwave Flash format files are also commonly referred to as Flash graphics.) Export artwork in the Flash format and then import it into the Flash application to add enhancements or optimize the files for Web delivery.

In FreeHand, you can save an individual still image such as the fish artwork by using the Export command and selecting the Flash (*.swf) format, the same way you can export GIF and JPEG files. Since Shockwave Flash graphics do not need to remain motionless, however, FreeHand also enables you to create and export animations.

An animation is a sequence of images, or frames, in which the artwork changes over time. In FreeHand, you can create artwork for each frame of an animation, or you can create two or more key frames that identify the beginning, end, and any important middle points of the desired change in shape or position; then use the Blend command, and FreeHand will automatically create the intermediate shapes required to complete the animation. In the next task you will explore the steps required to create a Shockwave Flash animation using key frames and Blend. You will start with a document where some of the work has already been done for you.

1] In FreeHand, open Flower.ft8, located in the Start folder within the Lesson9 folder.

379

This document contains several blends and paths, on and off the page, which you will use to complete the growing flower animation you previewed in a Web browser earlier in this lesson. You will use these elements to complete an animation of a flower growing as the sun rises in the sky along a curving path.

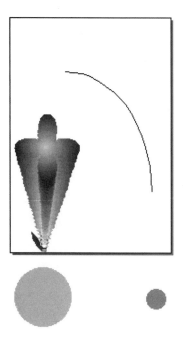

At the lower-left corner of the page you can see a red shape, which is a completed blend, transforming itself between a small ellipse at the bottom and a large flower shape at the top.

At the very bottom of the page, one green leaf is visible. That leaf is part of another blend, which is located directly behind the flower blend.

Now you will create a blend for the sun.

2] Select the two circles just below the bottom of the page and choose Modify › Combine › Blend. Then in the Object inspector, change the number of steps in this blend to 25.
All three blends in this document have 25 steps. These steps correspond to 25 frames in the animation you are creating.

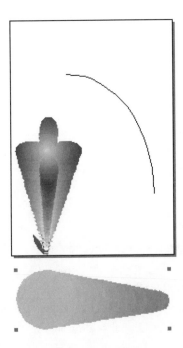

Next you will join the new blend to the curved path on the page, so the blending shapes will follow the curve.

3] With the sun blend still selected, hold down Shift and click the path that curves from the right side of the page up and over the flower blends. Then choose Modify › Combine › Join Blend to Path.

The sun blend now curves up and to the left, following the curve of the path it was joined to.

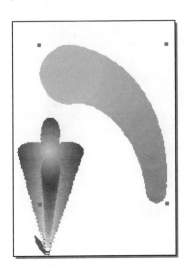

tip *You can join a blend to an open or closed path in any FreeHand document, not just those you are preparing for Web pages*

Now that the blends required for this animation are complete, you will change the way the elements in this document are organized. When exporting Flash graphics, you can have FreeHand animate artwork on a sequence of pages, where the artwork on page 1 is the first frame, the artwork on page 2 is the second frame, and so on. Alternatively, you can have FreeHand animate artwork on a sequence of layers, where each layer contains artwork for different frames in the animation. Here you will use layers.

4] Choose Edit › Select › All to select all three blends on the page. Choose Xtras › Animation › Release to Layers.

It may take a few moments to complete this step as FreeHand creates new layers and moves the individual shapes from each blend to the new layers. There are now 25 layers, because there were 25 steps in each of the blends. The first element of each blend is on one layer, the second element of each blend is on the next layer, and so on.

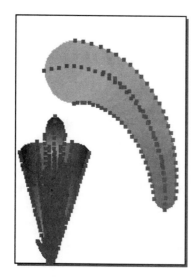

tip *Display the Layers panel to see all 25 layers.*

Now you are ready to export this sequence as a Shockwave Flash animation.

5] Choose File › Export and select Flash from the Format menu. Export this animation as *flower.swf* to your MyWork folder.

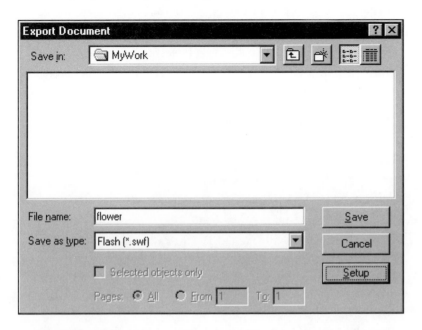

The default settings automatically export each layer as a separate frame and prepare the file to play the frames sequentially.

6] Open your new Flash graphic, *flower.swf,* in a Web browser or in the Flash Player application to see your results.

Your flower should grow as the sun rises in the sky.

Now that this artwork is a Shockwave Flash animation, you can import it into Macromedia Flash to add enhancements such as sound and interactivity. The Flash application also includes optimized compression routines that can save your Shockwave Flash graphic as a much smaller file than FreeHand can on its own. The Flash application can also save the animation as a digital video file or an animated GIF graphic.

You can learn more about Flash and Flash format graphics by visiting Macromedia's Web site (http://www.macromedia.com). In addition, a trial version of the Macromedia Flash application is included on the CD-ROM included with this book.

tip *Specify a custom page just large enough to accommodate the graphics in your Flash animations for best results. FreeHand uses the page size as the size of an exported Flash graphic.*

USING FREEHAND AND THE INSTA.HTML XTRA
TO CREATE WEB PAGES

Web pages are actually text files written in a specific language: HTML, or Hypertext Markup Language. You can create Web pages in a variety of ways, including by learning and writing HTML code in a text editor. Serious Web designers may combine that approach with a professional-strength visual layout and development tool such as Macromedia Dreamweaver.

For simpler needs or for prototyping a larger Web site, you may want to consider using FreeHand. With the addition of the Insta.html Xtra, FreeHand can be used not only to create Web graphics and animations, but also to create the HTML Web pages themselves. Insta.html is an Xtra for FreeHand that enables you to export FreeHand pages directly as HTML documents and automatically export the documents included on the FreeHand pages in the GIF, JPEG, or Flash format for the Web. Insta.html is included in Macromedia's Design in Motion Suite of applications, which also includes FreeHand and Flash, or you can purchase Insta.html separately.

To use Insta.html, you first design your Web page or pages in FreeHand. Then you use the Xtra to create links, specify the desired graphic file formats, and export the pages as HTML files. At the same time, the graphics can be exported to the designated formats to complete the Web pages.

In this task you will open a FreeHand document that has been designed as a small Web site. Much of the work has been already been done, so you can explore the specific steps required to export your FreeHand documents as HTML Web pages.

note *The CD-ROM that accompanies this book does not include a trial version of Insta.html In this task, you will learn how to prepare your document and export HTML pages using the Insta.html Xtra, but you will not actually need to export the document included in this lesson. If you do not have the Insta.html Xtra, simply read through the following steps to learn the process you can use to export your FreeHand layouts as HTML pages.*

1] In FreeHand, close all open documents and open Webfolio.ft8, located in the Start folder within the Lesson9 folder.

This four-page FreeHand document is designed as a four-page Web site that presents examples of the type of FreeHand artwork you have learned to create. The first page is the welcome page for the site, and it includes graphics for the buttons that will take viewers to see the other pages of the site.

Notice that the page size has been adjusted to represent a common viewing size for a Web browser.

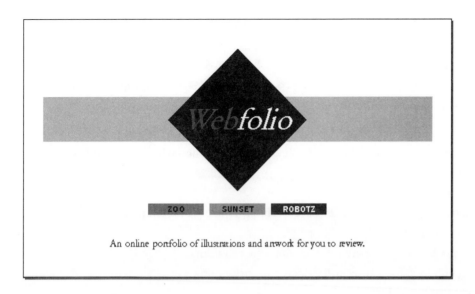

An online portfolio of illustrations and artwork for you to review.

2] Switch to page 2.

The second, third, and fourth pages contain elements similar to those on the first page to add visual consistency to the site and provide consistent navigation controls. This page contains the Greenville Zoo artwork you worked with earlier in these lessons.

The Greenville Zoo poster includes intricate tracing and special text effects including gradient fills and patterns pasted inside the paths.

3] Take a look at pages 3 and 4. Then return to page 1.

The artwork and text on these pages is complete. You will now create a link from an element on page 1 to the second page.

4] Choose Window › Xtras › URL Editor. Then use the Pointer tool to select the blue rectangle.

A Web page address is called a URL, or Universal Resource Locator. You will use this panel to make the blue rectangle and the word *Zoo* a link to another page by assigning the address of the desired page to those elements. In a Web browser, clicking that link will take you to the assigned page.

The word *Zoo* is grouped with the blue rectangle so they will be exported as one graphic.

5] Click Page 2 in the URL Editor to designate the blue rectangle group as a link to the second page.

The link has been assigned. When you select an item on a page that has a link assigned, the URL Editor will display the current link.

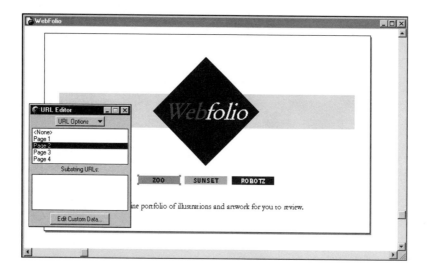

In creating your own Web pages, you would need to work through the entire document, assigning a URL to each element that should become a link to other pages or other Web sites. In this document, the other links have already been assigned.

If you want to create a link to a remote site, you can choose New from the Options menu at the top of the URL Editor. Then type the entire Web address, such as *http://www.macromedia.com* to create a link to Macromedia's Web site.

6] Close the URL Editor. Then choose Xtra › HTML › Insta.html.

The Insta.html Xtra provides the features you need to export your FreeHand document as individual Web pages.

If you don't have Insta.html installed, you will not be able to complete the rest of this lesson. Instead, just read the steps to learn how to perform these tasks.

First you will set a few preferences in the Insta.html Export Options menu.

7] Choose Preferences from the Insta.html Export Options menu.

You can specify default folders for saving your HTML Web pages and the graphics for those pages (you can assign the same location for both, if you want). The settings you make here apply to all new documents you work with from now on. You can also specify the location of your favorite text editor for making manual adjustments to HTML code and a Web browser for previewing your results.

In this task you are exploring the steps required to export your FreeHand documents as Web pages, but you will not actually export this document when you're finished. Therefore, you do not need to make any changes in this dialog box.

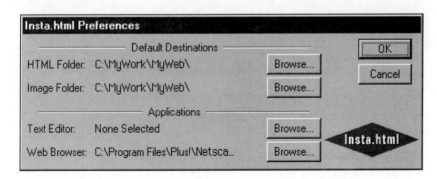

8] Click OK to close the Preferences dialog box. Then choose Document Properties from the Insta.html Export Options menu.

Document Properties contains options for this document only. You can identify locations for the HTML documents and graphics (which will override the defaults set in the previous step if you change the locations here). You can also specify colors for the background and links, as well as a background image to use for this site.

At the top of the dialog box, you can select individual pages from the Page Number menu to make changes to the name, title, location, or colors for any page within this document.

Again, no changes are necessary at this time.

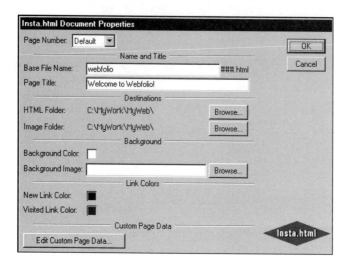

Notice that the Export Options menu also includes the URL Editor. This is the same panel you used before; it is provided here to make it even more accessible to you.

9] Change to page 2 and select the Zoo poster artwork. In the Insta.html panel, change the file format by choosing JPEG from the Format menu.

When you export these pages as an HTML document, you will have the option of exporting the graphics as GIF or Flash files. Specify the file format manually, as in this step, for any artwork that should be saved in a particular format. For instance, the JPEG format was assigned for this poster because it contains a wide variety of colors.

In this document, a name and Alt tag have also been entered for this element. Alt is a brief name or description of the selected element that will appear on the Web page if the image does not appear for any reason. For example, people who have slow modem connections to the Internet may instruct their browsers not to display images by default. In this case, the text entered in the Alt field will appear.

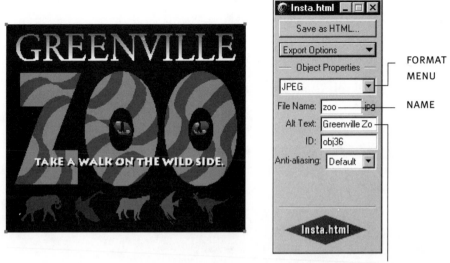

FORMAT MENU

NAME

TEXT THAT WILL APPEAR IF THE SELECTED ITEM DOES
NOT APPEAR IN THE WEB BROWSER FOR ANY REASON

Once all of the elements in the document have been assigned links, file formats, names, and Alt tags as desired, you are ready to export the pages.

10] Click the Save as HTML button at the top of the Insta.html panel.

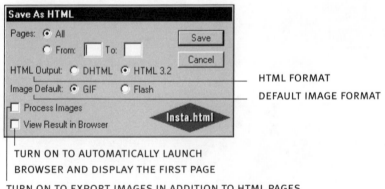

HTML FORMAT

DEFAULT IMAGE FORMAT

TURN ON TO AUTOMATICALLY LAUNCH
BROWSER AND DISPLAY THE FIRST PAGE

TURN ON TO EXPORT IMAGES IN ADDITION TO HTML PAGES

The first step in this dialog box is to specify which pages you want to export and then to select the HTML format. DHTML (Dynamic HTML) is a newer format that is supported only by the newer browsers (version 4 or later of both Netscape Navigator and Microsoft Internet Explorer). HTML 3.2 is compatible with older browsers, but it does not offer as much precision as the newer format. For example, the placement of elements in HTML 3.2 may not be as precise as in a DHTML document.

The Image Default setting you specify here will apply to all images in the document that do not have a specific format assigned.

Select Process Images to export graphic files along with the HTML pages. If you turn on View Result in Browser, the browser you specified in the Preferences dialog box will automatically open and display the first page of this new Web site.

11] Click Cancel to close the dialog box without exporting the Web pages. Then quit the FreeHand application.

This document has already been exported in HTML 3.2 format, with GIF as the default format and Process Images turned on to export the graphics along with the HTML pages. In the next task you will open the resulting pages in a browser.

VIEWING THE WEB PAGES IN A BROWSER

The final task in this lesson is to look at the results Insta.html produced when the Webfolio document was exported from FreeHand.

1] Open the Complete folder within the Lesson9 folder. Then open the Folio folder. Drag the webfolio.html document and drop it on the icon for your Web browser.

The opening page of the new Web site is displayed.

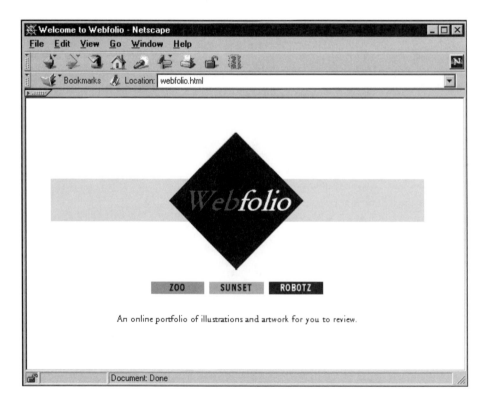

2] Click one of the buttons to view the other pages.

Each button is linked to the page displaying the appropriate artwork, and the Webfolio logo above the buttons will return you to the opening page.

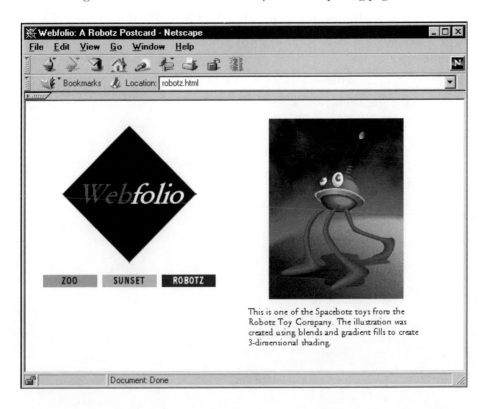

This is one of the Spacebotz toys from the Robotz Toy Company. The illustration was created using blends and gradient fills to create 3-dimensional shading.

3] When you have completed your review of these pages, quit all applications.

WHAT YOU HAVE LEARNED

In this lesson you have:

- Learned the difference between GIF and JPEG graphic formats [*page* **372**]

- Viewed Web pages and graphics in a Web browser [*page* **372**]

- Exported FreeHand artwork as GIF and JPEG files [*page* **375**]

- Created animated Shockwave Flash graphics in FreeHand [*page* **379**]

- Joined a blend to a path [*page* **381**]

- Learned how to use the Insta.html Xtra to export Web pages from FreeHand [*page* **384**]

CONCLUSION

Congratulations! You have just completed all the lessons in *FreeHand 8 Authorized*. In these lessons, you have created both simple and complex graphics and designed single- and multiple-page layouts containing text, graphics, and imported images. You've also used FreeHand's tracing tools to create paths, organized your documents using layers and styles, pasted artwork inside other paths, and created blends between paths.

You have learned how to apply advanced features to create sophisticated illustrations, and you've been introduced to Web page development techniques with FreeHand, Flash, and the Insta.html Xtra. We hope you enjoyed learning about FreeHand, and most of all, we hope the techniques in these lessons will help you in your own graphic design, page layout, illustration, multimedia, and Web design projects.

windows shortcuts

FreeHand offers lots of shortcuts that, once you learn them, will make your work easier. Many are described in the lessons in this book. This appendix is a quick reference to the default shortcuts in FreeHand for Windows computers.

KEYBOARD SHORTCUTS

FreeHand supports menu command shortcuts throughout the user interface. This section lists the default keyboard shortcuts for issuing commands. FreeHand 8's shortcuts can be customized by choosing File > Customize > Shortcuts. You can then select one of the predefined shortcut sets included with FreeHand, so you can use keyboard shortcuts you may already be familiar with from applications such as Adobe Illustrator, PageMaker, Corel Draw, or QuarkXPress. You can also assign new keyboard shortcuts to frequently used commands to suit your own individual needs. The Customize Shortcuts dialog box provides a Print button that enables you to print a complete set of the current keyboard shortcuts.

note   *O is the alpha character. 0 (zero) is the number.*

FILE MENU

Command	Shortcut
New	Ctrl+N
Open	Ctrl+O
Close	Ctrl+F4
Save	Ctrl+S
Save As	Ctrl+Shift+S
Import	Ctrl+R
Export	Ctrl+Shift+R
Print	Ctrl+P
Preferences	Ctrl+Shift+D
Customize Shortcuts	Ctrl+Alt+Shift+Z
Exit	Alt+F4

EDIT MENU

Command	Shortcut
Undo	Ctrl+Z
Redo	Ctrl+Y
Cut	Ctrl+X
Copy	Ctrl+C
Paste	Ctrl+V
Cut Contents	Ctrl+Shift+X
Paste Inside	Ctrl+Shift+V
Copy Attributes	Ctrl+Alt+Shift+C
Paste Attributes	Ctrl+Alt+Shift+V
Duplicate	Ctrl+D
Clone	Ctrl+Shift+C
Select All	Ctrl+A
Select All in Document	Ctrl+Shift+A
Find and Replace Text	Ctrl+Shift+F
Find and Replace Graphics	Ctrl+Alt+E

VIEW MENU

Command	Shortcut
Fit Selection	Ctrl+0 (zero)
Fit to Page	Ctrl+Shift+W
Fit All	Ctrl+Alt+0 (zero)
Magnification › 50%	Ctrl+5
Magnification › 100%	Ctrl+1
Magnification › 200%	Ctrl+2
Magnification › 400%	Ctrl+4
Magnification › 800%	Ctrl+8
Previous Custom View	Ctrl+Alt+Shift+1
Preview or Keyline	Ctrl+K
Fast Mode View	Ctrl+Shift+K
Toolbars	Ctrl+Alt+T
Panels	Ctrl+Alt+H
Page Rulers	Ctrl+Alt+M
Text Rulers	Ctrl+Alt+Shift+T
Snap to Point	Ctrl+Shift+Y
Snap to Guides	Ctrl+Alt+G

MODIFY MENU

Command	Shortcut
Object	Ctrl+I
Stroke	Ctrl+Alt+L
Fill	Ctrl+Alt+F
Text	Ctrl+T
Document	Ctrl+Alt+D
Transform: Scale	Ctrl+F10
Transform: Move	Ctrl+E
Transform: Rotate	Ctrl+F2
Transform: Reflect	Ctrl+F9
Transform: Skew	Ctrl+F11
Transform Again	Ctrl+Shift+G
Bring to Front	Ctrl+F
Move Forward	Ctrl+Alt+Shift+F
Move Backward	Ctrl+Alt+Shift+K
Send to Back	Ctrl+B
Align	Ctrl+Alt+A
Align Again	Ctrl+Alt+Shift+A
Join	Ctrl+J
Split	Ctrl+Shift+J
Blend	Ctrl+Shift+B
Join Blend to Path	Ctrl+Alt+Shift+B
Lock	Ctrl+L
Unlock	Ctrl+Shift+L
Group	Ctrl+G
Ungroup	Ctrl+U

TEXT MENU

Command	Shortcut
Smaller Size	Ctrl+Alt+1
Larger Size	Ctrl+Alt+2
Type Style › Plain	F5 or Ctrl+Alt+Shift+P
Type Style › Bold	F6 or Ctrl+Alt+B
Type Style › Italic	F7 or Ctrl+Alt+I
Type Style › Bold Italic	F8 or Ctrl+Alt+Shift+O
Effect › Highlight	Ctrl+Alt+Shift+H
Effect › Strikethrough	Ctrl+Alt+Shift+S
Effect › Underline	Ctrl+Alt+U
Align Left	Ctrl+Alt+Shift+L
Align Right	Ctrl+Alt+Shift+R
Align Center	Ctrl+Alt+Shift+M
Align Justified	Ctrl+Alt+Shift+J
Special Characters › Non-Breaking Space	Ctrl+Shift+H
Special Characters › Em Space	Ctrl+Shift+M
Special Characters › En Space	Ctrl+Shift+N
Special Characters › Thin Space	Ctrl+Shift+T
Special Characters › Discretionary Hyphen	Ctrl+_ (underscore)
Editor	Ctrl+Shift+E
Spelling	Ctrl+Alt+S
Run Around Selection	Ctrl+Alt+W
Flow Inside Path	Ctrl+Shift+U
Attach to Path	Ctrl+Shift+Y
Convert to Paths	Ctrl+Shift+P

WINDOW MENU

Command	Shortcut
New Window	Ctrl+Alt+N
Toolbox	Ctrl+7
Object Inspector	Ctrl+I
Stroke Inspector	Ctrl+Alt+L
Fill Inspector	Ctrl+Alt+F
Text Inspector	Ctrl+T
Document Inspector	Ctrl+Alt+D
Layers Panel	Ctrl+6
Styles Panel	Ctrl+3
Color List Panel	Ctrl+9
Color Mixer Panel	Ctrl+Shift+9
Tints Panel	Ctrl+Shift+3
Halftones Panel	Ctrl+H
Align Panel	Ctrl+Alt+A
Transform Panel	Ctrl+M
Xtras › Operations	Ctrl+Alt+O
Xtra › Xtra Tools	Ctrl+Alt+X
Cascade	Shift+F5
Tile	Shift+F4

DRAWING AND EDITING

Command	Shortcut
Clone	Ctrl+Shift+C
Cut Contents	Ctrl+Shift+X
Thinner Stroke	Ctrl+Shift+1
Deselect All	Tab
Group	Ctrl+G
Thicker Stroke	Ctrl+Shift+2
Paste Inside	Ctrl+Shift+V
Preview or Keyline	Ctrl+K
Select All in Document	Ctrl+Shift+A
Select All on Page	Ctrl+A
Snap to Guides	Ctrl+Alt+G
Snap to Point	Ctrl+Shift+Y
Ungroup	Ctrl+U

GENERAL

Command	Shortcut
Close Document	Ctrl+F4
Export	Ctrl+Shift+R
Import	Ctrl+R
Next Page	Ctrl+Page Down
New Window	Ctrl+Alt+N
Previous Page	Ctrl+Page Up
Zoom In Magnification	Ctrl+Spacebar+click
Zoom Out Magnification	Ctrl+Alt+Spacebar+click

396

FreeHand offers lots of shortcuts that, once you learn them, will make your work easier. Many are described in the lessons in this book. This appendix is a quick reference to the default shortcuts in FreeHand for Macintosh computers.

KEYBOARD SHORTCUTS

APPENDIX B

FreeHand supports menu command shortcuts throughout the user interface. This section lists the default keyboard shortcuts for issuing commands. FreeHand 8's shortcuts can be customized by choosing File > Customize > Shortcuts. You can then select one of the predefined shortcut sets included with FreeHand, so you can use keyboard shortcuts you may already be familiar with from applications such as Adobe Illustrator, PageMaker, Corel Draw, or QuarkXPress. You can also assign new keyboard shortcuts to frequently used commands to suit your own individual needs. The Customize Shortcuts dialog box provides a Print button that enables you to print a complete set of the current keyboard shortcuts.

note   *O is the alpha character. 0 (zero) is the number.*

FILE MENU

Command	Shortcut
New	Command+N
Open	Command+O
Close	Command+W
Save	Command+S
Save As	Command+Shift+S
Import	Command+R
Export	Command+Shift+R
Print	Command+P
Preferences	Command+Shift+D
Customize Shortcuts	Command+Shift+Control+K
Quit	Command+Q

EDIT MENU

Command	Shortcut
Undo	Command+Z
Redo	Command+Y
Cut	Command+X
Copy	Command+C
Paste	Command+V
Cut Contents	Command+Shift+X
Paste Inside	Command+Shift+V
Copy Attributes	Command+Shift+Option+C
Paste Attributes	Command+Shift+Option+V
Duplicate	Command+D
Clone	Command+=
Select All	Command+A
Select All in Document	Command+Shift+A
Find and Replace Text	Command+Shift+F
Find and Replace Graphics	Command+Option+E

VIEW MENU

Command	Shortcut
Fit Selection	Command+0 (zero)
Fit to Page	Command+Shift+W
Fit All	Command+Option+0 (zero)
Magnification › 50%	Command+5
Magnification › 100%	Command+1
Magnification › 200%	Command+2
Magnification › 400%	Command+4
Magnification › 800%	Command+8
Previous Custom View	Command+Option+1
Preview or Keyline	Command+K
Fast Mode View	Command+Shift+K
Toolbars	Command+Option+T
Panels	F12, or Command+Shift+H
Page Rulers	Command+Option+M
Text Rulers	Command+/
Snap to Point	Command+'
Snap to Guides	Command+\
Snap to Grid	Command+;

MODIFY MENU

Command	Shortcut
Object	Command+I
Stroke	Command+Option+L
Fill	Command+Option+F
Text	Command+T
Document	Command+Option+D
Transform: Scale	Command+F10
Transform: Move	Command+E
Transform: Rotate	Command+F13
Transform: Reflect	Command+F9
Transform: Skew	Command+F11
Transform Again	Command+,
Bring to Front	Command+F
Move Forward	Command+[
Move Backward	Command+]
Send to Back	Command+B
Align	Command+Option+A
Align Again	Command+Shift+Option+A
Join	Command+J
Split	Command+Shift+J
Blend	Command+Shift+B
Join Blend to Path	Command+Shift+Option+B
Lock	Command+L
Unlock	Command+Shift+L
Group	Command+G
Ungroup	Command+U

TEXT MENU

Command	Shortcut
Smaller Size	Command+Shift+‹
Larger Size	Command+Shift+›
Type Style › Plain	F5 or Command+Shift+Option+P
Type Style › Bold	F6 or Command+Option+B
Type Style › Italic	F7 or Command+Option+I
Type Style › Bold Italic	F8 or Command+Shift+Option+O
Effect › Highlight	Command+Shift+Option+H
Effect › Strikethrough	Command+Shift+Option+S
Effect › Underline	Command+Option+U
Align Left	Command+Shift+Option+L
Align Right	Command+Shift+Option+R
Align Center	Command+Shift+Option+M
Align Justified	Command+Shift+Option+J
Special Characters › Em Space	Command+Shift+M
Special Characters › En Space	Command+Shift+N
Special Characters › Thin Space	Command+Shift+T
Special Characters › Discretionary Hyphen	Command+ –
Editor	Command+Shift+E
Spelling	Command+Shift+G
Run Around Selection	Command+Option+W
Flow Inside Path	Command+Shift+U
Attach to Path	Command+Shift+Y
Convert to Paths	Command+Shift+P

WINDOW MENU

Command	Shortcut
New Window	Command+Option+N
Toolbox	Command+7
Object Inspector	Command+I
Stroke Inspector	Command+Option+L
Fill Inspector	Command+Option+F
Text Inspector	Command+T
Document Inspector	Command+Option+D
Layers Panel	Command+6
Styles Panel	Command+3
Color List Panel	Command+9
Color Mixer Panel	Command+Shift+C
Tints Panel	Command+Shift+Z
Halftones Panel	Command+H
Align Panel	Command+Option+A
Transform Panel	Command+M
Xtras › Operations	Command+Shift+I
Xtra › Xtra Tools	Command+Shift+X

DRAWING AND EDITING

Command	Shortcut
Clone	Command+=
Close a Cut Path	Control+Knife tool
Cut Contents	Command+Shift+X
Deselect All	Tab
Grabber Hand	Spacebar
Group	Command+G
Paste Inside	Command+Shift+V
Preview or Keyline	Command+K
Select All in Document	Command+Shift+A
Select All on Page	Command+A
Snap to Guides	Command+\
Snap to Point	Command+'
Thicker Stroke	Command+Option+›
Thinner Stroke	Command+Option+‹
Ungroup	Command+U

GENERAL

Command	Shortcut
Export	Command+Shift+R
Help Cursor	Help
Import	Command+R
Next Page	Command+ Page Down
New Window	Command+Option+N
Pause Screen Redraw	Command+.
Previous Page	Command+Page Up
Zoom In Magnification	Command+ Spacebar+click
Zoom Out Magnification	Command+Option+ Spacebar+click

FreeHand is designed to be easy to learn and use for people familiar with other graphic applications. This appendix is a quick reference to help you convert the terms and techniques found in other applications to the FreeHand equivalents.

BASIC TERMINOLOGY

Although the drawing and editing techniques you use in FreeHand are similar to those in other applications, there are differences in the terminology used to describe the tools and controls involved. This terminology is often the most confusing aspect an Adobe Illustrator or CorelDraw user will encounter when learning to use FreeHand. Here are some common terms that may help you understand FreeHand operations.

FEATURE	TERMINOLOGY		
	FreeHand	*Adobe Illustrator*	*CorelDraw*
Working with paths	Points	Points	Nodes
Adding color	Color Mixer, Tints Panel, Color List	Paint Styles palette Fill and Stroke	Colors
Clipping paths	Paste Inside	Mask	Power Clips
Effects and add-ins	Xtras	Filters	Effects
Path operations	Operations	Pathfinder Filters	Shaping
Gradients	Gradients	Gradients	Fountain Fills
View modes	Keyline, Preview	Artwork, Preview	Wireframe, Normal

KEYBOARD SHORTCUTS

Many of the keyboard shortcuts you are familiar with in other applications may have the same functions assigned in FreeHand by default (for example, Save, Print, and 100% View), and as you work with FreeHand you can easily learn the other shortcuts for the features you use frequently.

Perhaps the quickest way to take full advantage of the efficiency and power keyboard shortcuts can offer is to use the shortcuts you already know from another application. Choose File > Customize > Shortcuts and select one of the predefined shortcut sets from the menu at the upper right.

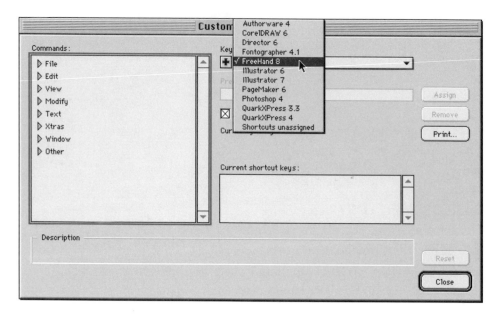

For example, if you are familiar with the keyboard shortcuts used in Macromedia Director, Authorware, Adobe Illustrator, Photoshop, PageMaker, CorelDraw, or QuarkXPress, select any of these from the Shortcuts Setting menu. Your familiar keyboard commands are now available, assigned to the equivalent functions and commands in FreeHand.

You can also assign your own keyboard shortcuts to frequently used commands to suit your individual needs. First, select a command from the list on the left. The current shortcut key or keys are displayed at the bottom right (if any are assigned). You can add your own shortcuts to this list or even delete any of the ones currently assigned and replace them with your own choice. By default, FreeHand will warn you if the shortcut you have entered is already being used by another command. (Make sure that the Go to Conflict on Assign button remains on so FreeHand can continue to provide these warnings.)

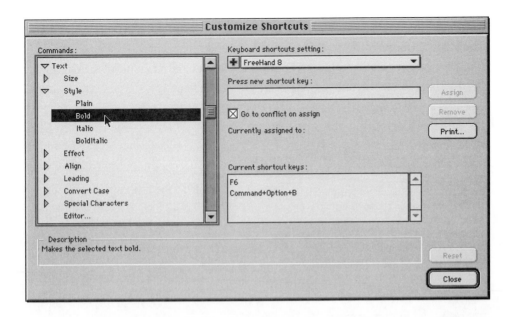

The Customize Shortcuts dialog box also provides a Print button which enables you to print a complete set of the current keyboard shortcuts.

FILE FORMATS FREEHAND SUPPORTS

You may have artwork created in other applications that you would like to convert to FreeHand. FreeHand provides extensive support for various graphic file formats on both Windows and Macintosh platforms. Here are the formats supported for each platform.

WINDOWS
Import File Formats
EPS; Illustrator 1.1, 88, 3.0, 4.0, 5.5, 6, and 7 (Windows and Macintosh); CorelDraw 7 Win; Photoshop 2.5, 3.0, and 4.0; Acrobat PDF; FreeHand 3, 4, 5, 5.5, 7, and 8 (Windows and Macintosh); DCS 1 and 2; DXF; RTF; ASCII; TIFF; GIF; JPEG; PNG; xRes LRG; Targa; BMP; WMF; EMF

Export File Formats
Macromedia Flash; Generic EPS (RGB and CMYK); EPS for Photoshop; EPS for Quark; Illustrator 1.1, 88, 3.0, 4.0, 5.5, 6, and 7 (Windows and Macintosh); FreeHand 3, 4, 5, 5.5, 7, and 8 (Windows and Macintosh); DCS 2; RTF; ASCII; TIFF; GIF; JPEG; PNG; Acrobat PDF; xRes LRG; Targa; BMP; WMF; EMF

MACINTOSH
Import File Formats

EPS; Illustrator 1.1, 88, 3.0, 4.0, 5.5, 6, and 7 (Windows and Macintosh); CorelDraw 7 Win; Photoshop 2.5, 3.0, and 4.0; Acrobat PDF; FreeHand 3, 4, 5, 5.5, 7, and 8 (Windows and Macintosh); DCS 1 and 2; DXF; PICT; PICT2; RTF; ASCII; TIFF; GIF; JPEG; PNG; xRes LRG; Targa; BMP

Export File Formats

Macromedia Flash; Generic EPS (RGB and CMYK); EPS for Photoshop; EPS for Quark; Illustrator 1.1, 88, 3.0, 4.0, 5.5, 6, and 7 (Windows and Macintosh); FreeHand 3, 4, 5, 5.5, 7, and 8 (Windows and Macintosh); DCS 2; PICT; PICT2; RTF; ASCII; TIFF; GIF; JPEG; PNG; Acrobat PDF; xRes LRG; Targa; BMP

If you ever encounter a file format that FreeHand does not directly support, check to see if your other application can import or export an intermediate file format that FreeHand can import or export.

index

3D images, 272–74
  pasting, 273
  positioning, 274
  renaming, 274
3D Rotation tool, 315
3D shading, 341–43

A

Add Guides dialog box, 219
Add to Color List dialog box, 86
alignment
  bleed area, 71
  to center, 75
  cursor, 154
  elements, 47, 142–44, 187–89
  graphic, 106
  group, 187–89
  horizontal, 48, 52, 75, 102, 143, 148, 364
  icon, 105
  performing, 52
  vertical, 48, 52, 75, 102, 143, 148, 364
Align panel, 47–48
  Align to Page option, 364
  Apply/Align button, 143, 148, 188
  displaying, 47, 75, 101, 143, 188, 364
  Horizontal Alignment menu, 48, 52, 102
  illustrated, 48
  preview grid, 364
  Vertical Alignment menu, 48, 52, 102
alpha channels, 375
Alt tags, 388–89
Angel.ft8, 140

animation
  blend steps, 380
  defined, 379
  exporting, 382–83
  frames, 379
  growing flower, 380
  Shockwave Flash, 379–83
Aquarium.ft8, 319
Aquarium sign, 298
  distorting, 323–24
  fish illustration, 300–311
  illustrated, 298
  lens fill, 326–29
  school of fish in, 313, 319–20, 329
Arc tool, 315
arrow keys, 284
artwork
  animating, 382
  exporting, 204–8
  moving in front/behind, 279
  picture frame for, 201–2
  positioning, 190–93
  reflecting, 200–201
  scaling, 194–201
  trimming, 190
  viewing, 201
Autotrace tool, 267
  Color Mode setting, 271
  crosshair cursor, 270
  double-clicking, 269
  illustrated, 11
  multiple layers with, 271
  preferences, 269–70
  selecting, 269
  tracing with, 270–71

B

background
- elements, 352
- text blocks, 96
- transparent, 376

Background layer, 155, 349
- clicking, 156
- hiding, 176
- hiding elements on, 176
- locking, 156
- nonprinting, 155
- *See also* layers

base color, 190

baseline
- characters hanging below, 225
- defined, 104, 225
- positioning ruler guide along, 104
- snapping to guide, 225

basic fills, 291
- defined, 42
- in text, 146
- *See also* fills

Beacon1.fh8, 273

Beacon2.fh8, 264

Beam layer, 275, 276, 277, 289

Bend tool, 315

Beziér curves, 112–13

Bezigon tool, 114, 140, 280, 291
- for adding points, 116–17, 125
- Alt/Option key with, 129, 132, 136, 140
- clicking, 129
- displaying, 117
- illustrated, 11
- learning, 114
- Shift key and, 127
- tracing with, 124–25

Bitmap Export Defaults dialog box
- illustrated, 375
- Include Alpha Channel option, 375
- More button, 376

bleed area
- aligning, 71
- defined, 66
- extending elements beyond, 223
- printing beyond, 91
- setting up, 223
- size of, 66, 213, 223

blending
- grouping and, 310
- shapes, 345
  - closed, 307
  - to create reflections, 286–90
  - to create shading, 307–10, 334–68
  - multiple, 280–85

blends, 78
- cloning, 79
- copying, 283, 346
- creating, 76–77, 337–41, 350
- creating in Keyline view, 289
- cutting, 343, 347
- defined, 75
- gaps in, 310, 338
- grouping, 80
- joining, 381–82
- moving, 311
- pasting, 346, 347
- pasting inside paths, 341–43
- paths in, 78
- positioning, 342
- selecting, 311, 382
- smooth, 283, 307, 339
- steps, 78, 283, 338
  - animation and, 380
  - changing, 339, 340, 350
- when to create, 356

BMP format, 206

business cards, 262

C

CD-ROM, 4
- fonts, 4, 145
- FreeHand training version, 8
- News Gothic T, 4
- URWGaramondTMed font, 99
- URW Garamond T Normal, 4
- Vladimir Script, 4

centerpoint
- adjusting, 357
- of circles, 331
- moving, 357, 358
- radial fill, 355, 356

characters
- formatting, 243
- modifying, 227
- nonprinting, displaying, 244
- space between, 226, 227, 232
- width of, 232
- *See also* text

Chart tool, 315

circles, 73
- centerpoint of, 331
- creating, 34, 49, 127, 169
- filling, 134
- radial fill, 46
- resizing, 50

clipping paths, 169
- adding elements to, 193–94
- creating, 169, 310–12
- defined, 401
- when to create, 356
- *See also* paths

cloning, 89–90, 183–84
  blends, 79
  defined, 79
  duplicating, 167
closed paths, 126, 131, 275
  creating, 126, 133, 163, 179
  filling, 163
  See also paths
closed shapes, 291
  blending, 307
  filling, 282
  selecting, 282
  verifying, 281, 291
CMYK colors, 138, 158
  creating, 277
  TIFF files, 260
  See also colors
Collect for Output feature, 261–62
color drop box, 86
Color List, 18–19, 21–23, 288
  active, 180
  adding bitmap image colors to, 253–55
  adding colors to, 19, 82
  adding tints to, 86
  color drop box, 86
  Current Stroke Color button, 338
  defined, 19, 137
  displaying, 18–19, 21, 46, 82, 96, 100, 137,
    180, 222, 302, 337
  dragging, 21
  Fill Selector, 232
  hiding, 20
  illustrated, 19, 82
  Options menu, 83, 84, 222
  swatches, 139
  Color Mixer, 17–18, 21–23, 131
  Add to Color List button, 37, 139
  CMYK button, 277, 281, 291
  color controls, 37
  color well, 37, 138, 203
  defined, 17, 137
  displaying, 17, 21, 36, 137, 203
  hiding, 18
  HLS button, 37
  illustrated, 18, 37, 38
  Process Color button, 37, 138
  RGB button, 37
  System Color Picker button, 37
  Tint button, 286
color percentages, 138–39
color ramp, 44, 46, 198, 351
  dragging swatches up, 355
  dropping swatches on, 356

colors
  adding from bitmap images, 253–55
  adding to Color List, 19, 82, 253–55
  applying, 137–40
  base, 190
  CMYK, 138, 158, 281
  computer monitor, 83, 221
  creating, 281, 291
  defining in Color Mixer, 37
  documents, 36
  dragging, 37–38
  dropping, 37–38, 97
  fill, 100, 358
  importing, 159, 222
  for layers, 202–3
  naming, 139
  PANTONE, 83–85
  process, 138, 158–62
  selection box, 202–3
  spot, 158
  stroke, 89, 109, 338, 340, 358
  text, 96–102, 241, 277–78
  Web Safe, 375
Colors panel, 20
  displaying, 159
  illustrated, 159
composite paths
  applying gradient fill to, 302–5
  combining shapes into, 301
  creating, 300–302
  defined, 300
  selecting, 311
  See also paths
computer monitor colors, 83, 221
connector points, 117
control handles, 133, 136
  adjusting, 133
  corner point, 133, 134, 252
  curve point, 119, 129, 179, 185
  defined, 119
  displaying, 179
  dragging, 134
  illustrated, 119
  manipulating curves with, 131–34
  Paste Inside, 343
  using, 119
  viewing, 133
Control key
  in dropping swatches, 302, 305
  gradient fills and, 305
  in selecting, 304
copying
  blends, 283, 346
  cloning, 167
  elements, 26
  pages, 213
  shapes, 293

corner points
adding, with Bezigon tool, 125, 129, 132
adding, with Pen tool, 162, 178
changing to curve point, 118
control handles, 115, 133, 134, 252
defined, 117
moving, 118
positioning, 128
representation of, 117, 118
selected, 117, 118
selecting, 134
See also points
crop marks, 258
crosshair cursor, 126, 270
cursors
aligning, 154, 177
blinking, 92, 231
crosshair, 126, 270
four-direction arrow, 349
import, 248, 249
magnifying glass, 29
snap, 225
curve points
adding, 129
changing corner point to, 118
control handles, 119, 129, 179, 185
defined, 117
placing, 136, 140
positioning, 128
removing, 119
representation of, 118
selecting, 133
See also points
curves
Beziér, 112–13
manipulating with control handles, 131–34
paths, creating, 178–80
Customize Shortcuts dialog box, 393, 397
illustrated, 365, 403
Keyboard shortcuts setting menu, 365
opening, 365
Press new shortcut key box, 365
Reset button, 366
Customize Toolbars dialog box, 366–68
Button display, 366
buttons, dropping, 367
command selection, 367
Commands list, 367
illustrated, 366, 367, 368
opening, 366
Reset button, 368
triangle, 367
custom page sizes, 212–13, 262, 266–67, 362, 383
custom views
changing, 128, 131
creating, 126
defined, 126

D

Darken lens fill, 360, 363
dashed lines
adding, 107–10
characteristics of, 109
selecting type of, 109
deleting
elements, 27
guides, 220
layers, 195
points, 119, 128
distorting, 323–26
groups of objects, 323
objects, 323
process, 324–25
dithering, 376
docked panels, 22–23
hiding/displaying, 23
illustrated, 23
moving, 23
panel dock, 22, 23
See also panels
Document Inspector, 16, 65–67, 266–67
Bleed Area option, 65, 213
defined, 16
displaying, 16, 65, 152, 212, 266
illustrated, 17, 65, 152, 212
Landscape Orientation option, 152, 153, 212, 267
Options menu, 212, 234
Page Dimensions display, 212
Page Size menu, 65, 66, 152, 153, 212
Portrait Orientation option, 152, 212
printer resolution, 213
Thumbnail Magnification buttons, 212, 235
thumbnail preview, 212, 235
See also Inspectors
Document Report window, 261
documents
adding traced elements to, 141–42
creating, 8–9
creating custom-sized, 64–67, 152–53, 266–67
multiple-page, 234–36
naming, 36
open, list in Window menu, 342
organizing into layers, 201
printing, 256–59
restoring, 204
saving, 35–36, 213
sizing, 153
template, 124
documents window, 64, 114
illustrated, 236
Next Page button, 236
Page Selector field, 235, 236
Page Selector menu, 236
Previous Page button, 236
Dynamic HTML (DHTML), 389

E

Edit menu
Clone command, 89, 166, 183, 186, 200, 229
Copy command, 26, 51, 141, 283, 313, 342
Cut command, 171, 193, 310, 312
Duplicate command, 26, 167, 199
Links command, 260
Paste command, 26, 51, 141, 283, 310, 314, 342, 348, 361
Paste Inside command, 169, 171, 193, 312
Redo command, 70
Select All command, 29, 47, 59, 80, 169, 184, 187, 189, 312, 382
Undo command, 27, 38, 39, 68, 70, 96, 120, 233
Edit Style dialog box, 191–92
angle dial, 191
Fill option, 192
illustrated, 192
opening, 191
elements
actions applied to, 24–27
adding, 49–52, 81
to clipping paths, 193–94
to existing layout, 319–23
aligning, 47, 142–44, 187–89
arranging, 189
background, 352
cloning, 89–90
combining with Paste Inside command, 169–72
combining with path operations, 183–84
converting to guides, 216
copying, 26
creating, 24–27, 184–87
creating with Pen tool, 162–65
deleting, 27
deselecting, 81, 131, 161, 165, 188, 189, 228, 272, 286, 302, 311, 328, 342, 357
dimensions of, 71
grouping, 51, 135, 169
highlighted, 349
mirror image of, 55–57
moving, 25, 33
moving between layers, 155
pasted, positioning of, 310
positioning, 91–92
rotating, 57–59
scaling, 90–91, 142–44
selecting, 6, 47, 311
sizing, 25
traced, adding to documents, 141–42
Zoo ad, 135–37

ellipses
aligning, 74–75
blended, 76, 346–47
constraining, 127
copying, 352
creating, 73–74
cutting, 354
drawing from center out, 134
in Keyline view, 289
pasting, 354
positioning, 352
ring, 352
selecting, 74, 197, 345, 358
for shading, 344
sizing, 73
Ellipse tool, 134, 169
Alt/Option key and, 49, 134, 169
displaying, 34, 49, 73
illustrated, 11
Shift and, 34, 49, 134, 197
using, 34, 286, 287
embedded graphics, 260
Envelope Xtra, 323–26
defined, 323
opening, 324
Presets menu, 324, 325
preview window, 325
Reset button, 325
window, 324
EPS format, 205
default, 207
files, 208
Photoshop, 207
QuarkXPress, 207–8
with TIFF preview, 208
See also formats (export)
Expand Stroke dialog box, 308
Export Document dialog box, 205, 378, 383
export file formats
Macintosh, 404
Windows, 403
exporting
artwork, 204–8
formats, 205–8
Eyedropper tool, 253–54
positioning, 253
selecting, 253

F

Fast Keyline mode, 172, 173
changing to, 173, 349
defined, 172
Fast Preview mode
changing to, 174, 332
defined, 172
embedded graphics and, 260

File menu
Close command, 120, 123
Collect for Output command, 261
Customize submenu
Shortcuts command, 365, 393, 397, 402
Toolbars command, 366
Export command, 204, 208, 375, 378, 383
Import command, 102, 154, 177, 195, 237,
248, 267, 273, 363
New command, 9, 64, 114, 152, 212, 266
Open command, 31, 124, 141
Preferences command, 14, 27, 116
Print command, 256
Revert command, 204, 324
Save command, 35, 46
files
collecting for output, 259–62
font, 4
formats supported by FreeHand, 403–4
linked, 260
Shockwave Flash, 370, 379
Fill Inspector, 16, 43–46, 87–88
center point control, 198
Centerpoint option, 331
Color menu, 147
color ramp, 44, 46, 198, 351
displaying, 43, 87, 160, 164, 291, 326
Ending Color menu, 87
Fill Type menu, 87, 147
Gradient Direction Angle, 87
Gradient Direction dial, 87
Graduated button, 44
illustrated, 43, 44, 45, 87
Objects Only option, 332
Radial button, 44, 45
Snapshop option, 332
Starting Color menu, 87
See also Inspectors
fills
applying, 87–89
applying to text, 96–102
basic, 42, 291
changing, 97, 164, 198, 288, 346, 350
colors, changing, 100, 358
control angle, 291
defined, 36
gradient, 42–46, 291
graduated, 44
lens, 275
radial, 44, 45, 46, 198
transparency, 276
viewing, 229
Fisheye Lens tool, 315

fish illustration
black element, 300
body fill, 307
body stroke, changing, 312
dragging/dropping swatches on, 302–3
gradient fills on fins, 304, 305
moving blend into body of, 310–11
yellow shapes, 300–301
See also Aquarium sign
Flash graphics
animated, creating, 379–83
defined, 379
importing, 383
Flash Player application, 383
FlexBotz2.ft8, 368
FlexBotz.fh8, 335
folders
creating on hard drive, 8
Fonts, 4
PrintSet, 257
fonts, 95
CD-ROM, 145
changing, 96, 99, 145
files, 4
license, 261
multiple displayed, 226
News Gothic T, 4
selecting, 145
TrueType, 4
URW Garamond Demi, 245, 246
URW Garamond Regular, 242
URWGaramondT, 145
URWGaramondTMed, 99, 277
URW Garamond T Normal, 4
Vladimir Script, 4
Foreground layer, 155, 320–21
active, 156, 319
creating, 175–77
double-clicking, 274, 285
pasting, 283, 293
removing, 272
renaming, 274
selecting, 272
See also layers
formats (export), 205–8
application-specific, 208
BMP, 206
EPS, 205, 207–8
GIF, 206, 207
JPEG, 206
PICT, 206
PNG, 206
TIFF, 206, 208

formatting
    character, 243
    local, 243, 245
    text block, 243
    viewing, 246
four-direction arrow cursor, 349
Frame.fh8, 202
Frame layer, 201–2
Freeform tool, 114
    default mode, 121
    displaying, 121
    double-clicking, 122
    dragging, 122
    illustrated, 11
    learning, 123
    manipulating paths with, 120–23
    options, 122, 137
    positioning, 121
    practicing with, 123
    Push/Pull mode, 121, 122, 136
    Reshape Area mode, 121, 122, 136
    size of, 121
    using, 120–23, 136–37
FreeHand
    CD-ROM training version, 8
    EPS formats, 205
    file format support, 403–4
    screen, 8
    terminology, 401
    version 8, 1
Freehand tool, 11
Front Fish layer, 329

G

GIF files
    color selection, 375
    creating, 375–77
    defined, 373
    extension, 376
    importing, 377
    uses, 373
GIF format, 206, 207
    for small icons, 373
    Web page, 370
    See also formats (export)

GIF Options dialog box, 207, 376
gradient fills, 134, 192, 291, 355
    adding colors to, 46
    angle, 87, 164, 351, 359
    applying, 42–46, 353
    applying by dragging/dropping colors, 302–5
    changing to, 147
    color ramp, 44, 46, 198, 351
    Control key and, 305
    defined, 42, 401
    defining, 45
    direction of, 44, 303
    ending color, 46
    flow of, 192
    graduated, 44
    linear, 44, 359
    modifying, 43
    radial, 44, 45, 46, 198, 354–57
    starting color, 46
    sunshine look, 193
    swatches, 44
    text, 144–49
    See also fills
graduated fills, 44
Graphic Hose panel, 316–18
    closing, 320
    Contents menu, 316
    Hose menu, 316, 317
    illustrated, 317
    opening, 316
    Options button, 320
    Paste In button, 318
    Rotate menu, 320
    Scale menu, 320
Graphic Hose tool, 313–18
    defined, 313
    double-clicking, 316, 320
    dragging, 316
    opening, 316, 329
    options, 316–17
    rotate factor, 320
    scale factor, 316, 320
    spacing, 316
    using, 316–17, 320
Graphic Interchange Format. *See* GIF files;
    GIF format

graphics
 aligning, 106
 animated Flash, 379–83
 creating, 223–29
 distorting, 249
 embedded, 260
 exporting, 376
 finishing touches to, 134–35
 GIF, 372
 importing, 102–7, 248–50, 267–72, 363
 JPEG, 372
 moving, 105
 picture frame, 202
 positioning, 104, 202, 363
 resizing, 103, 106
 Shockwave Flash, 374
 vector, 7
 Web page, 206, 372
 wrapping text around, 250–53
Ground.ft8, 290
Ground layer, 294
ground shape, 292–93
 coordinates, 292–93
 copying, 293
 filling, 292
 positioning, 292
grouped paths, 75, 115
 behavior of, 115
 creating, 140
 defined, 75
 See also paths
grouping
 blends, 80
 elements, 51, 135, 169, 184
 paths, 140
groups
 aligning, 187–89
 blending and, 310
 changing shapes of, 323
 selecting, 187
guides
 adding, 219
 converting elements to, 216–17
 deleting, 220
 in Guides list, 219
 location of, 219
 manipulating, 218–20
 releasing, 220
 repositioning, 220
 ruler, 104, 197, 214–18
 snapping to, 225
 types of, 219
Guides dialog box, 218–20
Guides layer, 155, 217
 hiding, 217
 locking, 217
 moving, 217
 moving elements to, 217
 path to, 220

H

handles
 control, 119, 133–34
 dragging, 115
 smaller, 116
 text block, 252
 transform, 165
Help menu, FreeHand Help command, 60
help system
 displaying, 60
 experimenting with, 60
 features, 61
highlighted elements, 349
Hills layer, 177, 190, 193, 194
Hill style, 182, 186
Hose dialog box, 317, 318
hoses
 creating, 313, 316
 current, 316
 objects in, 317–18
 options, 316–71
 See also Graphic Hose tool
HTML (Hypertext Markup Language), 384
 3.2 format, 390
 code adjustments, 387
 Dynamic (DHTML), 389
 format, 389
 Web pages, 372, 384

I

images. *See* graphics
import cursor, 248, 249
import file formats
 Macintosh, 404
 Windows, 403
importing
 colors, 159
 Flash graphics, 383
 GIF files, 377
 graphics, 102–7, 248–50, 267–72, 363–64
 JPEG images, 267, 269
 PANTONE process colors, 221–23
 picture frames, 201–2
 text, 236–37
 tracing pattern, 154–55
Info bar
 displaying, 214
 hiding, 218
 illustrated, 214
 using, 215
insertion point, 92, 231
Inspectors, 16
 displaying, 17
 Document, 16–17, 65–67, 266–67
 Fill, 16, 43–46, 87–88, 160, 164
 hiding, 17
 Object, 15–16, 31–33, 68–74, 78, 216
 Stroke, 16, 40–41, 88–89, 109, 160
 Text, 16, 95, 225

Insta.html, 384–90
  defined, 384
  document properties, 388
  illustrated, 387, 389
  opening, 386
  preferences, 387
  using, 384
Insta.html Document Properties dialog box, 388
Insta.html Preferences dialog box, 387–88
interlacing, 376
Intersect operation, 183–84, 186

J
joining blends, 381–82
Joint Photographic Experts Group. *See* JPEG files;
    JPEG format
JPEG files
  creating, 378–79
  defined, 373
  extension, 376, 378
  image quality, 378
  uses, 373
JPEG format, 206
  choosing, 378, 388
  compression, 373, 377
  images, importing, 267, 269
  uses for, 267
  Web page, 370
  See also formats (export)
JPEG Options dialog box, 378

K
keyboard shortcuts, 393–400, 402–3
  assigning, 365, 402
  Command+=, 166
  Command+A, 29, 169, 312
  Command+D, 167
  Command+F, 50, 305
  Command+G, 48, 140, 169, 312
  Command+N, 9, 64, 114, 152
  Command+Option+M, 98, 197
  Command+R, 102, 154, 267
  Command+S, 35
  Command+Shift+W, 29, 98, 153, 267
  Command+Z, 68, 233
  Ctrl+A, 29, 169, 312
  Ctrl+Alt+M, 98, 197
  Ctrl+D, 167
  Ctrl+F, 50, 305
  Ctrl+G, 48, 140, 169, 312
  Ctrl+N, 9, 64, 114, 152, 266
  Ctrl+R, 102, 154, 267
  Ctrl+S, 35
  Ctrl+Shift+C, 166
  Ctrl+Shift+W, 29, 98, 153, 267
  Ctrl+Z, 68, 233
  customizing, 365–66, 393, 397
  drawing, 396, 400
  editing, 396, 400
  Edit menu, 394, 398

File menu, 394, 398
  general, 396, 400
  Macintosh, 397–400
  Modify menu, 395, 399
  printing, 393, 397
  switching, sets, 365
  Text menu, 395, 399
  View menu, 394, 398
  Window menu, 396, 400
  Windows, 393–96
Keyline mode, 202
  changing to, 172, 228, 233, 248, 289, 309
  creating blends in, 289
  defined, 172
  experimenting with, 203
  layers in, 203
  ruler guides and, 228
  See also views
Knife tool, 11

L
landscape orientation, 152, 153, 212, 267
layers, 150–80
  active, 156, 157, 195
  adding, 155
  Background, 155, 156, 176, 349
  Beam, 275, 276, 277, 289
  checking, 171
  check mark next to, 194, 321
  color coding, 202–3
  creating, 157, 175–77, 269, 272–73
  defined, 150
  deleting, 195
  displaying, 162
  dragging, 176, 285
  Foreground, 155, 175–77, 272, 274, 293, 319
  Frame, 201–2
  Front Fish, 329
  Ground, 294
  Guides, 155, 217, 220
  hiding, 162, 175, 294
  Hills, 177, 190, 193
  Lighthouse, 286
  locking, 156, 177, 322, 327
  moving elements between, 155, 175
  multiple, 271
  naming, 157, 171, 269, 285
  nonprinting, 155
  organizing documents into, 201
  Reflection, 289
  renaming, 175, 194–95, 201, 289
  reordering, 285, 289
  Sky, 161, 162, 170, 171, 190, 193, 201, 269
  Sun, 161, 170
  Trees, 195, 202, 203
  Type, 320, 323
  viewing, 203, 382
  Water, 285, 289
  Waves, 321, 322

Layers panel, 19–20, 155–58
    controls, 202–4
    displaying, 19, 155, 161, 170, 319, 382
    dragging, 20
    gray circle, 203
    hiding, 177
    illustrated, 19, 155
    layer names in, 171
    Lock icon, 156, 177
    Options menu, 157, 161, 175, 194, 195, 269, 272, 289
    separator line, 155, 176, 269
layouts
    adding elements to, 319–23
    adding text to, 92–95
    creating guides for, 214–18
    printing press, 66
leading, 242, 277
    fixed, 277
    specifying, 242
lens fills, 275
    applying, 326–29, 360
    Darken, 360, 363
    default, 326
    defined, 326
    exploring, 296
    Lighten, 327
    Magnify, 328, 330–32
    object, 332
    performance and, 326
    selecting, 322
    snapshot, 332
    spot colors viewed through, 275, 276
    Transparency, 322, 326, 360
    types of, 326
    See also fills
library styles, 42
Lighten lens fill, 328
Lighthouse layer, 286
linear gradient fills, 44, 359
Line tool
    dragging with, 108
    illustrated, 11
    Shift key and, 108
    using, 108
Link box, 237, 238, 239
linked files, 260
linking text blocks, 238–39
locking layers, 156, 177, 322, 327

M

Macintosh file formats, 404
Macintosh keyboard shortcuts, 397–400
    customizing, 397
    drawing and editing, 400
    Edit menu, 398
    File menu, 398
    general, 400
    Modify menu, 399
    printing, 397
    Text menu, 399
    View menu, 398
    Window menu, 400
    See also keyboard shortcuts
Macromedia Authorized training courses, 1–4
    defined, 3
    lesson plans, 3
    lessons, this book, 1–2, 3–4
    minimum system requirements, 5
Macromedia Flash, 379
magnification, 29
    changing, 239
    factor, 331
    menu, 30
    setting, 31
    See also Zoom tool
Magnification menu, 338
Magnify lens fill, 328, 330–32
    adjusting, 330
    centerpoint, 331
    factor, 331
    See also lens fills
main toolbar
    Color List button, 19, 46, 82, 100, 222
    Color Mixer button, 17, 36, 85
    defined, 10
    docking, 13
    dragging, 13
    Group button, 59
    illustrated, 10
    Layers button, 217, 319
    Object Inspector button, 15
    Save button, 35
    tool names, 10
    Ungroup button, 115
    See also toolbars
marquee, 28
measurement units, 32, 64, 109
    changing, 152, 266
    entering, 212
Mirror tool, 55–57
    clicking, 57
    displaying, 56
    reflection axis, 56

Modify menu

Align command, 47, 75, 101

Arrange submenu

Bring to Front command, 47, 50, 189, 251, 305, 351

Move Backward command, 47, 189

Move Forward command, 47, 189

Send to Back command, 47, 134, 188, 189, 279, 311, 363

Combine submenu

Blend command, 78, 282, 288, 309, 338, 340, 380

Intersect command, 184, 186

Join Blend to Path command, 381

Fill command, 43

Group command, 48, 51, 55, 59, 82, 140, 169, 184, 186, 189, 271, 292, 312

Join command, 301

Stroke command, 40

Ungroup command, 76, 115

moving

blends, 311

centerpoint, 357, 358

corner points, 118

elements, 25

graphics, 105

Guides layer, 217

shapes, 349

spirals, 233

text, 227

text blocks, 97–98, 100

multiple-page documents, 234–36

page sizes and, 262

printing, 259

See also documents

N

naming

colors, 139

documents, 36

layers, 157, 171, 269, 285

object styles, 182

paragraph styles, 240, 241

views, 306

Normal style, 181, 184, 193

O

Object Editing Preferences dialog box, 68

Object Inspector, 31–33, 68–74

Automatic option, 118

Corner radius value, 71

Curve button, 118

displaying, 15, 31, 68, 78, 216, 274

h value, 70

illustrated, 15, 32, 33

measurements, 68

negative values, 71

object information display, 68

values, 33

w value, 70, 73

x value, 69, 70, 71, 216, 268, 294

y value, 69, 70, 72, 216, 268, 294

See also Inspectors

object-oriented programs, 6–7

objects

deselecting, 41

distorting, 323

distributing, 143

selecting, 24, 68

selecting multiple, 51

snapping to guide, 225

object styles

defined, 181

defining, 181–83

power of, 193

opacity settings, 322

opening, 8

orientation

landscape, 152, 153, 212, 267

portrait, 152

printing, 258

Outline.ft8, 336

P

page rulers

displaying, 98, 197, 214

hiding, 218

pages

active, 235

arrangement on pasteboard, 235

bleed area of, 66

business card, 262

custom size of, 212–13, 262, 362, 383

dimensions of, 153, 267

duplicating, 213, 234–36

orientation of, 267

size of, 152–53, 267, 362, 383

panel dock, 22, 23
panel groups, 16
panels, 15–20
    Align, 47–48, 75, 101, 143, 188
    aligning, 21–22
    closing, 73
    Color List, 18–19, 21–23, 96, 137, 180
    Color Mixer, 17–18, 21–23, 131, 137
    Colors, 20, 159
    defined, 15
    dialog boxes vs., 15
    docked, 22–23
    docking, 22
    dragging, 21
    floating, 214
    Graphic Hose, 316–18
    grouping, 20
    hiding, 23
    Inspector. *See* Inspectors
    Layers, 19–20, 155–58, 161, 170, 319
    opening, 73
    Shift-dragging, 22
    snapping, into position, 21
    Styles, 42–43, 181–83
    Tints, 18, 38–39, 85
    Transform, 79–80, 142
    undocking, 23
    ungrouping, 20
    Xtra Tools, 55–56, 230, 253
PANTONE colors, 83–85
    adding to Color List, 84
    Coated color libraries, 83
    for process color, 159, 221–23
    for spot color, 158
    Uncoated color libraries, 83
    See also colors
PANTONE Process color library dialog box, 222
paper sizes, 258
paragraph marks, 244
paragraphs, selecting, 242
paragraph styles, 181, 240–43
    defined, 181
    defining, 240–47
    naming, 240, 241
    text color, 241
Parts.ft8, 336
pasteboard
    clicking with Text tool, 144
    defined, 9
    illustrated, 9
    page arrangement on, 235
pasted elements, 310
Paste Inside feature, 169–72
    benefits of, 172
    control handles, 343
    for pasting blends inside paths, 347
    using, 171–72, 190

paths
    adding points to, 116–17
    adjusting, 133, 136
    attaching text to, 230–33
    automatic adjustment of, 118
    in blends, 78, 338
    clipping, 169, 193–94, 310–12, 356
    closed, 126, 131, 133, 163, 179, 275
    combining with Blend command, 75–78
    composite, 300–302
    converting to text, 146
    creating, 117
    curved, 178–80
    defined, 75
    deforming, 122
    deselecting, 179
    grouped, 75, 115
    grouping, 140
    manipulating with Freeform tool, 120–23
    modifying, 116
    open, 75
    overlapping, 300
    pasting blends inside, 341–43, 347
    points, 75
    starting, 178
    tracing, 131
    ungrouped, 116
    viewing, 76
path segments
    clicking on, 117
    constraining, 127
    defined, 112
    horizontal, 127
    pulling, 121
    pushing, 121
    vertical, 127
Pen tool, 114, 151, 280, 291
    adding corner points with, 162, 178
    clicking, 162
    creating curved paths with, 178–80
    for creating elements, 162–65
    dragging, 162, 178
    illustrated, 11
    positioning, 163
    selecting, 163
    Shift key and, 179
    tracing with, 185
    using, 114, 162, 178–80
Photoshop EPS format, 207
PICT format, 206
picture frames
    graphic, 202
    importing, 201–2
Plane.fh8, 63, 102
PNG format, 206

Pointer tool, 326, 338, 348, 354
clicking on empty screen, 137
for deselecting objects, 41
double-clicking with, 57
illustrated, 11
returning to, 35
selecting, 69
Shift+clicking with, 183, 184
Shift key and, 74, 106, 199, 227
using, 24–25
points
adding, 116–17
adjusting, 136
connector, 117
control handles, 133
corner, 117
curve, 117
defined, 75
displaying, 117
dragging, 116
manipulating individual, 115
nudging, 127
removing, 119, 128
selecting, 76–77
See also paths
Polygon tool, 11
portrait orientation, 152
PostScript printers, 256
preferences
Autotrace tool, 269–70
customizing, 14–15
Insta.html, 387–88
Spiral tool, 230
tool, 53–55
Preferences dialog box
General tab, 14
opening, 14
Redraw tab, 14–15, 155
Preview mode, 353
changing to, 174, 228, 233, 248, 249, 289, 310, 350
defined, 172
layers in, 203
See also views
Print dialog box, 256–57
Cancel button, 259
illustrated, 256
opening, 256
Print button, 259
Print Setting menu, 256, 257
Setup button, 256
printers, 256
PostScript, 256
resolution, 213

printing, 256–59
bleed area and, 91
crop marks, 258
documents, 256–59
invisible characters and, 245
keyboard shortcuts, 393, 397
multiple-page documents, 259
orientation, 258
paper sizes, 258
process color, 158
service bureau, 259, 261
setting up, 256–59
PrintSet folder, 257
Print Setup dialog box, 257–59
illustrated, 257, 258, 259
Imaging tab, 258
opening, 256
Paper Setup tab, 258–59
Save Settings button, 257
Separations tab, 257
process colors, 138, 158–62
defined, 158
defining, 158–62
importing, 221–23
libraries, 158
names of, 160
PANTONE for, 159, 221–23
printing, 158
See also colors

Q
QuarkXPress EPS format, 207–8

R
radial fills, 44, 45, 46
adding dimension with, 354–57
Alt/Option key and, 305
applying, 304, 358
centerpoint, 355, 356
changing to, 198
creating, 355
shading with, 356
See also fills
rectangles
constraining, 127
converting to guide, 217
copying, 26
creating, 24, 31, 33, 67–68, 157, 221
deleting, 27, 30
handles, 115
moving, 25, 27, 33
positioning, 68–73
resizing, 25, 115
rounded, 54, 71
using, 67–68

Rectangle tool, 157, 216
  Alt/Option key and, 49
  Corner radius option, 54
  displaying, 24, 67
  double-clicking, 53
  illustrated, 11
  Shift and, 34
  using, 24, 114
reflection
  artwork, 200–201
  axis, constraining, 200
  blending shapes for, 286–90
Reflection layer, 289
Reflect tool
  illustrated, 11
  Shift key and, 200
  using, 200
requirements, minimum system, 5
RGB TIFF files, 269
Rich Text Format (RTF) files, 236–37
Road style, 183, 186, 192
Robot1.fh8, 31
Robot.fh8, 7
Robot.ft8, 377
Robot illustration
  adding blends to, 345
  antenna, 357–59
  background image, 361
  blend creation for, 337–41
  centering on page, 364
  completing, 357–59
  illustrated, 334
  parts, 336–37
  for postcard, 361–64
  radial fills, 354–57
  shading
    for bottom of sphere, 348–51
    for cylindrical ring, 351–54
    for top of sphere, 344–47
  shadow, 360
  template, 336
Robotz.fh8, 211
Robotz.rtf, 237
Rotate tool
  clicking, 166
  double-clicking, 79, 165
  illustrated, 11
rotation
  angle, 166, 167
  around center point, 58
  center of, 166
  copies, 79–82
  elements, 57–59
  with Graphic Hose tool, 320
  spiral, 230
  with transform handles, 165
  with Transform panel, 79–80

Roughen tool, 315
rounded corners, 54, 71
ruler guides
  creating, 214–18
  defined, 104
  dragging, 197, 215
  horizontal, 215
  illustrated, 197
  intersection of, 197
  Keyline view and, 228
  nonprinting, 197, 215
  positioning, 106
  removing, 104
  using, 104, 106, 197
  vertical, 215, 219
  viewing, 228
rulers
  dragging ruler guides from, 215
  horizontal, 215
  page, 98, 197, 214
  text, 93
  vertical, 215
Run Around Selection dialog box, 251

S

Save As dialog box, 35, 36, 262
Save As HTML dialog box, 389
saving
  documents, 35–36
  templates, 336
Scale tool
  displaying, 142
  double-clicking, 90
  illustrated, 11
scaling
  artwork, 194–201
  elements, 90–91, 142–44
  options, 143
  percentage, 142
  proportions, 91
  uniform, 91, 142
school of fish, 313
  manipulating, 323
  moving, 322
  on Foreground layer, 319
  rotating, 320
  See also Aquarium sign
screens. *See* tints

selecting
blends, 311, 382
closed shapes, 282
composite paths, 311
Control key and, 304
corner points, 134
curve points, 133
ellipses, 74, 197, 345, 358
fonts, 145
groups, 187
lens fills, 322
objects, 24, 51, 68
paragraphs, 242
points, 76–77
shadows, 360
shapes, 301
Shift key and, 307
styles, 42, 192
text, 94, 100, 101, 145, 224, 227, 241
through element stack, 304
transparent fill, 322

selection boxes
around group, 48
colors of, 202–3
defined, 24
illustrated, 24
matching swatches, 203

selection marquee
defined, 76
dragging, 270

service bureau, 259, 261

shading
blends and, 356
clipping paths and, 356
creating with blended shapes, 307–10, 334–68
for cylindrical ring, 351–54
with radial gradient, 356
realistic, 344–47
for sphere bottom, 348–51
for sphere top, 344–47
three-dimensional, creating, 341–43

shadows, 360

Shadow tool, 315

shapes
adding with templates, 290–95
blending, 280–90, 307–10, 345
closed, 281, 282, 291
closing, 127
combining into composite path, 301
coordinates, 292–93
copying, 293
creating, 31–35
elliptical, 301
gaps between, 310
ground, 292–93
joining, 301–2
manipulating, 114–20
moving, 349
multiple, blending, 280–85
opacity settings, 322
overlapping, 301
pasting, inside paths, 346
positioning, 349
ring, 352–53
rounded ends on, 308
selecting, 301
shadow, 360
tracing, 124, 132–34

Shift key
Bezigon tool and, 127
Ellipse tool and, 34, 49, 134, 197
Line tool and, 108
Pen tool and, 179
Rectangle tool and, 34
Reflect tool and, 200
selecting with, 307
sizing with, 200, 314

Shockwave Flash
animation, 374, 379–83
defined, 370
files, 370, 379
FreeHand with, 370
graphics, 374, 379–83
plug-in, 372
technology, 206

sizing
circles, 50
documents, 153
elements, 25
ellipses, 73
Freeform tool, 121
graphics, 103, 106
rectangles, 25, 115
Shift key and, 200, 314
text, 95, 145, 146, 224
toolbox, 12

Skew tool, 11
Sky layer, 161, 162, 170, 171, 175, 190, 193, 269
    displaying, 201
    hiding, 194
Smudge tool, 315
snapping
    cursor, 225
    defined, 21
    disabling, 22
Snap to Guides feature, 225
spacebtz.tif, 248
Spelling window, 247
spirals
    direction of, 230
    drawing, 231
    moving, 233
    rotations of, 230
    text wrap around, 231–32
    types of, 230
Spiral tool, 230–31
    double clicking, 230
    preferences, 230
spot colors
    defined, 158
    libraries, 158
    names of, 160
    PANTONE for, 158
    viewed through lens fill, 275, 276
    See also colors
squares, creating, 127
standoff, 250
Stroke Inspector, 16, 40–41, 49, 50, 88–89
    Dash Type menu, 109
    displaying, 40, 88, 109, 160, 165
    illustrated, 40
    Stroke Color menu, 89, 109
    Stroke Type menu, 41, 88, 89, 109, 160
    Width menu, 40, 89, 109
    See also Inspectors
strokes
    applying, 87–89
    color of, 89, 109, 338, 340, 358
    defined, 36
    expanding, 308
    multiple, changing, 41
    removing, 88
    types of, 109
    viewing, 229
    width of, 89, 109, 308

styles, 181–208
    default, 42, 181
    defined, 150
    defining, 181–83
    definition, changing, 191–92
    double-clicking, 182
    editing, 190–93
    Hill, 182, 186
    naming, 182
    Normal, 181, 184, 193
    object, 181–83
    paragraph, 181, 240–43
    presets, 42
    Road, 183, 186, 192
    selecting, 42, 192
    Title, 240, 246
    types of, 181
Styles panel, 42–43, 181–83
    displaying, 42, 181, 191, 240
    illustrated, 42, 43
    Options menu, 42, 43, 181, 182, 191, 240
Sun layer, 161, 170
swatches
    Alt/Option key and, 304
    books, 82
    Color List, 139
    Command key and, 305
    Control key and, 302, 305
    Ctrl+Shift and, 305
    defined, 39
    dragging, 85–86, 100, 139, 164, 180, 254,
        302–3, 305
    dropping, 86, 100, 139, 180, 254, 302–3
    gradient fill, 44
    releasing, 96
    selection boxes matching, 203
    white, 355
    See also colors

T
Tab key
    deselecting with, 175, 179, 184, 188, 189, 191,
        195, 200, 269, 272, 286, 305
    text block editing and, 247
tabs
    custom, 93
    displaying, 244
    setting, 92
templates, 124–31
    for adding shapes, 290–95
    for blending shapes, 280–85
    file extension, 124
    file format, 336
    opening, 336
    Robot illustration, 336
    saving as, 336
    tracing and, 132
    tracing pattern, 154

terrabtz.tif, 249

text
adding to layouts, 92–95
applying color fill to, 96–102
attaching to paths, 230–33
baseline, 104, 225
basic fills in, 146
bold, 242
capitalization, 95
centering, 148
color of, 241, 277–78
converting to paths, 146
creating, 223–29
deselecting, 278
double-clicking, 241
extending, 232
flowing, 237–39
fonts, 95, 96, 99, 145
formatting, 94, 99
gradient-filled, 144–49
highlighting, 223
importing, 236
insertion point, 92
leading, 242, 277
moving, 227
overflow, 238
positioning, 148, 278
ruler, displaying, 93
selecting, 94, 100, 101, 145, 224, 227, 241
size, display of, 226
sizing, 95, 145, 146, 224
spell-checking, 247
spiral, 231–32
style, 95
viewing, 94
See also text wrapping

text blocks, 92
background, 96
creating, 144, 237
dragging, 98
editing, 96, 224, 247
formatting, 243
handles, 252
linking, 238–39
moving, 97–98, 100
opening, 96
positioning, 100
selecting, 94, 100, 225, 238, 239
Tab key and, 247
typing in, 93

Text Editor, 243–47
closing, 246
defined, 243
illustrated, 244
opening, 243
scrolling in, 245
Show Invisibles option, 244
text display, 244
using, 243–47

Text Inspector, 16, 95
Adjust Columns button, 226
Character button, 226
Column and Rows button, 226
displaying, 225
Horizontal Scale, 225, 226, 232
illustrated, 226, 227
Leading Options menu, 242
Leading value, 242
Paragraph button, 226
Range Kerning option, 226, 232
Spacing button, 225, 226
See also Inspectors

Text menu
Attach to Path command, 231
Convert Case command, 95, 145
Convert to Paths command, 146
Editor command, 243
Run Around Selection command, 250
Spelling command, 247

Text tool, 277
clicking, 99, 223
dragging, 223
illustrated, 11
selecting, 92, 96

text toolbar
defined, 10
docking, 13
dragging, 13
illustrated, 10
Leading Options menu, 277
using, 99, 223
See also toolbars

text wrapping, 250–53
assigning, 250, 251
standoff, 250

thumbnails
defined, 234
displaying, 234
double-clicking, 235
preview, 212, 235

TIFF format, 206, 208
CMYK files, 260
images, 259
RGB files, 269
See also formats (export)

tints
adding in Color Mixer, 286
adding to Color List, 86
base color for, 39
creating, 85
default name of, 190
defined, 18, 85
display of, 39, 85
See also colors

Tints panel, 18, 49
    Add to Color List button, 86, 190
    Base Color menu, 86
    Color List menu, 39
    Custom Tint Control slider, 86
    defined, 18
    displaying, 17, 38, 85, 190
    hiding, 18
    illustrated, 18, 39
    swatches, 39, 85–86
Title style, 240, 246
toolbars
    customizing, 366–68
    main, 10, 13
    text, 10, 13
toolbox, 10–11
    defined, 10
    docking, 10, 13
    dragging, 11–12, 13
    illustrated, 11
    resizing, 12
    size box, 12
    tool preferences, 53–55
    tools, moving, 13
    See also specific tools
Trace1.ft8, 124
tracing, 124–31, 132–34, 179
    adjustments and, 132
    around shapes, 132, 179, 185
    with Autotrace tool, 270–71
    with Bezigon tool, 124–25
    images, 267–72
    with Pen tool, 185
    process, 128–31
    techniques, practicing, 140
    templates and, 132
tracing patterns, 135
    importing, 154–55
    template, 154
transformations
    center, 57
    duplicating, 151
    tools for, 59
transform handles, 57, 58, 165
Transform panel, 79–80, 165
    displaying, 79, 90, 142, 165
    illustrated, 79, 80
    Rotate controls, 79–80, 166–67
    Scale controls, 90–91
transparency
    alpha channels and, 375
    background, 376
    effects, 275–79
Transparency lens fill, 322, 326, 360
Trees layer, 195, 202, 203
TrueType fonts, 4
Type layer, 320
    activating, 323
    locking, 327

U
ungrouped paths, 116
uniform scaling, 91, 142
Units menu, 32, 64, 65
    illustrated, 152
    Inches, 266, 362
    Picas, 214
units of measure, 32, 64, 109
    changing, 152, 266, 362
    entering, 212
URL Editor, 386, 388
URLs (Universal Resource Locators), 386

V
vector graphics, 7
View menu (document window)
    Fast Keyline command, 173
    Fast Preview command, 172, 260
    Keyline command, 172, 228
    Paths command, 306
    Preview command, 172, 228
View menu
    Custom command, 126, 127, 306, 338
    Fit All command, 29, 238
    Fit Selection command, 29
    Fit to Page command, 9, 29, 98, 100, 106, 110,
        148, 153, 213, 267, 362
    Guides command, 218
    Magnification command, 94, 100, 104, 213, 239
    Page Rulers command, 98, 197, 214
    Snap to Guides command, 225
views, 338
    changing, 28–30, 172–75, 315, 339, 340
    custom, 126, 128, 131
    defining, 306–7
    Fast Keyline, 172, 173, 349
    Fast Preview, 172, 174, 260, 332
    Keyline, 172, 202, 228, 233, 248, 289, 309
    of layers, 203, 382
    modes, 401
    naming, 306
    Preview, 172, 174, 228, 233, 248–49, 289,
        310, 353
    reducing, 238

W
Water.ft8, 280
Water layer, 285, 289
Waves layer, 321, 322
Web browser
    checking graphics in, 377
    defined, 372
    HTML names and, 376
    launching, 372–73
    software, obtaining, 372
    viewing Shockwave Flash graphics in, 374
    viewing Web pages in, 390–91

Webfolio.ft8, 384
Web graphics, 206
Web pages, 370
    creating with Insta.html, 384–90
    formats, 370, 379
    graphics, 372
    graphic types, 372–74
    HTML, 372, 384
    URLs, 386
    viewing in browser, 390–91
Web Safe color library, 375
Welcome Wizard, 8–9
Window menu
    Inspectors submenu, 17
        Document command, 65, 152, 212, 266
        Fill command, 43, 87, 160, 164
        Object command, 15, 68, 78
        Stroke command, 40, 109, 160
    open document list, 342
    Panels submenu, 20
        Align command, 47, 143, 148, 188, 364
        Color List command, 18, 82, 96, 137, 180
        Color Mixer command, 17, 36, 131, 137
        Colors command, 159
        Layers command, 319
        Styles command, 42, 181, 191, 240
        Transform command, 79, 142
    Toolbars submenu
        Info command, 214
        Main command, 10
        Text command, 10
        Toolbox command, 11
    Xtras submenu
        URL Editor command, 386
        Xtra Tools command, 55, 230, 253, 315
Windows file formats, 403
Windows keyboard shortcuts, 393–96
    customizing, 393
    drawing and editing, 396
    Edit menu, 394
    File menu, 394
    general, 396
    Modify menu, 395
    printing, 393
    Text menu, 395
    View menu, 394
    Window menu, 396
    See also keyboard shortcuts
Wolf.ft8, 135
workspace, organizing, 21–23
World.fh8, 63
wrapping text, 250–53

X

Xtras menu
    Animation command, 382
    Create Blend command, 282
    Distort Envelope command, 324
    HTML command, 386
    Path Operations command, 308
Xtra tools
    3D Rotation, 315
    Arc, 315
    Bend, 315
    Chart, 315
    Eyedropper, 253–54
    Fisheye Lens, 315
    Graphic Hose, 313–18
    Mirror, 55–57
    Roughen, 315
    Shadow, 315
    Smudge, 315
    Spiral, 230–31
Xtra Tools panel
    displaying, 55, 230, 253, 315
    Eyedropper tool, 253
    Graphic Hose tool, 315, 329
    illustrated, 56, 230, 253
    Mirror tool, 56
    Spiral tool, 230

Z

Zoo.fh8, 113
Zoom tool, 280, 291, 352
    with Alt/Option key selected, 28, 107
    clicking, 107
    dragging with, 125
    illustrated, 11
    opening, 28
    plus/minus sign, 29
    using, 28–29, 107
    zooming out with, 107
    See also magnification
ZooStart.ft8, 141